WRITING
AND
PRODUCING
TELEVISION
NEWS

WRITING AND PRODUCING TELEVISION NEWS

From Newsroom to Air

ALAN SCHROEDER
Northeastern University

New York Oxford
Oxford University Press
2009

Oxford University Press, Inc., publishes works that further Oxford University's objective of excellence in research, scholarship, and education.

Oxford New York
Auckland Cape Town Dar es Salaam Hong Kong Karachi
Kuala Lumpur Madrid Melbourne Mexico City Nairobi
New Delhi Shanghai Taipei Toronto

With offices in
Argentina Austria Brazil Chile Czech Republic France Greece
Guatemala Hungary Italy Japan Poland Portugal Singapore
South Korea Switzerland Thailand Turkey Ukraine Vietnam

Copyright © 2009 by Oxford University Press, Inc.

Published by Oxford University Press, Inc.
198 Madison Avenue, New York, New York 10016
http://www.oup.com

Oxford is a registered trademark of Oxford University Press

Art credits: page 1: © Ann Johansson/Corbis; pages 2, 19, 22, 51, 79, 110, 133, 136, 158, 196, 214, 238: © iStockphoto.com; page 6: © David Stluka/Getty Images; page 8: © Jeff Greenberg/PhotoEdit; page 15: © Louise Gubb/CORBIS SABA; page 21: © Eric Robert/CORBIS SYGMA; page 28: courtesy of WCPO Television Cincinnati, OH; page 33: © Katja Heinemann/ Aurora/Getty Images; page 50: © Ken Cedeno/Corbis; page 52: © Alex Wong/Getty Images for Meet the Press; page 55: © David Paul Morris/ Getty Images; page 78: ©AP Photo/Bob Anez; page 84: © Jeff Greenberg/PhotoEdit; page 89: © AFP/ Getty Images; page 109: © David McNew/Getty Images; page 111: © Scott de Freitas-Draper/Santa Maria Times/Corbis; page 116: © Najlah Feanny/CORBIS SABA; page 118: © Skip Bolen/WireImage.com/ Getty Images; page 120: © John Moore/Getty Images; page 135: © Attar Maher/CORBIS SYGMA; page 137: © David McNew/Getty Images; page 140: © Mike Theiss/Ultimate Chase/Corbis; page 146: © 2006 Kim Karpeles. All Rights Reserved; page 157: © Jeff Greenberg/PhotoEdit; page 162: © Roger Hutchings/Alamy; page 174: © Tim Pannell/Corbis; page 195: courtesy of BBC Points West, photo by Maurice Flynn; page 197: © David Young-Wolff/PhotoEdit; page 200: © Kim Karpeles/Alamy; page 213: courtesy of BBC Points West, photo by Maurice Flynn; page 219: © David Young-Wolff/PhotoEdit; page 225: © David Young-Wolff/PhotoEdit; page 229 © Richard B. Levine; page 237: © Colin Young-Wolff/ PhotoEdit; page 241: © Mario Tama/Getty Images; page 243: © David Young-Wolff/PhotoEdit

Library of Congress Cataloging-in-Publication Data

Schroeder, Alan, 1954—
    Writing and producing television news : from newsroom to air / by Alan Schroeder.
        p. cm.
    ISBN-13: 978-0-19-531193-8 (alk. paper)
    1. Television broadcasting of news—Authorship.   2. Television broadcasting of news.   3. Television—Production and direction.
I. Title.
    PN4784.T4S34 2009
    808'.06607—dc22   2008018586

Printing number: 9 8 7 6 5 4 3 2 1

Printed in the United States of America
on acid-free paper.

CONTENTS

PART ONE
WRITING AND REPORTING

PART TWO
PRODUCING

CHAPTER SIX

NEWS JUDGMENTS   135

CHAPTER SEVEN

NEWSCAST PRODUCING   157

CHAPTER TEN

TELEVISION NEWS ON THE WEB 237

Tune in to a typical newscast, and what you'll see is a fairly straightforward-looking presentation: anchors and reporters delivering a mix of stories, some that originate in the studio and some that originate in the field. You'll find hard news, features, weather, sports, and entertainment, all bundled into a visually appealing package that is fast paced and audience friendly. Behind this superficially simple exterior, however, lies a complex process involving dozens of personnel making literally hundreds of decisions. The newscast might be the product that rolls off the assembly line, but only after many hours and a good deal of effort by the journalists whose job it is to put the pieces together, ingredient by ingredient.

That brings us to the purpose of this book. For students with an interest in television journalism, *Writing and Producing Television News: From Newsroom to Air* has two main goals: first, to acquaint you with the basic challenges and skills faced by professional practitioners of television news; and second, to put these principles into practice through realistic exercises and assignments. The book functions both as a textbook and a workbook, allowing you to experience firsthand the work of a television journalist.

Writing and Producing Television News concentrates on the process of storytelling—storytelling as it is practiced in the newsroom, the studio, and the field. This text provides a step-by-step guide to the nuts and bolts of writing and producing television journalism. We approach TV news as an organic process made up of various components, from scriptwriting to graphic design to on-camera reporting. Underlying these mechanics are the news judgments and ethical considerations that TV journalists face on a daily basis.

This book will immerse you in the everyday challenges of being a journalist in a professional television newsroom. To accomplish this, we have created a fictional city in which all the exercises and examples are set. A key difficulty for students seeking to learn about TV news is replicating the real-life circumstances under which television journalists operate. *Writing and Producing Television News* addresses that problem directly by putting you, the student, in the role of decision maker, confronting the sorts of situations that news producers and writers regularly face.

This text contains dozens of original examples, exercises, and assignments. Each topic area—news judgment, program producing, story writing, promotion, graphics, and so on—is complemented by assignments designed to closely approximate the work of professional television journalists. These exercises cover a wide spectrum of material, from breaking news to features. They introduce a range of story formats, from simple anchor readers and voice-overs to more complicated structures like sound-bite stories and news packages. In addition to scriptwriting, the exercises and assignments extend to such ancillary areas as graphics, headlines, teases, newscast organization, live reporting, web-based journalism, and anchoring, as well as news judgment and ethical decision making.

Because most beginning TV journalists launch their careers in local news, it is the local level on which we focus. You will function as producers and reporters in a setting that allows you to prepare a range of rundowns and stories for local newscasts. Our fictional city is called Lakedale. At the end of the text you will find a detailed profile of this community, including a directory of Lakedale's key institutions and players that will serve as a useful reference as you undertake the various assignments.

Last but not least, *Writing and Producing Television News* draws on the insights and experiences of a select group of dedicated professionals who represent the best of TV news: reporters, anchors, producers, assignment editors, web journalists, graphic artists, and newsroom executives, who work at local stations around the country. Although they represent a wide variety of markets and job descriptions, these individuals have one thing in common: They all had to learn the ins and outs of television journalism. Now it's your turn.

ACKNOWLEDGMENTS

This book would not have been possible without the cooperation of a number of talented professionals in the television news field. I would like to extend my particular thanks to the staff of WBZ-TV, the CBS affiliate in Boston, who allowed me to observe them in operation and who shared generously of their time and knowledge. Many individuals in the WBZ newsroom offered their assistance, but let me single out a few who made special contributions: former news director Jennifer Street; managing editor Tim White (who has since moved to WPRI-TV in Providence, R.I.); web journalist Chuck McKenney; graphic artist Gary Stout; producer Megan Fazio; assignment editor Jason Laverty; and anchors Paula Ebben and Scott Wahle. Thanks, too, to WBZ staffers Jim Priest, Ken Tucci, Pat Kreger, and Ro Dooley-Webster.

A huge debt of gratitude is owed to the producers, reporters, and anchors around the country who provided written answers to my questions and whose quotes are included in this book. In alphabetical order they are: Jen Berryman of WCVB-TV in Boston; Mary Bubala of WJZ-TV in Baltimore; Anna Crowley of WCNC-TV in Charlotte; Matt Gaffney of WTTG-TV in Washington, D.C.; Katie Hammer of KFSN-TV in Fresno; Larry Hatteberg of KAKE-TV in Wichita; Sean Kelly of WCVB-TV in Boston; Beth Parker of WTTG-TV in Washington, D.C.; and Tim Tunison of WBAL-TV in Baltimore. Most of these individuals are my former students, and they do me proud. Other contributors to whom I am grateful are Glenn Counts of WCNC and Steve Chaggaris of the CBS News Washington Bureau.

I am deeply indebted to my graduate research assistant at Northeastern University, Mike Beaudet, who brought a sharp and critical eye to this manuscript. Mike's background as an investigative reporter at Boston's WFXT-TV made him a valuable contributor to the project.

At Oxford University Press I would like to thank executive editor Peter Labella, assistant editor Chelsea Gilmore, project editor Christine D'Antonio, copyeditor Teresa Horton, and marketing assistant Deborah Gross. I'd also like to thank the following reviewers: Ralph Beliveau, University of Oklahoma; Cassandra Clayton, University of Maryland, College Park; Jerry Dunklee, Southern Connecticut State University; James A. Gorham, Midwestern State University; Terry Likes, Western Kentucky University; David C. Ogden, University of Nebraska at Omaha; and Larry Stuelpnagel, Northwestern University.

Thanks also go to Bob Steele of the Poynter Institute and Barbara Cochran of the Radio–Television News Directors Association.

Finally, a tip of the hat to the many colleagues with whom I worked during my career as a television producer. The list is too long to offer every name, so let me cite two favorites: from KAKE-TV in Wichita, Ron Loewen; and from WBZ-TV in Boston, Francine Achbar. May everyone who uses this textbook be privileged to work for such great bosses.

WRITING

AND

PRODUCING
TELEVISION
NEWS

CHAPTER ONE

THE NEWSROOM

TOPICS DISCUSSED IN THIS CHAPTER

- The Newsroom Atmosphere • Jobs in a TV Newsroom
- Day-to-Day Operations in a TV Newsroom • Working in TV News
- Diversity in TV Newsrooms • Checklist of Key Points

ASSIGNMENTS/ANALYSIS

THE NEWSROOM ATMOSPHERE

The managing editor strides briskly through the newsroom, announcing in a loud voice that a downtown subway station is under evacuation following the discovery of a suspicious package containing an unidentified white powder. "We're going live with this in two minutes," he says, then quickly doles out various assignments: an anchor to deliver the news, a writer to assemble the script, a graphic artist to create a map of the location, a helicopter pilot to feed back a live aerial shot of the scene, and a web journalist to post the story on the newsroom's internet site. The atmosphere in the room palpably changes, from relative calm to the intensity of a beehive.

At the appointed time the station goes live from the anchor desk, and viewers throughout the area learn of the story. By the time the next scheduled newscast airs an hour later, the closing of the subway stop remains the lead item, but the incident is over, and operations have returned to normal. The suspicious substance was nothing more than baby powder spilling out of a dropped shopping bag. Another day, another tale from the city.

Although the vast majority of stories on local television news stations do not warrant a breaking on-air update, the suspicious package episode illustrates the degree to which TV journalists must be able to roll with the punches and respond quickly. Immediacy is the hallmark of TV news, and the people who work in television newsrooms regularly find themselves operating against the clock, juggling the need to get it fast with the need to get it right.

A TV newsroom is no place for the faint of heart. The work is intense, difficult, challenging, and easy to get wrong. Everything happens at warp speed.

When most people think of television news, they think of the anchorpersons and reporters who constitute its on-camera face. Important as these individuals are, they represent only the most visible part of the newsroom work force. Behind the cameras producers, writers, photographers, editors, graphic artists, technicians, and management personnel team up to deliver the day's news.

JOBS IN A TV NEWSROOM

The jobs in a television newsroom range from the familiar—on-air anchors and reporters—to positions that would baffle average consumers of TV news. In this chapter we take a look at the key players in TV news, with a particular emphasis on the jobs that take place behind the scenes. Chapter 5, "The On-Camera Journalist," deals more specifically with the work of reporters and anchorpersons.

The Assignment Desk

The nerve center of any television newsroom is the *assignment desk,* often referred to simply as "the desk." This is where assignment editors track the news of the day, keeping a close eye on unfolding events. At the same time they also develop nonbreaking story ideas and look ahead to events that will happen down the line.

In addition to tracking stories, the assignment desk is charged with dispatching reporters, photographers, and electronic newsgathering (ENG) crews into the field to report the stories that will appear in the station's newscasts and on its website. For large-market newsrooms this presents an especially significant challenge. At WBZ-TV, Boston's CBS affiliate, for example, about 7 to 10 reporters are available on average (fewer during nights and weekends), along with some 14 or 15 photographers, plus three or four live shot crews and production vehicles. During the 4 p.m.–6:30 p.m. news block, it is not uncommon for the station to air six live shots. A great deal of effort goes into coordinating these individuals, who on a given day are scattered throughout metropolitan Boston and beyond.

Whatever the market size, assignment editors are expected to keep close tabs on the day's news. They accomplish this in a variety of ways: They monitor other media like newspapers, radio, internet sites, and rival TV stations. They take phone calls and written suggestions from viewers. They sift through mountains of press releases sent by public relations professionals who hope to gain coverage for various organizations, events, and causes.

Assignment desk personnel keep an eye out for breaking stories by monitoring scanners from local law enforcement agencies, fire departments, and ambulance services. In larger cities, where scanner traffic is intense, newsrooms might subscribe to a service that provides regular e-mail updates about scanner activity. When a story breaks on the scanner—a homicide, for instance, or a major traffic accident—the assignment desk whips into action, making follow-up phone calls and dispatching crews to the scene to jump-start the reporting process in the field.

Beyond breaking news, assignment editors also make routine phone calls to key contacts at law enforcement agencies, district attorneys' offices, city hall, the state capitol, and so forth. Assignment desk personnel usually make the same round of calls every day. Over time this allows for relationships to develop, relationships that come in handy when major news breaks.

A large percentage of the assignment desk's work is conducted over the telephone. When viewers call a TV newsroom with story tips, the first person they are likely to talk to is an assignment editor. Although the majority of these tips do not result in stories, part of the assignment editor's skill is being able to sort through the chaff and recognize potentially viable ideas.

The assignment desk keeps what are known as "futures files" of upcoming stories. Many of these are perennial (opening day at the ballpark, the town Fourth of July concert, local and state fairs, etc.) and are covered year in and year out. Others are one-time events that are scheduled in advance. Because the assignment desk deals with both breaking and nonbreaking news, it is the responsibility of assignment editors to follow everything that happens in a community. Larger newsrooms may include a specialized type of assignment editor called a planning editor, whose job it is to concentrate on major upcoming events like election night coverage.

Assignment editors also generate what are known as *enterprise stories*: original, non-breaking news stories that other media have not covered. Journalists with a reputation for aggressiveness and creativity do not sit back and wait for the news to happen; they dig up interesting stories on their own.

What qualities are required to work successfully on an assignment desk? Communication skills, flexibility, aggressiveness (especially with reluctant sources), level-headedness, and an ability to multitask are all useful. "The best assignment editors are people persons," says Tim Tunison, assistant news director of WBAL in Baltimore, who stresses the value of building relationships between the assignment desk and the organizations that are regularly covered in TV newscasts.

It has been said that assignment editors tend to be "journalism people," which means tenacious pursuers of information who enjoy going after a story like a dog chasing a bone. The assignment desk might not be the most glamorous post in the newsroom—to viewers at home it's probably the most invisible part of the process—and it certainly isn't the calmest work environment. Furthermore, when something goes wrong, assignment editors are often the first to be blamed. For anyone who loves to chase news, however, the desk is a stimulating and rewarding place to be. It is no exaggeration to call assignment editors the unsung heroes of the newsroom.

Newscast Producers, Writers, and Web Journalists

In a word, *producers* are organizers. They organize the material that goes into TV newscasts, coordinate the various individuals who contribute to the effort, and make sure that every element of a program is ready when it comes time to air. Those who specialize in putting together newscasts are sometimes called show producers or line producers to distinguish them from field producers, whose work takes place on location. Newscast producers operate exclusively from the newsroom.

Chapter 7, "Newscast Producing," deals with the specifics of preparing a newscast, but in a nutshell the job involves choosing which stories will air and in which order; timing the program to make sure everything fits; and arranging live shots, graphics, and other production elements of the newscast. An important part of the producer's job is to communicate changes with the various members of the production team, both in advance of the program and while it is on the air. In the control room, this means talking with the director and other technical personnel, as well as anchors and reporters in the field. Because of the complicated nature of the process, producers need strong communication skills.

Above all else, producers need to be able to handle last-minute changes. Breaking news often changes a producer's carefully made plans, creating the need for a top-to-bottom restructuring of the program against a looming deadline. The pressure can be intense.

"A good producer needs to stay calm under pressure (there's a lot of it every day) and be prepared to redo large parts of a show or dump it altogether for breaking news," says Matt Gaffney, executive producer for WTTG-TV in Washington, D.C. Gaffney adds that the best producers know how to "take a fresh approach every day and not follow a stringent formula. They need to know when a story or a piece of video is so compelling that they just stay with it, knowing that the viewer at home wants to see it too."

WBAL's Tim Tunison stresses how important it is for producers to stay on top of the news locally, nationally, and around the world. "The producer has the responsibility of selecting how many of those stories will fit in his or her newscast. Essentially, the producer is deciding what the audience learns about the world. I don't think many producers understand how awesome a responsibility that is."

The work is often grueling, and the rigors of producing newscasts day in and day out can take a toll. A recent study of local TV news producers in Texas found that one-fifth were experiencing burnout or were at risk for burnout. Almost half the producers surveyed reported high levels of exhaustion, and two-thirds scored high on cynicism. On the other hand, an overwhelming majority of respondents felt they were effective in their jobs.

Writers concentrate exclusively on writing scripts for the newscast. In smaller markets the producer of a newscast is likely to write most of the stories, perhaps with help from the show's anchors and reporters. Larger market news operations have staff writers who do not get involved in the producing. Their job is to write a variety of studio-based news stories, often from wire copy or other outside sources. Writers also put together package intros and write scripts for teases and billboards. Like everyone else in a TV newsroom, writers must work quickly under intense deadline pressure.

What makes a good television news writer? According to Jennifer Street, former news director of WBZ-TV in Boston, the best writers "know what to distill, know what the lead is, and know how to use active language." Like many newsrooms around the country, WBZ runs occasional writing seminars for its journalists to help them polish their skills.

Web journalists, the newest additions to the TV news team, execute many of the same functions as traditional producers and writers. The key difference is that their efforts are devoted to preparing content for the organization's website. Again, the ability to work quickly and efficiently is critical. Chapter 10, "Television News on the Web," examines in detail the work of these online journalists.

Web-based journalism is one of the growth areas of television news. Jennifer Street points out that the best online producers and writers are those who understand content. The basic requirements of the job? "Great writing and great storytelling," she says. "That doesn't change for the web."

On-Camera Journalists

In Chapter 5, "The On-Camera Journalist," we take a detailed look at the job requirements of news anchors and reporters, including interviewing, covering breaking news,

Interviewing on camera is one of the better-known functions of television journalists, but behind the scenes a crew of producers, videographers, sound people, directors, and other technicians is also working to get the product on the air.

beat reporting, and going live from the field. For now, we quickly summarize the principal roles of news professionals who work in front of the camera.

Television reporters cover a wide range of subject matter. *General assignment reporters* can be sent out on virtually any kind of story, depending on what develops. When a general assignment reporter shows up for work, he or she has no idea what lies ahead. More often than not, these reporters will spend the day covering breaking news.

By contrast, *beat reporters* work within a narrower range. Beat reporters are specialty journalists, assigned to a regular topic area: politics, crime, entertainment, health, consumer news, features, and the like.

News anchors are a news organization's public face and first-line communicators. In addition to delivering the news, they may also serve as reporters, interviewers, and writers. Beyond their work in the newsroom, anchors function as a news organization's public relations representatives.

Most, but not all, anchors start off as reporters. Some newsrooms split the job into anchor-reporter, with part of the person's work schedule devoted to the anchor desk and the rest to reporting. Weekend anchors, for instance, often spend their other workdays as reporters. For most people in this job, however, anchoring the news is a full-time occupation.

Specialty Units

Especially in larger television markets, newsrooms may devote *specialty units* to a particular area such as investigative stories, consumer reports, medical news, or entertainment stories.

The size and scope of these units varies greatly. In the Boston market, to cite one example, all the major TV news operations run *investigative units*, usually consisting of at least one or two full-time producers, plus a staff of reporters who either work exclusively for the unit or alternate between investigative work and general assignment reporting. The key difference between daily journalism and investigative journalism is time.

Because of the more complex subject matter, investigative reporters and producers are given more lead time to track down information and file stories. By the same token, the stories themselves frequently run in a longer form than the standard minute-and-a-half package, sometimes taking shape as multipart series or magazine pieces. Investigative units are typically staffed by the station's most aggressive and experienced reporters, who have proven themselves capable of handling more complicated assignments.

Specialty units in other topic areas—consumer affairs, health, entertainment, and the like—tend to be smaller, often with only a single producer and single reporter. A slightly different category is the *special projects unit*, which tackles a variety of assignments, many of which fall outside the realm of daily journalism. A station's special projects unit may be in charge of coordinating election coverage or other events that receive widespread local coverage. Special projects might also generate high-profile material for regular newscasts. Unlike other specialty units, special projects teams do not generally have full-time reporters. Instead, they are staffed by producers.

Specialty units tend not to be found in small- and medium-market TV stations, where staffs are much smaller.

Sports and Weather

In addition to the journalistic specialties, TV newsrooms generally include sports and weather teams. The most visible components of these operations are the on-camera *sports anchors, sports reporters,* and *weatherpersons* who present the newscasts' sports and weather segments. Stations in larger markets might supplement on-air positions with full-time producers, especially for sports. These producers function in much the same way as the newscast producers, but their work is limited to a specific portion of the program.

At some TV stations weatherpersons may contribute science and environmental stories to news programs in addition to their meteorological reports. Weatherpersons are also responsible for producing their own regular segments in the newscast.

Photographers and Editors

Like reporters, *photographers* (sometimes called videographers or video journalists) do most of their work in the field. Every day, in coordination with the assignment desk, photographers team up with reporters to cover whichever stories are on the agenda. Rarely do photographers know in advance what they will be shooting, which means they must be able to handle any kind of assignment.

In addition to having highly developed visual skills, photographers need to work fast, particularly in the case of breaking news, where there might be no second chance to get a shot. Like everybody else in a TV newsroom, photographers must have the ability to work collaboratively. Another job requirement is strong communication and negotiating skills, because photographers often find themselves in situations where people might not want to have their pictures taken.

It is not unusual in smaller markets for reporters to do their own shooting, an arrangement called the "one-man band." Doing double duty as a reporter and videographer poses

News videographers never know what kind of story they may be assigned to shoot. They must be prepared for every kind of subject matter and every kind of work situation.

a number of challenges, especially when the journalist has to shoot him- or herself in an on-camera stand-up. It is similarly difficult to conduct interviews from behind the camera, as the tendency of the interviewee is to want to look at the reporter while answering questions, a tricky matter when the questioner's face is hidden behind a viewfinder.

Beth Parker, a reporter at WTTG-TV in Washington, D.C., shot her own stories as part of her first TV news job in Harrisonburg, Va. "It felt like torture at the time," she recalls, "but I am eternally grateful that I shot for myself for that first year or so. It really laid a foundation for becoming a successful storyteller. You simply can't tell a TV story well unless you appreciate how to meld pictures, sounds, and words."

Most medium and large markets do not require reporters to shoot their own stories, freeing the journalist to concentrate on gathering information and interview bites without also dealing with camera angles, lighting, and audio. Even so, journalists generally involve themselves to some degree in suggesting shots and making sure the video matches the contents of the script. If reporters and photographers are not in synch, problems are bound to occur when it comes time to edit the story.

Unlike photographers, *editors* are almost always based in the studio. Working from a reporter's script, the editor takes raw footage that has been shot in the field and fashions it into a coherent story. The hallmarks of a good editor are creativity, a sharp eye, and an ability to turn around a finished product under intense deadline pressure, in some cases just minutes before the piece hits the air.

In larger TV markets video editors do nothing but edit tape. The situation varies in small and medium markets, where the photographer who has shot the story could also be the person who edits it. The reporter who writes the script might also be called on to handle the editing. With a one-man-band arrangement, the reporter-photographer might have the additional responsibility of editing the story once he or she gets back to the station.

However challenging the exercise, journalists gain valuable insight from knowing how to put together a story in the editing room. Sean Kelly, a reporter at Boston's WCVB-TV, got his start at a small-market TV station in Fayetteville, Ark. "I've done my own shooting and a lot of my own editing. I think knowledge of both is vital to telling better stories. Especially with editing, you need an understanding of how the video and writing flow together."

Newsroom Executives

Although often overlooked in discussions of newsroom personnel, management figures play a leading role in setting the tone and direction of a TV station's news operation. Let's take a look at a few of the key positions.

The top management figure in a television newsroom is the *news director*, the person charged with overseeing every aspect of the news operation. In a large newsroom the responsibilities of the news director might be divided among several individuals, with the top position somewhat removed from the day-to-day mechanics of getting news programs on the air. In small to medium markets the news director is likely to take a more hands-on approach. All news directors deal with issues of personnel and hiring, financial management of the newsroom, and maintaining journalistic integrity. All news directors also coordinate with other departments at the television station.

Much of the news director's energy goes toward providing leadership, a difficult and amorphous task whatever the size of the operation. In markets large and small, the news director sets the prevailing tone. "It's the news director's responsibility to communicate the TV station's message to the entire newsroom and make sure it's followed," says WBAL-TV's Tim Tunison. "Smaller market news directors spend the majority of their time training the younger members of their staff. Large market news directors spend the majority of their time managing problems with staff members and balancing budgets, two things they don't teach you in Journalism 101."

News directors generally work their way up through the newsroom ranks, many of them beginning as producers or assignment editors. It is less typical for on-air personnel like reporters and anchors to make the transition into management, although not unheard of. Staffers on the technical side of the newsroom (photographers, editors, satellite coordinators, etc.) are also less likely to advance into management positions. The management skills required of assignment editors and newscast producers make these backgrounds more applicable to news directorships.

Larger newsrooms often supplement the news director with supporting management positions. The most common job titles are *assistant news directors, managing editors,* and *executive producers.* Responsibilities can vary from newsroom to newsroom, but in each case these executive-level managers have direct oversight of the daily news product.

The first two categories, assistant news directors and managing editors, contribute to the process in several ways: making news judgments, running the daily planning meetings, coordinating with the various players involved in the newscast production, and serving as front-line decision makers when issues need to be resolved. In some newsrooms the title of managing editor is given to the anchorperson. This means different things in different news organizations, but because the anchor has other responsibilities, the anchorperson–managing editor is likely to take a less hands-on approach than a managing editor with no on-camera role.

The exact job description of executive producer varies greatly from shop to shop. Executive producers might be assigned to a single newscast, or they might oversee more than one program. At some stations the executive producer reviews scripts and rundowns before the newscast goes on the air. In others the executive producer does essentially the same thing as any other newscast producer.

Other News Jobs

Depending on the market, television newsrooms might employ other staffers with differing job responsibilities. Some of these positions are technical—the ENG crews who handle the production side of the day's live shots, for example. Others are artistic in nature, like the *graphic designers* who create and execute the visuals that supplement TV newscasts. Chapter 9, "TV News Graphics, Titles, and Supers" takes an in-depth look at this increasingly important element of television journalism.

Larger newsrooms might also employ full-time *archivists* or librarians, who save all the stories that air and integrate them into a searchable database for future reference. A high percentage of news stories unfold over time, giving reporters and producers reason to revisit previously shot footage as new developments occur. A newsroom archivist is the person who facilitates this process by cataloguing the stories that air on the various newscasts.

Promotions/Creative Services

With the exception of the routine teases that run within newscasts, promotional spots are frequently written and produced by nonnews personnel who specialize in marketing. Although these individuals are not journalists per se, they work closely with the newsroom to generate viewership and bring positive attention to the product. This part of the organization is called different things in different shops: the department might go by the name promotions, creative services, or something similar.

Promotions producers offer a range of support for TV news organizations. They may create campaigns that highlight individual newscasts and anchor teams or specific phases of the operation such as the investigative unit, weather, or sports. These types of promotional messages fall under the umbrella heading of generic spots.

They might also produce topical spots that emphasize specific stories, multipart series, or perhaps a prestigious award the newsroom has won. In larger markets the promotions department might get involved in putting together a newscast's opening billboards or preshow teases, the portions of the program designed to draw audiences into watching.

Another common type of promotional message is the proof of performance spot, which reminds viewers that a news operation has broken a big story. The copy for these messages usually goes something like this: "When such-and-such an event took place, Channel 2 News was first to bring you the story," accompanied by visuals from the event in question. Although these self-congratulatory promos can be useful in reinforcing a station's commitment to breaking news, they sometimes run the risk of appearing to take advantage of an unfortunate situation.

DAY-TO-DAY OPERATIONS IN A TV NEWSROOM

Although no two days are exactly alike in a television newsroom, the fixed timetable of newscasts dictates a set structure for the day's activities. Key deadlines revolve around airtimes, which at most local stations fall into four general periods: early morning, noon, late afternoon, and late evening, either at 10 p.m. or 11 p.m. Not every station will carry news in every available time slot, and a less intensive schedule of news programming runs on the weekends.

With a full lineup of daily and weekend newscasts and constant updates on the web, news personnel work virtually around the clock, seven days a week, 365 days a year. Newsrooms are at their busiest, however, Monday through Friday from about 9 a.m. to 6:30 or 7 p.m. This is when the bulk of the news staff works, although other individuals are on duty at other times. For early-morning newscast producers the workday might begin at midnight and end at 8 a.m. Late-evening newscast producers start work early in the afternoon and leave late at night when their programs go off the air.

Staffers with the most normal schedules (if anything about TV news can be called normal) are those who work on the late-afternoon shows. More reporters and photographers are on duty during the day than at night or on weekends, because that's when most nonbreaking news gets covered. Newsroom executives also tend to work according to a regular daytime schedule. Of course, everyone's hours are subject to the demands of the day. All TV news personnel are on permanent standby in the event of major breaking news, and when there's a big story to cover, the entire staff is expected to pitch in.

During the week the workday in a TV newsroom generally begins with a planning meeting. The purpose of this meeting is to discuss story ideas, and it brings together a range of individuals: news executives, assignment editors, newscast and web producers, reporters, technicians, designers, and anyone else who needs to be in the big-picture loop. Because television news is a group effort, it is important for staff members with different responsibilities to communicate with each other, not just in the meeting, but throughout the day. Plans change quickly in a TV newsroom, and everyone must operate from the same playbook.

The morning meeting deals primarily with lining up material for the afternoon newscasts. In this meeting stories are discussed and pitched. Reporters and photographers are assigned to the topics deemed worthy of coverage. Stories are allocated among the various newscasts. Live shots are designated. Naturally, unscheduled events will come along to alter these plans—sometimes radically so—but the morning meeting gets the day off to an organized start.

It is likely that an early afternoon meeting will also be held in which the process is refined, both for the afternoon newscasts and the late-evening news. The process here is much the same: Assignments are made, stories are added to the rundown, and crews are dispatched. Reporters already in the field will have checked in with updates for the assignment desk, giving program producers a clearer idea of how these stories in progress should be played in the newscasts.

Throughout the workday, assignment editors continue to track breaking events, as producers for the various newscasts lay out their program rundowns and write their scripts. Out in the field, reporters and photographers shoot the interviews and cover footage they will need to put together news packages. All the participants, those at the station and those in the field, operate with an eye toward the looming deadlines. The pace steps up as airtime nears, and by the time the newscasts go on the air, the day's plans will have taken shape as a coherent product.

In addition to planning meetings, many stations conduct regular postmortems, during which the day's newscasts are analyzed. At Boston's WBZ-TV, for instance, the key participants meet for a 6:30 p.m. session that looks back at the 4 p.m., 5 p.m., and 6 p.m. newscasts. A less formal postshow meeting is held after the 11 p.m. newscast with the late-night executive producers, anchors, and producers. In each case the goal is to examine what went right and what went wrong, not as a means of punishing mistakes, but to learn lessons for the future.

WORKING IN TV NEWS

Television newsrooms attract a certain personality type: individuals who thrive on pressure, who work well as collaborators, who know how to communicate with each other and with the broader public, and who genuinely love the thrill of competition. Curiosity and patience are other key ingredients for anyone hoping to succeed in this dynamic and challenging field.

Everyone who works in a television newsroom is a slave to the clock. Although deadlines are an inescapable fact of life for all journalists, the pressures of delivering a live telecast in front of thousands and thousands of viewers makes TV news considerably more stressful than other forms of journalism. Newspaper reporters and editors face a single daily deadline. Magazine deadlines are even more generous. Web journalists work with a never-ending deadline, but if a story isn't ready it doesn't matter greatly if they post it 10 or 15 minutes late. Television offers no such luxury. When it's time to go, it's time to go, and the alternative to not being prepared is dead air.

The pressure isn't just about deadlines. The reality of TV news is that all plans are constantly subject to change. Breaking news can happen at any moment, and if it's a big enough story, a complete shift in priorities must occur. This can happen an hour before air, five minutes before air, or even while a program is in progress. Everyone involved—producers, reporters, photographers, editors, assignment editors—must keep a cool head to successfully navigate the situation.

Of course there's more to working in a TV newsroom than having the right personality. Equally important are the journalistic skills that come with this territory: writing, reporting, interviewing, making news judgments, and understanding ethics and legalities. The same qualities required of print journalists are also demanded by television news organizations. "TV stations are hungry for journalists," says Tim White, former managing editor of Boston's WBZ-TV. White sees a need for reporters and producers who "understand the power of the pictures, who know how to make contacts and how to search for documents."

In other words, the time-honored objectives of the profession—the ability to uncover, gather, and communicate information of value to the public—are still the best calling cards.

A common misconception about TV news is that it is a high-paying occupation. Although big salaries might be the norm for major-market anchors, reporters, and executives, the reality for most television journalists is quite different. Each year the Radio–Television News Directors Association (RTNDA), in association with Ball State University, conducts a salary survey of America's TV journalists. Results published in 2007 show a vast range of incomes, determined largely by market size. The bigger the market, the higher the salary. With more than 200 markets in the United States, the figures run from paltry to impressive.

Salaries for news directors started at $11,000 a year and topped out at $300,000. The average news director salary stood at $84,900, with the median at $74,000 (meaning half of the news directors surveyed made more than this figure, and half made less). For anchors the range was even greater: $8,500 at the low end and $1.2 million at the high end. The average for anchors was $72,400 and the median $60,000. News reporter salaries varied from $10,000 a year to $275,000, with an average of $35,600 and a median of $29,500.

In large-market newsrooms, producers rank among the highest-paid employees, attesting to the value placed on this critical position. At the top end of the spectrum, according to the RTNDA–Ball State survey, producers earned an annual income of $120,000, with the bottom end coming in at $9,500. The average producing salary was $31,900, with a median of $30,000. Assignment editors ranged from $11,000 to $80,000. Photographer salaries ran from a low of $7,000 to a high of $82,000.

As these figures show, television journalists in nonurban markets make surprisingly little money. It is not unheard of for TV reporters in small towns to take second jobs to cover their rent. Because most recent graduates start in these low-paying markets, newcomers to the field can expect to live modestly as they launch their careers.

The RTNDA–Ball State survey specifically examined salaries for starting hires with no previous full-time experience, and found that most newcomers to the profession can expect annual incomes in the low $20,000 range. The highest average starting salaries went to assignment editors and producers at $23,600. Averages for the other major positions—came in slightly lower than this figure.

Only by proving their skills and advancing into larger markets can television journalists hope to substantially increase the amount of money they make. Traditionally, this is the pattern TV news professionals have followed: taking their first job in small or medium-sized city, earning low wages, and gaining experience that prepares them to move up. Not everyone follows this path. Some television journalists start in entry-level positions in urban areas, and others prefer to spend their careers away from the big-city spotlight. The breadth of local television news in the United States offers an array of possibilities.

In the final analysis, for most practitioners the choice to work in TV news has little to do with money. Those who pursue this profession do so because they love the excitement, the challenge, and the psychological rewards that come from doing good journalism. There's another factor worth noting: Television newsrooms are vibrant places full of creative and interesting people. However intense it might be, the work is rarely dull. Most days it can be a great deal of fun.

"I am convinced you must be a little crazy to succeed in TV news," says Anna Crowley, a reporter who started off in market 169 (Utica), advanced to market 80 (Syracuse), and now works at WCNC-TV in Charlotte, the country's 25th largest market. "You get in this business because you are excited about it. There are going to be some highs and there are going to be some pretty painful lows." Crowley's advice to would-be TV journalists: "Have patience, don't take things personally, and hang in there."

DIVERSITY IN TV NEWSROOMS

What kinds of people pursue careers in television journalism? Increasingly the field is becoming a female domain. The old days of TV news as a boys' club, comically depicted in the Will Ferrell movie *Anchorman: The Legend of Ron Burgundy,* have vanished into history. Today women outnumber men in many key newsroom jobs, especially on camera. A 2005 survey by the RTNDA and Ball State University found that 57.2 percent of local TV news anchors and 57.8 percent of reporters were female. Similar numbers applied to off-camera positions like executive producers (54.9 percent), news producers (65.9 percent), and news writers (55.6 percent).

In the highest echelon jobs, however, men continue to dominate: According to the RTNDA–Ball State survey for 2006, men accounted for about three-quarters of the nation's news directors, although women held a higher percentage of these jobs in the largest markets.

Other newsroom positions remain largely male-dominated. In 2005 a whopping 93.4 percent of TV news photographers were men. So were 68 percent of tape editors, 92.8

Television news combines work created and produced in a studio environment with work created and produced in the field, as in this interview by Ed Bradley for the long-running news magazine *60 Minutes.*

percent of sports anchors, 89.5 percent of sports reporters, and 79 percent of weathercasters. It remains to be seen how rapidly women will increase their participation in these traditionally male positions.

Gender offers one index of newsroom diversity. Television news organizations also strive for ethnic and racial diversity in their staffing, although some stations show better results than others. According to the 2006 annual survey by RTNDA and Ball State University, minorities made up 22.2 percent of local TV news staffs around the United States. Among news directors—the top newsroom position—the percentage of minorities stood at 13.2.

Big-city TV stations are more likely than their small-town counterparts to have minorities on staff. In the top 25 U.S. markets, nearly a third of the employees were African-American, Hispanic, Asian-American, or Native American. This rate reflects national population estimates, which show that 33.6 percent of the American population is non-Caucasian.

Why is diversity important in television newsrooms? "To effectively cover our communities, the people who work in our newsrooms and manage our operations must reflect various viewpoints and life experiences," wrote Chris Berry in the *Communicator*, the official publication of the RTNDA. "By having a diverse staff covering the news that affects our entire audience, our listeners and viewers will be better informed, and they might just learn something new about their neighbors."

A number of national organizations devote themselves to furthering diversity in the newsroom, including the following:

- The Asian American Journalists Association
  Website: www.aaja.org

- The National Association of Black Journalists
  Website: www.nabj.org

- The National Association of Hispanic Journalists
  Website: www.nahj.org

- The National Lesbian and Gay Journalists Association
  Website: www.nlgja.org

- Native American Journalists Association
  Website: www.naja.com

- Unity: Journalists of Color, Inc. (This organization is an alliance of the Asian American Journalists Association, National Association of Black Journalists, National Association of Hispanic Journalists, and the Native American Journalists Association.)
  Website: www.unityjournalists.org

- American Women in Radio and Television
  Website: www.awrt.org

A visit to the websites of these organizations provides an excellent introduction to each group and what it does. Of particular relevance to students are the sections about scholarships, workshops, and career networking opportunities. The associations also post news items of interest to their communities, along with job listings, links to journalistic resources, and industry updates. Each organization holds an annual national convention, as well as numerous local gatherings, and many of these events feature programs for student journalists.

It bears mentioning that Hispanic TV stations are a particular growth area for local television news, with increasing numbers of local Spanish-language newscasts popping up around the United States. As the national population grows more diverse, such trends are likely to continue.

CHECKLIST OF KEY POINTS

Although on-camera jobs are the most visible positions in a TV news operation, most of the work in a newsroom takes place behind the scenes. Here are the main jobs:

- The assignment desk is the nerve center of the newsroom, where assignment editors keep on top of breaking news, plan for upcoming events, and dispatch reporters and crews to cover stories.

- Newscast producers, writers, and web journalists generate content that appears on the station's news programs and website. Whether their work appears online or on the air, producers must be well organized, quick, and skilled at making news judgments.

- On-camera journalists fall into two principal categories: reporters and anchors. General assignment reporters cover the day's breaking news, whereas beat reporters concentrate their work in specific topic areas. Anchors deliver stories from the news desk, and also report from the field.

- Big-market television newsrooms are likely to have specialty units that produce in-depth content such as investigative journalism and other news-related special projects.

- Sports and weather personnel specialize in their particular areas, either on camera or off, and are considered an integral part of the news team.

- Photographers and editors represent the technical side of television journalism. Photographers accompany reporters as they cover events in the field, and editors turn raw video into polished stories back at the station or sometimes from remote editing facilities. In smaller markets, reporters might be expected to shoot and edit their own stories.

- News executives are responsible for the management side of the operation, providing oversight of journalistic content as well as administrative oversight of budgets, personnel, and long-range planning. The lead person in any TV newsroom is the news director. Many stations also have other management positions, with titles like assistant news director, managing editor, and executive producer.

- Other newsroom positions include a range of specialties: ENG crews, who oversee production from remote locations; graphic artists, who design the news graphics that appear in newscasts and on the website; and archivists, who catalog news materials for easy referencing. Promotions producers focus on creating advertising and marketing campaigns for the station's news product.

- Television journalism is a round-the-clock effort, with a timetable dictated by the station's schedule of newscasts. Key newsroom personnel meet for regular planning meetings to discuss the day's coverage. They also hold postnewscast critiques.

- Working in a TV newsroom requires flexibility and a level head. Events change constantly, and the process unfolds against relentless deadlines. TV news is a fiercely competitive arena where the basic skills of journalism—writing, reporting, and interviewing—get a constant workout.

- Although TV journalism can be lucrative for on-air personalities in large cities, salary levels as a general rule are not particularly high. Compensation varies greatly from job to job and market to market, with stations in larger cities paying substantially better than those in small towns.

- Increasingly television news is becoming a female-dominated field, especially among reporters, anchors, and producers. More and more women are joining the ranks of news executives, although other jobs (photographers, sports anchors, and weathercasters) remain overwhelmingly male.
- Television newsrooms seek to assemble staffs that are racially and ethnically diverse. News is something that affects all communities in the viewing audience, and diversity in hiring helps bring diversity in coverage.

ASSIGNMENTS/ANALYSIS

- Determine from the job descriptions in this chapter which of the various newsroom positions you find most intriguing. Contact a professional TV journalist in your area who works in that position to find out more about his or her job.
- Visit the websites of your local TV news operations and study the biographies of the journalists who work there. See what trends you can discern about careers in TV news.
- Using the internet, conduct an informal survey of job openings at television news operations around the country. From these postings write a brief report on what kind of employees are being sought and what news directors are looking for in potential staffers. If you have a particular area of interest (anchoring, reporting, producing, shooting, etc.) concentrate your analysis on those listings.

WRITING
AND REPORTING

CHAPTER TWO

THE LANGUAGE OF TELEVISION NEWS

TOPICS DISCUSSED IN THIS CHAPTER

- Writing in a Two-Track Language
- Writing for TV Versus Writing for Other News Media
- Writing in a Conversational Style
- Using the Parts of Speech in TV News Scripts
- Other TV Newswriting Issues • Checklist of Key Points

ASSIGNMENTS/ANALYSIS

- Assignment: Television Newswriting Style • Analysis

WRITING IN A TWO-TRACK LANGUAGE

On the surface, television newswriting may seem like a fairly basic craft. It involves fewer words than print journalism, there are pictures to facilitate the reporting, and the stories themselves are short and to the point. In reality, though, writing for TV news is just as difficult as writing for other any other form of journalism. In some ways, it can be even more daunting.

What sets TV newswriting apart is that it operates according to a two-track language: the language of pictures and sound. The fundamental challenge for anyone writing in this dual language is to take full advantage of what both tracks offer. As you learn to do this, you will see that the choices are more varied and complicated than they might initially seem.

The visual side of the two-track language generally means video: moving imagery recorded in the field to illustrate the story in question. However, visuals can also take the form of still images, graphics, animation, archival footage, maps, lists, charts, or any other visual elements that are contextually appropriate. Creative storytellers take advantage of a range of visual opportunities, pressing into service whatever works best to make the information comprehensible and interesting.

The audio side of the equation divides into two basic categories: sound that has been recorded in the field at the location of a story, and written narration that is delivered by a reporter or an anchor. Sound recorded in the field can be either sound bites—quotes from an interviewee—or natural sound, which is noninterview audio that helps tell the story. Natural sound (often abbreviated as nat sound or natsot, for natural sound on tape) can consist of anything from music or applause to traffic noise or the sound of hammers at a construction site. Narration from the reporter or anchor involves words that are written specifically for the story. These can be read live during a newscast or recorded in an audio booth and edited into the taped product.

In this two-track language, pictures and sound serve as complementary layers, each delivering something unique to the audience. TV newswriters must properly use these layers to convey the maximum amount of information within the allotted time and structure. At the same time, the writing must follow the guidelines of good journalism.

Like other languages, the dual-track language of pictures and sound observes its own grammar. Mastering this grammar is the key to functioning successfully as a television newswriter. Over the next few chapters you will learn how to combine written language, interview sound bites, natural sound, and a variety of visuals to create TV news stories. Before introducing the full range of visual and sound elements that go into TV newswriting, let's concentrate on the mechanics of written language in television news.

WRITING FOR TV VERSUS WRITING FOR OTHER NEWS MEDIA

Writing for a television newscast is profoundly different from writing for print. Unlike print journalism, which typically comes across as impersonal and disembodied, television news has a human face. An individual—either an anchor or reporter—is telling the audience the news of the day. TV news represents a personal transaction between the journalists who deliver the information and the viewers who watch.

Because of this, television news stories are written for the ear, as well as for the eye. Where print stories allow readers to control the pace, TV news unfolds according to its own schedule. Audience members have only one opportunity to hear the information and assimilate it (unless, of course, they're watching on the web). Writers of television news scripts must be sure the story makes complete sense the first time it is delivered.

TV newswriting follows a straightforward, uncomplicated tone. This means simple sentence structure, less use of detail in the text, and a writing style that is conversational yet authoritative. If the script is anything less than completely clear, there's a good chance of confusing the audience.

Unlike print stories, TV news scripts do not adhere to the inverted pyramid structure, in which all the important details come in the first paragraph. In a television context this would be impossible. Instead, each sentence in a TV news script adds a new piece of information, so that the accumulated facts make sense by the end of the story. The brevity of TV news scripts—often they are only a few sentences in length—challenges the writer to omit all extraneous details.

Print journalism emphasizes relatively minor facts, such as street addresses, ages, precise times, and so forth. Because TV news stories are so short, some of this detail must inevitably be omitted. A television news script distills a story down to its essence, forgoing many of the particulars that appear in a typical newspaper account. When it comes to TV, the general rule is this: Less is more. Remember that in television much of this extra detail emerges through the use of visuals. Furthermore, details that are not included in the story can be incorporated into story introductions or tags, or posted on the TV station's website.

As a medium for storytelling, television has one enormous advantage over print, according to veteran journalist Larry Hatteberg of KAKE-TV in Wichita: it transmits "experience." "The newspaper can give you every 'fact' you ever wanted to know about a subject. But only television can give you a 'feeling' for a person or an event," Hatteberg says. "Newspaper writers will disagree, but not until you have looked into someone's eyes and heard him speak can you make up your mind about his character. Television does that more effectively than any other medium."

In its structure and tone, television newswriting more closely resembles radio news-writing than print journalism. At the same time, because of its pictorial nature, TV news has parallels to filmmaking, especially in its use of visual grammar. Whatever the similarities and differences, one common denominator runs through all journalistic writing: the need for accuracy, balance, and objectivity. This is as true of TV news as it is for print, radio, and online journalism.

WRITING IN A CONVERSATIONAL STYLE

Television news is delivered by human beings, not as a disembodied collection of paragraphs on a page. This calls for a writing style more conversational in tone than the omniscient language of print journalism. Another way of looking at this is to remember that TV news involves writing words that will be heard, rather than read, by the audience.

With that in mind, here are a few pointers.

TV News Scripts Speak Directly to Viewers

The content of television news stories is communicated from journalists to viewers in a direct and personal way. Therefore it is perfectly acceptable in TV newswriting to use contractions in your scripts, because that's the way people talk.

> **Print style**
> Police do not have any suspects in the case, and they have not released a description of the intruder.

> **TV style**
> Police don't have a suspect in the case. They haven't released a description of the intruder.

One word of caution, however, about using contractions: Certain contractions—shouldn't, wouldn't, and couldn't—can sound confusing when spoken aloud. In those cases, stick with both words: should not, would not, and could not.

The use of the second-person "you" is also common in TV news, unlike print, where directly addressing the audience would seem out of place. A TV news script might say something like this: "Authorities recommend that you stock up on basic supplies before the blizzard arrives." The idea is to relate the information to the viewer, again, because it is being delivered by a person, not a disembodied paragraph.

A conversational style does not mean language that is overly casual or off-the-cuff. After all, anchor and reporter scripts are written in advance for a reason, so that they will be accurate and to the point. You can think of TV news style as representing a compromise between written English and spoken English.

TV News Scripts Favor Clear, Straightforward Language

This guideline also stems from the conversational tone of television news scripts. Given a choice between a fancy word and a simple word, go for the simple word. When in doubt, ask yourself how you would say something if you were relaying the story to a friend. Would you tell your friend that "10 people are deceased after a tornado struck," or that "10 people are dead"? Would you refer to a "three-story edifice" or a "three-story building"? Inevitably the less pretentious language works best.

Here are a few more examples of fancy words and their conversational counterparts: prior to/before, subsequent to/after, utilize/use, possess/have, erroneous/wrong, initiate/begin, commence/begin, terminate/end, encounter/meet, inform/tell, purchase/buy, ascertain/determine. The list goes on, but in each case the TV news writer is better off with the more straightforward term.

By the same token, try not to use foreign words or phrases that might be unfamiliar to your audience. Find a substitute in plain English.

Weak
The mayor will host a soiree for the visiting dignitaries.

Better
The mayor will host a party for the visiting dignitaries.

Weak
One of the speakers made an embarrassing faux pas.

Better
One of the speakers made an embarrassing error.

TV News Scripts Follow Simple Sentence Construction

A good rule of thumb in structuring your sentences is to follow an S/V/O pattern: subject, verb, object. "Fire struck a downtown cathedral" is about as simple as a sentence can be, which makes it perfect for someone to read out loud. The S/V/O construction is not only more concise, it also casts the sentence in active voice.

To the extent possible, avoid compound sentences and clauses within your sentences. If you find yourself using either of these structures, take the secondary part of the information and make a new sentence out of it. As a general guideline, each sentence should be limited to a single thought.

The following sentence contains an internal clause:

The Capitol building, which has not been renovated in 50 years, will get a face-lift beginning next summer.

Rewriting this for a TV news script, we can improve the text by expressing the information in two parts. Try reading both versions out loud, and you will hear the difference:

The Capitol building will get a face-lift beginning next summer. It was last renovated 50 years ago.

Similarly, compound sentences will probably work better as two separate sentences. Here's a sentence that's too long for a TV news script:

Police arrested 10 suspects at the scene of the demonstration, and court appearances have been set for next week.

Yet that same information reads fine as two sentences, especially out loud:

Police arrested 10 suspects at the scene of the demonstration. Court appearances have been set for next week.

When presenting a series of details, it is usually best to separate the information into several short sentences. Think of this as the principle of "bite-sized chunks." Short sentences might feel choppy on the page, but when they are read out loud, they make perfect sense.

Here's an example of a sentence that works better in print than it would in a TV news script:

The suspects, both of whom were residents of the dorm where the burglaries occurred, will be charged in county court with theft and trespassing, and will face judicial charges from the university.

For television, let's break this down into three short sentences, or, bite-sized chunks:

Both suspects are students in the dorm where the burglaries occurred. They'll be charged in county court with theft and trespassing. The university has filed separate judicial charges.

Do you hear the difference?

TV News Scripts Avoid Too Much Negation

Because TV journalists write for the ear, it is preferable to cast sentences in the positive form rather than the negative. This makes the information easier to understand.

Weak
The donation represents a not insubstantial gift to the school.

Better
The donation represents a substantial gift to the school.

Weak
The accident scene lies not five miles from where a similar event took place last year.

Better
The accident scene is less than five miles from where a similar event took place last year.

The same rule applies to the subject of your sentences.

Weak
No one knows for certain how long the highway will remain closed.

Better
The highway will remain closed for an indefinite period of time.

TV News Scripts Place Attribution at the Beginning of the Story

In TV and radio news stories the source typically is given before the information, giving audience members an opportunity to evaluate the source's credibility. This is not necessarily the case in print journalism.

Print style
The suspect was dressed in an Easter bunny costume, eyewitnesses told police.

TV/radio style
Eyewitnesses told police the suspect was wearing an Easter bunny costume.

As in print journalism, the most common verb used in making an attribution is "to say." Don't substitute other verbs in an attempt to sound more official. TV news style generally calls for the present-tense form of the verb.

Wrong
The attorney general declared he would file charges next week.

Right
The attorney general says he'll file charges next week.

Similarly, don't confuse "to say" with "to explain." Just because something is said doesn't mean it's explained.

Wrong
The governor explained that he will make the announcement in Finchester.

Right
The governor says he'll make the announcement in Finchester.

By the same token, avoid the temptation to come up with fancy synonyms for say: state, declare, aver, and the like.

Wrong
The police chief declared that armed robberies have declined dramatically from last year.

Right
The police chief says armed robberies have declined dramatically from last year.

TV News Scripts Make Frequent Use of Transitions

Newscasts and individual news stories present a wide range of information in a short amount of time, which means they can feel disjointed. Adding transitions to your scripts helps viewers make the shift, and makes things easier on the anchors, who might look uncomfortable when asked to execute an awkward segue.

Transitions are particularly helpful when the content veers dramatically from one subject to another. Such expressions as "Closer to home," "Back in this country," and "In local news" are useful in signaling a shift in geographical location. Sometimes the transitions are time-related: terms like "meanwhile," or "earlier in the day." Transitions can also indicate a shift in topics: "Turning to medical news" or "From the world of sports." Whenever possible, use transitions to soften sharp turns within newscasts.

TV News Scripts Avoid Homophones

Because the audience hears, but does not read, the script, steer clear of homophones, words that, when spoken, sound like other words. Several examples from the religious

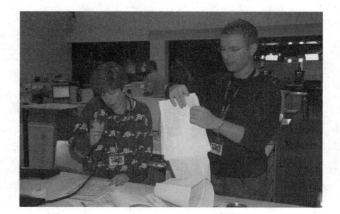

Writing television news stories demands a great deal of attention to detail. A mistake-riddled script could result in confusion on the air.

realm make the point: *sects* is not the same as *sex*, however similar they might sound. *Pray* does not mean *prey*. *Wholly* does not mean *holy*. A good habit to get into as you write television news scripts is to read the copy out loud to yourself. You'll hear problems that might not be apparent on the page.

Here are a few more examples of potentially troublesome homophones: magnet/magnate, sole/soul/Seoul, dam/damn.

Using that last pair, let's consider how easy it might be for viewers to hear the story wrong. Suppose this was the sentence:

The dam-building is expected to be complete next month.

To the audience it might sound as if the anchor had just referred to a "damn building." The problem can easily be fixed with a rewrite:

Construction of the dam is expected to be complete next month.

USING THE PARTS OF SPEECH IN TV NEWS SCRIPTS

By parts of speech we mean the different categories of words and phrases that make up the building blocks of written and spoken language: verbs, nouns and pronouns, adjectives, adverbs, conjunctions, and interjections. With the exception of the last two, these parts of speech are of particular relevance in television newswriting.

Verbs

To the extent possible, TV news writers should employ action verbs; that is, vivid verbs that paint a word picture or emphasize activity. Use a high ratio of verbs to nouns. If you want to improve your writing, check your verbs first. Make sure they are as active as the situation allows, and that there are enough of them.

Here are a few other guidelines for using verbs in TV news scripts.

Active Versus Passive Voice. Write in active voice, not passive voice. In other words, it works better to say "Fire destroyed a downtown church today" than "A downtown church was destroyed by fire today." In the first example a thing (the subject) does something (the action) to something (the object). The second example, written in passive voice, lacks punch. Active voice strengthens your sentences by emphasizing the action (verb) and its cause (subject).

Another way to think about this is to follow the S/V/O sentence construction described earlier. "Flood waters devastated an Oklahoma town this morning" packs a stronger punch than "An Oklahoma town was devastated by flood waters this morning," and it has the added benefit of being shorter.

Take a look at two additional examples of active versus passive voice, and see how writing in the active voice improves the structure:

Weak
The award for best costume was presented to an 80-year-old great-grandmother.

Better
An 80-year-old great-grandmother won the award for best costume.

Weak
Authorities say the rockets were fired by guerillas from half a mile away.

Better
Authorities say guerillas fired the rockets from half a mile away.

Present-Tense Leads. Most TV news stories are written with a present-tense lead to bring the story as up-to-the-minute as possible. The idea is to convey to viewers that what they are hearing is the absolute latest information. Once you've established the present-tense lead, you can then shift into past tense for the rest of the story.

The following past-tense lead is factually accurate, but not exactly fresh:

Vandals did extensive damage to a statue of George Washington in City Park last night. Police have not made any arrests.

By bringing the lead forward into the present tense, the script emphasizes what is current about the story:

Police are looking for the vandals who damaged the statue of George Washington in City Park last night. So far they haven't made any arrests.

Be careful that you are writing a true present-tense lead, not just a lead with a present-tense verb. This means finding the latest angle on the story and incorporating it into the lead. Here's a lead with a present-tense verb that is not as up-to-the-minute as it could be:

A semi trailer crashes on the interstate this morning, critically injuring the driver.

A better version of this is to add a fresh detail to the lead sentence:

The driver of a semi trailer is in critical condition at this hour after an early morning crash on the interstate.

Almost any lead can be written in the present tense, even when the situation appears to be over and done with. Consider the following sentence:

A local policeman died in a downtown shootout this afternoon.

Even if no new developments have occurred, the lead can easily be brought into the present tense:

A local policeman is dead tonight following a shootout downtown.

Rewriting "to Be" Verbs. Because the verb "to be" is such a common ingredient of language, it tends to get overused. The problem in a TV newswriting context is that the various forms of "to be"—is, am, are, was, were, be, being, and been—describe a state of existence rather than action. See if you can find a more active way to express your meaning without relying on a form of the verb "to be."

These examples show how a stronger verb makes for a punchier sentence:

Weak
The parade is the first in a week-long series of centennial events.

Better
The parade kicks off a week-long series of centennial events.

By the same token, avoid writing sentences that begin with "there is" and "there are." These are also lackluster verbs that can usually be replaced with something more vibrant. It is better to say "A plane crashed near Denver today" than "There was a plane crash near Denver today." In the first version the verb does much of the sentence's heavy lifting, and it also benefits by being shorter. The second version feels watered down and overlong.

Here are a few more examples:

Weak
There were burial services in Ohio today for the victims of a school bus crash.

Better
Burial services took place in Ohio today for the victims of a school bus crash.

Weak
There are 25 additional police officers assigned to security at the arena.

Better
Twenty-five additional police officers will handle security at the arena.

Weak
There was a derailment in San Francisco this morning involving a commuter train.

Better
A commuter train ran off the tracks in San Francisco this morning.

Other Problem Verbs

Certain other verbs should raise a red flag for TV news writers.

"To Continue." This is a weak verb that cues the audience that nothing new is going on in the story. Find another way to express the information.

Weak
Protests continue to cause headaches for American diplomats in the Middle East.

Better
A new round of protests is complicating diplomatic efforts in the Middle East.

"To Force" or "To Be Forced." News writers commonly misuse this verb. It should be reserved for occasions when actual physical force is involved.

Weak
Promoters were forced to cancel tonight's concert because of slow ticket sales.

Better
Promoters cancelled tonight's concert because of slow ticket sales.

"To Try." When following "try" with another verb, use the word "to," not "and."

Wrong
Inspectors will try and find the cause of the crash.

Right
Inspectors will try to find the cause of the crash.

Nouns

Be careful not to overuse nouns when verbs will carry some of the load for you. Sentence constructions that rely on a high proportion of nouns to verbs employ what is called a *nominal style*. Nominal style creates unnecessarily long sentences and downplays the importance of verbs.

Here's an example of a sentence written in nominal style:

Outside the school there is a statue of a man who became the first African-American senator from our state.

Here's a better way to write the sentence:

A statue of the state's first African-American senator stands outside the school.

The second version uses only a single verb and is several seconds shorter. Let's look at another example:

Weak
There is a supermarket in the downtown area that had to be destroyed by bulldozers because the building's roof collapsed due to heavy snow.

Better
Crews bulldozed the downtown supermarket after heavy snow caused the roof to collapse.

Adjectives and Adverbs

In general TV news writers use fewer adjectives and adverbs than their counterparts in print journalism. The reason for this is simple: With so many visuals helping to tell the story, descriptive words like adjectives and adverbs become less necessary. You don't need to say the truck is red, for example, because viewers can make that determination for themselves.

Adjectives can be problematic in TV news scripts when they cue the viewers about how they are supposed to feel. Be on guard against these subjective adjectives, which more often than not come across as clichés: *shocking, tragic, gut-wrenching, unbelievable,* or *heart-breaking.* Let the facts speak for themselves. If a story is tragic or shocking, audience members are smart enough to figure that out on their own.

Similarly, you might find yourself throwing in adverbs that add nothing to the meaning of the sentence, words like *literally, actually, definitely,* and *incidentally.* If you use one of these adverbs, ask yourself if the sentence loses anything without it.

Wrong
The snow fell nonstop for literally 24 hours.

Right
The snow fell nonstop for 24 hours.

Wrong
This is the first time that anyone has actually won the scholarship.

Right
This is the first time anyone has won the scholarship.

OTHER TV NEWSWRITING ISSUES

A number of other recurring issues face television news writers. Some of these deal with style, some with grammar, and some with the journalistic side of the process. Try to keep these points in mind as you write your television news scripts.

Abbreviations

Avoid abbreviations that are not widely understood, or that could confuse the audience. FBI and CIA are well-enough known that they can be used in a news story with no problem. The same is true of AFL-CIO, IRS, NATO, PTA, and YMCA. By contrast, DOJ (Department of Justice), DOT (Department of Transportation), ADA (American Dental Association or American Dairy Association), and others need clarification.

Wrong
According to the ADA, most Americans don't bother to floss.

Right
According the American Dental Association, most Americans don't bother to floss.

Absolutes

Absolutes are words that indicate a superlative state. News writers must be careful about using these unless they can be certified as true. If you can't attribute the claims to a

Television newswriters become proficient at using all the building blocks of visual storytelling: images, sound bites, natural sound, and reporter narration.

source, avoid them. Examples are words like *unique, unprecedented, oldest, youngest, biggest, smallest, first, most important,* and so on.

Wrong
The woman has a unique home—she lives on her own island.

Right
The woman has an unusual home—she lives on her own island.

Wrong
The giant cake will be the world's largest.

Right
Event sponsors say the giant cake will be the world's largest.

Age

Television and radio news style places a person's age before the name. In print the age goes after the name. TV and radio news stories do not routinely cite ages the way print stories do. If the age is particularly relevant to the story, or if there's something unusual about the person's age, it should be included.

Wrong
Bob Jones, 23, turned himself in to police several hours after the shooting.

Better
Twenty-three-year-old Bob Jones turned himself in to police several hours after the shooting.

Best
Bob Jones turned himself in to police after the shooting.

Wrong
Among today's skydivers was Jerome Sunday, 90.

Right
Among today's skydivers was 90-year-old Jerome Sunday.

Agreement of Subject and Verb

The subject and verb of a sentence must grammatically agree. If the subject is singular, the verb must be singular. If the subject is plural, the verb must be plural. Take particular care with prepositional phrases, as in these examples:

Wrong
A busload of students are headed for the coliseum.

Right
A busload of students is headed for the coliseum.

Wrong
The troupe of actors are in town for a benefit performance at the Majestic Theater.

Right
The troupe of actors is in town for a benefit performance at the Majestic Theater.

Note also that either and neither are considered singular when followed by a singular subject, and therefore take singular verbs.

Wrong
Neither the landlord nor the tenant have a criminal record.

Right
Neither the landlord nor the tenant has a criminal record.

Agreement of Subject and Pronouns

Make sure you have grammatical agreement between a subject and its related pronouns. A subject that is singular—everybody, everyone, each person, and so on—takes the singular pronoun his or her, not their. A subject that is plural calls for the plural pronoun their.

Wrong
Everyone has their favorite restaurant.

Right
Everyone has his favorite restaurant.

Better
Everyone has a favorite restaurant. (This version is both grammatically correct and gender-neutral.)

Wrong
If a person wants to own a gun they should have that right.

Right
If a person wants to own a gun he should have that right.

Wrong
The company announced they will lay off 200 workers.

Right
The company announced it will lay off 200 workers.

Burying the Lead

Burying the lead means placing critical information in a news story after less important information. Generally, the goal is to deliver the most significant details right from the start.

Wrong
Police are searching for clues at a home in southwest Libertyville this morning. Last night neighbors discovered the bodies of a man and woman who had been murdered there.

Right
The double murder of a Libertyville couple has police searching for clues this morning.

Characterizing the News

Don't cue the audience's response to a news story by including words that characterize how they should feel, such as tragic or unfortunate. Let the information speak for itself.

Wrong
Three people died in the tragic overnight fire.

Right
Three people died in the overnight fire.

Words that characterize don't have to indicate an emotional state. You should also be careful about subjective adjectives like interesting, amazing, bizarre, mysterious, and so on.

Poor
Doctors at Harvard University Medical School have released an interesting report.

Better
(Rewrite the sentence to tell what's in the report.)

Poor
Spectators saw an amazing show involving a dozen parachute jumpers.

Better
Spectators watched 12 parachute jumpers skydive over the airfield.

Let the audience decide whether to be amazed.

Clichés

Strive to avoid clichés in your writing. You can always find a more original way to make the same point. Clichés are particularly problematic in stories that deal with death, injury, or other sensitive matters, because they tend to make a sentence sound too casual. Examples include back to the drawing board, ballpark figure, bite the bullet, last but not least, lock horns, smoking gun, and 24/7.

Weak
Relief workers declined to give a ballpark assessment of how many storm victims remain unaccounted for.

Better
Relief workers declined to estimate the number of missing storm victims.

Generalizations

Take care not to make sweeping generalizations in your news copy, even when the subject matter seems uncontroversial.

Weak
Everybody loves a parade.

Better
Most people love a parade.

The first example might be correct, but it might not be. You're better off going with the less definitive statement.

Imprecise Language

Steer clear of wishy-washy qualifiers that don't help the audience understand your meaning. These include words like rather, quite, kind of, sort of, and somewhat.

Weak
The National Weather Service says it will be quite snowy today.

Better
The National Weather Service expects heavy snowfall today, with up to six inches of accumulation possible.

Weak
Hotels are expected to be rather busy this weekend because of the convention.

Better
Hotels are expected to be fully booked for this weekend's convention.

Inflated Language

Don't overstate the facts by using inflated language. Your word choice shouldn't be boring, but it must not exaggerate.

Weak
Medical researchers have made a major breakthrough in the war against cancer.

Better
Medical researchers report progress in the war against cancer.

Weak
The governor declared war on homeowners who don't pay their taxes.

Better
The governor took a stand against homeowners who don't pay their taxes.

Jargon and Slang

Don't overdo jargon and slang in your news copy, especially with subject matter of a serious nature. Sports metaphors, for instance, are inappropriate for stories about politics and natural disasters.

Weak
The two candidates will go to the mat in tonight's debate.

Better
The two candidates will meet face to face in tonight's debate.

Weak
Mother Nature gave the Gulf Coast of Florida a knockout punch today.

Better
Hurricane-force winds struck the Gulf Coast of Florida today.

Although TV news style is conversational, too much slang sets an overly casual tone.

Weak
The cops say they'll keep looking for the suspect.

Better
Police say they'll keep looking for the suspect.

Misplaced Modifiers

Make sure your adverbs and adjectives are in the right spot in the sentence.

Wrong
The candidate is only outspending his rivals in the states of Iowa and New Hampshire.

Right
The candidate is outspending his rivals only in the states of Iowa and New Hampshire.

Mistaken Meaning

Some words don't mean what you think they might. Make sure you are using precisely the right term for the occasion.

Mass murder, for example, is not the same as serial murder. The first involves the deaths of a large number of people, and the second refers to a series of consecutive homicides.

Wrong
Police are looking for a mass murder suspect after a series of homicides in downtown Lakedale.

Right
Police are looking for a serial killer after a string of homicides in downtown Lakedale.

Here's another example: Notorious (or the noun notoriety) does not mean famous. Instead it carries a negative connotation of fame for the wrong reasons.

Wrong
The notorious war hero will speak to high school students tonight.

Right
The celebrated war hero will speak to high school students tonight.

Here is one more example of mistaken meaning: Presently does not mean at present or at this moment; it means soon.

Wrong
Police say there are no suspects in the case presently.

Right
Police say there are no suspects in the case right now.

News Clichés

A number of phrases can be considered news clichés because of their overuse. They should be avoided.

"As Expected." This phrase makes the story sound unimportant and cues the listener to tune out the information.

Wrong
As expected, Congress passed the legislation today.

Right
Congress passed the legislation today.

"In the News." It isn't necessary to write that a story is in the news—what else could it be if it turns up in a newscast? Along similar lines, avoid the phrase "making headlines."

Wrong
The high price of housing is in the news today.

Right
A new government report is warning of higher housing prices.

"Only Time Will Tell." This is perhaps the most idiotic of all news clichés, although it can frequently be found in the closing lines of stories. Resist the temptation.

Weak
What's ahead for the space shuttle program? Only time will tell.

Better
Anything.

Numbers

Be precise, but don't go overboard with statistical information in TV news stories. Spell out numbers on a script to make it easier for the anchor to read.

Wrong
The tax increase is expected to generate $3.5 million.

Right
The tax increase is expected to generate three-point-five million dollars.

Punctuation

Punctuation for TV news scripts is less formal than punctuation for other types of prose. Commas are infrequently used, and semicolons and colons are almost never used. Dashes and ellipses sometimes take the place of commas to indicate a pause.

Wrong
The building will be completed in March; already it has become the city's tallest landmark.

Right
The building will be completed in March. It has already become the city's tallest landmark.

"Quote, Unquote"

In TV newswriting you don't need to use the words "quote, unquote." Instead, either play the person's words as a sound bite or paraphrase the words on the script. Do not punctuate the copy with quotation marks.

Wrong
The million-dollar lottery winner says she is, quote, "happy beyond belief," unquote.

Right
The million-dollar lottery winner says she is happy beyond belief.

"Reason Why"

Don't put these words back to back in a sentence. One or the other of them is usually sufficient to make your point. It might work better to restructure the sentence, especially if you can make it shorter.

Wrong
Police do not know the reason why the gunman fired into the crowd.

Right
Police do not know why the gunman fired into the crowd.

Wrong
Safety officials say the recent school bus crash is the reason why a new traffic light was installed.

Right
Safety officials say they installed the new traffic light because of the recent school bus crash.

Redundancy

Take particular care in writing TV news scripts to avoid redundancies. Examples of these include phrases like total strangers, armed gunman, unsolved mystery, free giveaway, unexpected surprise, past history, or past record. It is also redundant to refer to something happening at 6 a.m. this morning; use either 6 a.m. or 6 this morning, but not both.

Wrong
The hotel was filled to capacity at the time of the explosion.

Right
The hotel was full at the time of the explosion.

Wrong
The singer arrived in a chauffeured limousine.

Right
The singer arrived in a limousine.

Repetitive Language

Try to vary your word choice so as not to repeat the same word over and over within a sentence or news story.

Weak
Police say the accident injured five people, none seriously. The accident occurred at 11 a.m. This is the second accident at this intersection this month.

Better
Police say the accident injured five people, none seriously. The crash occurred at 11 this morning. Another wreck took place at the same intersection two week ago.

"Special"

Special is one of those cheesy TV words that are best avoided. The word is so overused that it has lost its meaning.

Wrong
The board members presented their chairman with a special birthday cake.

Right
The board members presented their chairman with a birthday cake.

"That" as a Relative Pronoun

A relative pronoun is a connecting word within a sentence. As a general rule in TV newswriting, you should omit relative pronouns. In the following sentence "that" acts as a relative pronoun: "Officials say that the road will reopen in the morning." The sentence flows more easily without "that": "Officials say the road will reopen in the morning."

Weak
The senator says that the bill will be passed next week.

Better
The senator says the bill will be passed next week.

Weak
Forecasters predict that the snow will end before midnight.

Better
Forecasters predict the snow will end before midnight.

Titles

In general, job titles and honorifics precede the name in TV newswriting. This is not always the case in print newswriting.

Print style
John Anderson, chairman of the committee, will report to the city council next month.

TV style
Committee chairman John Anderson will report to the city council next month.

Unnecessary Time References

Be careful of time-related words that add nothing to the sentence, including upcoming, earlier, later, and so on.

Wrong
The upcoming event is expected to attract thousands of visitors.

Right
The event is expected to attract thousands of visitors.

Wrong
The city council will meet later this morning.

Right
The city council will meet this morning.

Wrong
The accident occurred earlier this morning.

Right
The accident occurred this morning.

Wrong
The closed-door session lasted a full hour.

Right

The closed-door session lasted an hour.

Wordy Phrases

Tighten up phrases that contain unnecessary words. Your goal as a news writer should be to whittle down the sentence to its bare bones. Here are a few examples of wordy phrases: in order to, so as to, in the process of, the fact that, whether or not.

Wrong

Motorists will be rerouted in order to avoid the flood zone.

Right

Motorists will be rerouted to avoid the flood zone.

Wrong

Legislators are in the process of revising the amendment.

Right

Legislators are revising the amendment.

Wrong

The fact that the factory had a history of safety violations is what led officials to close it down.

Right

Safety violations led officials to close the factory.

CHECKLIST OF KEY POINTS

- Television news operates according to a two-track language: the language of pictures and sound. The objective for writers of TV news stories is to take full advantage of both tracks, observing the principles of storytelling with pictures and sound.

- Writing news stories for television differs from other forms of journalism. TV news is a spoken form of communication, closer in structure to radio than print. Scripts for TV news stories do not include as much written detail as print reports, in part because the visuals provide much of the descriptive information.

- TV news scripts are tightly written. Get rid of all unnecessary language in your copy, especially wordy phrases, gratuitous time references, repetitive terms, and redundancies.

- TV news is written in a conversational style. Language should be simple and straightforward. Contractions and use of the second-person "you" are acceptable. Homophones are not.

- Complicated sentence structures should be avoided. Your best bet is almost always a basic S/V/O structure: subject, verb, and object. Compound sentences or sentences with internal clauses should probably be divided into two separate sentences.

- Good TV newswriting employs a high ratio of verbs to nouns. Action verbs work best, especially as replacements for forms of the verb "to be."

- Avoid passive voice in constructing sentences. "Fire destroyed a downtown church" packs more of a punch than "A downtown church was destroyed by fire." In addition, it's shorter.

- Strive for present-tense leads. Your lead paragraph should emphasize the latest developments in a story to make the news sound as fresh as possible.

- Don't overdo adjectives and adverbs. Remember that in TV news the visuals carry much of the descriptive load for you.

- Attribution of sources usually comes before the information in TV news scripts.

- Be careful not to indulge in generalizations, inflated language, jargon and slang, foreign phrases, news clichés, or words that cue viewers about how they are supposed to feel about a story. The job of the news writer is to spell out the facts. Audience members can decide for themselves how they will react.

- Keep the needs and interest of your audience in mind as you write scripts. Remember that viewers don't know as much about the story as you do.

ASSIGNMENTS/ANALYSIS

Assignment: Television Newswriting Style
Rewrite the following sentences to fix the writing problems.

Abbreviations
Dr. Jones was a member of the ADA.

The carnival will be held in the courtyard of the Young Men's Christian Association.

Absolutes
Lakedale schools are expected to remain closed through the end of the week because of the unprecedented snowfall.

St. Monica's College is the site of a truly unique sculpture—a polar bear carved entirely of ice.

Today the committee will question its most significant witness, a former school district official from Rock City.

Rounding out the festivities will be a one-of-a-kind contest to see who can eat the most corn dogs.

Today's hailstorm is the kind that's seen only once in a lifetime.

There has never been a sadder love story than the tale of Romeo and Juliet.

Active Versus Passive Verbs

The bus was struck by an oncoming train.

Authorities say the building was knocked down by hurricane-force winds.

The new rescue vehicles were purchased by the police department as part of a federal grant.

Age

Mel Clayton, 43, a Lakedale lawyer, will be sworn in as the state's new Secretary of Education.

A 29-year-old man is being treated for smoke inhalation after fire engulfed his Lakedale home.

Police arrested the driver of the vehicle, Kevin Brown, 26, of Lakedale Heights.

Agreement

The chorus of singers are scheduled to visit 10 countries.

Each candidate will have their own opportunity to speak.

The caravan of students are expected to arrive from Chicago tomorrow.

Every person has their own assigned seat on board the plane.

Police said neither the boy nor his sister were in any danger.

The hospital will open their new wing next week.

Attribution

The suspect was wearing only a diaper, according to police.

The bank president embezzled millions of dollars—so says a key witness in the Henderson trial today.

Lottery officials explained that last night's drawing produced no winner.

The mayor stated that the city does not expect a budget shortfall this year.

John Smith's attorney declared that his client was innocent of the charge.

Burying the Lead

Lakedale Central High School was evacuated this afternoon after the principal's office received a phone call warning of a bomb inside the building. Students were sent home for the day. No bomb was found, school officials say.

A passenger jet was headed from New Orleans to San Juan, Puerto Rico. There's where the pilot made a crash landing after an engine caught fire.

Police are searching for clues at a downtown bank this morning. The bank was held up at 10 a.m. by a gunman wearing a George W. Bush mask.

The governor welcomed the ambassador to Mexico at a Cinco de Mayo luncheon today. The governor also made a surprise announcement: that he will not run for re-election.

Characterizing the News

Tragically, both victims died at the hospital an hour after the shooting.

The explosion occurred at 10 in the morning. Fortunately, no one was in the building at the time.

Two Lakedale residents are lucky to be alive after a head-on collision on the Downtown Loop this morning.

Clauses and Compound Sentences

The house, which was located across from Prospect Park, had been designated a historic landmark.

The students, ranging in age from kindergarten through sixth grade, took part in National Work-Out Day, which is held every year on May the first.

The farmers market opened in 1979 and has expanded in recent years to include hundreds of vendors, including booths that sell fresh produce and a variety of other products.

Clichés

The sheriff provided a ballpark assessment of the number of casualties.

Democrats and Republicans are locking horns again today.

Senator Jones and her advisers remained huddled behind closed doors this weekend.

A Florida town is wrestling with the aftermath of a hurricane this morning.

Contractions

Negotiators say they do not expect a breakthrough any time soon.

The freeway closing will not go into effect until after the holiday.

Rescue workers have not been able to reach the stranded miners. The miners have not been heard from since last night.

According to the report, health officials are not prepared for this year's flu season.

Authorities say they do not have a suspect at this time.

Fancy Words

The 40-story edifice will become the city's highest.

The pageant commenced shortly after sundown.

The meeting took place prior to an appearance in district court.

The new library replaces a building that has served the town for more than seven decades.

The city recently acquired new firefighting equipment for utilization in high-rise fires.

Arson investigators hope to ascertain the cause of the conflagration.

Foreign Words

The peace accord promises to bring a rapprochement between the two countries.

The leaders and their translators later held a private tete-a-tete at the palace.

The candidate is an aficionado of the Boston Red Sox.

Generalizations

The people in our town enjoy nothing more than a bright, sunny day.

California is known as the land of flakes—and here's another story that confirms that reputation.

All over the world kids love candy.

Homophones

The sole survivor of the crash was a man from Seoul, South Korea.

According to police, the reverend preyed upon his congregation for several years.

The ruling applies to fund-raising efforts by a number of religious sects.

Imprecise Language

According to Red Cross reports, the tidal wave resulted in numerous deaths.

Forecasters say we can expect a rather humid day tomorrow.

Inflated Language

The Lakedale Public Library plans to hunt down people who don't return overdue books.

The governor will make a major announcement confirming his intention to run for reelection.

Members of Congress are waging war in a bitter debate on the House floor.

Jargon and Slang

According to local cops, gang activity is on the increase.

What's up with the gasoline prices? We'll have the story when we continue.

The candidates will step into the arena this evening for a televised debate.

Undercover officers busted three perps today on charges of selling pot.

Misplaced Modifiers

The mandatory recycling ordinance only applies to residents within the city limits.

Formally the suspect was charged with assault and battery at a court hearing last week.

Mistaken Meaning

The team gained notoriety as the best basketball players in the country.

Lawyers are meeting presently to work out details of the plea bargain.

The suspect confessed to a series of 10 homicides over a five-year period. He will be sentenced next week in connection with the mass murders.

Negation

The State Supreme Court ruled that no victim of discrimination can sue for more than $1 million in damages.

Rescue teams are at work in a town not far from Halifax, Nova Scotia.

Father John Malone says the new bell tower is not unlike the one it replaces.

News Clichés

As expected, the President sent his bill to Congress today.

The price of gasoline continues to make news—consumers can expect to pay more at the pump.

In the headlines today, a report from the British intelligence agency says terrorist attacks are being planned for the London subway.

Nominal Style

Inside the choir loft is a pipe organ that was imported from Germany.

There's a street in the downtown area where high school students gather every weekend to go cruising in their cars.

As part of the concert there will be an opening number by a group of performers who make music with glass bells.

Numbers

The renovations are expected to cost about $11.2 million.

The flooding left some 400 people temporarily homeless.

The country has a population of about 10,000,000.

Present-Tense Leads

Last night's explosion broke windows in several downtown skyscrapers. This morning clean-up crews have begun clearing away the shattered glass.

The water tower toppled to the ground at around 1 p.m. today. No one was injured. Fire officials have been called in to investigate.

The train derailed this morning just before noon, and 10 people were sent to the hospital. Five of them are still there at this hour with serious injuries.

An armed robbery occurred last night at Lucky Joe's convenience store in downtown Lakedale. Police arrested two suspects. The suspects will appear in court this morning.

Problem Verbs

Candidates in the race continue to speak out about high unemployment, blaming the White House for the poor economy.

The search for a missing Lakedale boy continues this evening. Authorities say they have no new clues in his disappearance.

The polar habitat is an important addition to the zoo because it is home to a new colony of penguins.

Flags were at half-staff during the funeral services today.

Coalition forces are using artillery against the rebels.

Because of heavy fog, airlines have been forced to cancel all flights scheduled through noon today.

Health officials say they will try and contact everyone who might be affected by the announcement.

Punctuation/"Quote, Unquote"

A local man has come forward with the winning lottery ticket; it is said to be worth $2,000,000.

The tax increase comes as bad news for one group in particular: homeowners.

The governor says he will not—quote—participate in any witch hunt—end quote.

The district attorney says the defendant's criminal record "speaks for itself."

"Reason Why"

The defendant's previous behavior is the reason why he has been detained.

According to police, safety is the reason why the bridge has been closed.

Redundancy

Each member of the panel presented his own individual report on the allegations.

The planes collided in midair in the skies over central Missouri.

The revelation comes as an unpleasant embarrassment for the White House.

The First Lady gave her own personal assessment of the campaign so far.

The train derailed shortly after 1 p.m. this afternoon.

Repetitive Language

The fire started in the church basement. Firemen arrived on the scene around 2 p.m. and put out the fire within 10 minutes. Damage from the fire was confined to a small area.

Lieutenant Governor Sally Jones could become the first female to be elected to lead the state. If elected, her governorship would begin next January. She has held the post of lieutenant governor for the past two years under Governor Chet Smith.

"Special"

Coming up tonight—a special homecoming reunites twins who haven't seen each other in 20 years.

A special reception will be held tonight to honor the award recipients.

"That" as a Relative Pronoun

The actor promised that he would return for the sequel.

Spokesmen for the company say that the product has been recalled and that consumers will receive replacement items at no cost.

There Is/There Are

There are three new buildings on the campus that will open next month.

With the arrival of spring there are new worries for allergy sufferers.

There's something new on the campus of Lakedale University—a five-story parking garage.

There are two major freeways leading into the town. Both have been closed.

Titles

Quentin Tarantino, the film director, announced today he is retiring from the movies.

Jill Anderson, the head of consumer relations, says a new product line will be announced next week.

Tony Sanchez, who serves as an adviser to Governor Chet Smith, will speak at Lakedale University tomorrow.

Unnecessary Adverbs

In sports, the Lakedale University Lions literally slaughtered Centerville College last night.

Retailers are reporting that this holiday season was actually one of the worst on record.

In court news, the suspect in a local murder case was found definitely guilty today.

Unnecessary Time References

The committee held an emergency meeting to discuss the action earlier this morning.

The fireworks display lasted a full two hours.

Governor Smith will meet up with Democratic leaders later this morning at the state capitol.

The accident happened earlier this morning, at around 8 a.m.

The House is rushing to finish up its legislative business before the holiday.

The candidates will participate in one more debate before the upcoming New Hampshire primary.

Wordy Phrases

Fire officials are attempting to learn the cause of a mysterious explosion that occurred downtown today.

Police closed the road in order to protect motorists.

Negotiators are in the process of finalizing an agreement between the two countries.

The sheriff announced his candidacy despite the fact that his recent poll ratings have been overwhelmingly negative.

The head of the congressional committee voiced criticism against the President's health plan.

The district attorney is trying to decide whether or not to seek charges against the suspect.

Analysis

- Find 10 stories from the local newspaper and rewrite them in TV news style. Pay particular attention to present-tense leads, attribution, and deleting unnecessary details.
- Record a variety of local and national TV newscasts and critique the writing. Pay particular attention to the use of verbs and nouns.

CHAPTER THREE

WRITING STUDIO-BASED NEWS STORIES

TOPICS DISCUSSED IN THIS CHAPTER

- Overview of Studio-Based TV News Stories • Anchor Readers
- Voice-Over or Reader/Voice-Over Stories
- Voice-Over/Sound on Tape Stories • Setting Up a Sound Bite
- Using Natural Sound Full • Referencing: The Challenge of Writing to Video
- Checklist of Key Points

ASSIGNMENTS/ANALYSIS

- Assignment: Writing Anchor Readers • Assignment: Writing VOs
(Afternoon Newscast) • Assignment: Writing VOs (Evening Newscast)
- Assignment: Writing VO/SOT Stories (Noon Newscast)
- Assignment: Writing VO/SOT Stories (Afternoon Newscast)
- Analysis: Studio-Based TV News Stories

OVERVIEW OF STUDIO-BASED TV NEWS STORIES

Although TV news stories depict events in the field, they reach viewers via the controlled environment of a television studio. This is where the scriptwriter comes into play.

TV news scripts are written in four basic formats: the anchor reader, voice-over, VO/SOT/VO, and package. The first three of these story formats are delivered live in a studio by an anchorperson or reporter. Packages, which are not done live, are dealt with separately in Chapter 4.

Studio-based news stories account for a sizable percentage of any newscast's content. The advantage of these stories is that they are short, which means a producer can run a lot of them. Typically these shorter stories deal with subject matter that does not warrant a full reporter package.

ANCHOR READERS

The anchor reader, also called simply a reader, is the shortest and most basic form of studio-based TV news story. It is read by an anchorperson who remains on camera for the duration of the script. Because these stories are so brief—usually in the 10- to 20-second range—writers must relay the key points in only a few sentences. This means boiling the story down to its essence.

Producers use anchor readers when no visual material exists, as in the case of a late-breaking story for which video is not yet available. Sometimes graphic elements, either still or animated, are included in the shot as the anchorperson delivers the story. With or without graphics, in a reader the anchor is shown on camera for the full story.

Although readers might seem out of date in the hypervisual context of modern TV news, they continue to have a place. "Reader stories can be nice pacers," says Tim Tunison, assistant news director at WBAL-TV in Baltimore. "On generic stories I'd much rather see the anchor with a nice graphic over the shoulder instead of generic file video."

Script Format for an Anchor Reader

Here's a sample script for an anchor reader. We'll adapt this story—the Lakedale Tomato Bomber—to the different newswriting story formats in this chapter and the next.

(VISUALS)	(SOUND)
One-Shot of Anchor	---------------------Anchor---------------------
Graphic Box: Tomato Bomber Suspect	A SEARCH IS ON FOR THE SO-CALLED LAKEDALE TOMATO BOMBER.
	POLICE SAY THEY HAVE FEW CLUES IN THE CASE, WHICH INVOLVES A MAN THROWING TOMATOES AT SHOPPERS IN LOCAL SUPERMARKETS.
	VICTIMS HAVE DESCRIBED THE TOMATO BOMBER AS A YOUNG WHITE MAN WEARING NAZI STORM TROOPER BOOTS.

As with all TV news scripts, the page is split into two columns. Visual elements—in this example, a one-shot of the anchor with a graphics box—are listed in the left column. The column on the right contains the sound elements—in this case, the copy read by the anchorperson. Each sentence is indented as a new paragraph.

Note that the anchor copy is written in all caps and double-spaced to make the text as easy as possible for the presenter to deliver on camera. Everything about the script is designed to make it easy to follow for the anchors, the producer, the director in the control room, the audio engineer, and everyone else involved in the production of the newscast. A TV news script functions like an architectural blueprint. It's a detailed plan that helps bring the product into being by giving all the participants a common frame of reference.

Different newsrooms take different approaches to formatting news scripts, with each shop conforming to a "house style." The formats used in this chapter are not engraved in stone, but they do give you a basic idea of what the scripts should look like. If anything, the sample scripts in this textbook probably include more detail than most actual TV news scripts. The idea is to get you in the habit of thinking about the full range of elements that go into a script.

TV news scripts serve as the blueprint for what goes out over the air. Here Tim Russert begins another edition of *Meet the Press*.

VOICE-OVER OR READER/ VOICE-OVER STORIES

Voice-over stories (VOs) or reader/voice-overs (R/VOs) add a visual layer to the storytelling by incorporating video, full-screen graphics, or other illustrations to the anchorperson's words. Despite the inclusion of visuals, voice-overs are typically quite brief, usually in the 10- to 30-second range. Because TV is a visual medium, producers use video or other visuals as extensively as possible, even for a short VO story. The brevity of VO stories may allow for only a handful of shots, but those few seconds of pictures can bring a story to life.

Nonetheless, it is important to use images that accurately depict the situation and that add to the viewer's understanding of the story. "A VO should contain compelling video and not random locator video that isn't specifically referenced in the script," says Matt Gaffney, executive producer of WTTG-TV in Washington, D.C. Gaffney also warns against shots of people talking in VO stories, because these do not juxtapose well against the anchorperson's narration.

The structure for VO stories can take several basic forms. A standard R/VO story begins exactly like a reader, with the anchorperson on camera. As with a reader, a graphics box might appear over the anchor's shoulder. Shortly into the story, usually after the first sentence has been delivered on camera, full-screen visuals kick in. This is indicated on the script by a roll cue, the line that tells the director when it's time to cut away from the studio and take the video or graphics full.

Although it is possible to cut back to an anchorperson for the last sentence or so of a VO story, the usual structure calls for the video to play through to the end of the text. The exception would be a story for which few visuals exist. In that case it might make sense to return to the anchor for a final sentence or two. Normally, however, VO scripts are written with the video extending to the end of the narration.

Script Format for an R/VO Story

(VISUALS)	(SOUND)
	----------------------Anchor----------------------
One-shot of Anchor Graphic Box: Tomato Bomber Suspect	A SUSPECT IS UNDER ARREST TONIGHT IN THE SO-CALLED LAKEDALE TOMATO BOMBER CASE.
--------------------VIDEO/VO-----------------	---------------VO/Natsot Under)----------------
Suspect w/cops at supermarket Locator super: "Downtown"	POLICE APPREHENDED 25-YEAR-OLD SAM WITHERS THIS AFTERNOON IN THE PRODUCE SECTION OF A DOWNTOWN FOOD-MEISTER SUPERMARKET.
Elderly Victim	POLICE SAY HE WAS TACKLED TO THE GROUND BY A 90-YEAR-OLD WOMAN HE HAD HIT IN THE BACK WITH A TOMATO.
	CHARGES WILL BE FILED TOMORROW.

In this case the script begins exactly as it did for the reader, with a one-shot of the anchor and a graphics box. After the first sentence, the video starts, continuing through to the end of the story. The last few words of the first sentence serve as the roll cue, indicating to the director that he or she needs to cut away from the anchor to the video.

Notice that in the left column—the visual column—the script briefly indicates the shots that accompany the anchor's copy. Once the script is written, these shots will be edited together in the appropriate order and timed so that the images on screen coincide with the anchor's narration. (By the time the copy reaches the anchorperson, these shot details will probably be omitted, but when first writing the script, it's a good idea to provide visual details.)

Also in the left column, just as the video begins, is a locator super that says "Downtown." This simply means that the director will superimpose the word "Downtown" over the screen at that point in the story. Locator supers are routinely used to inform viewers where stories are taking place. Supers are visual elements, so they belong in the left column.

The right side—the audio column—contains the text that the anchorperson reads. At the point where the video begins, the right half of the script says "VO/natsot under," meaning that as the script is being read aloud, natural sound from the tape is also playing under the anchor's words at low volume.

Script Format for a Video-Only VO Story

A video-only VO features full-screen visuals throughout the anchorperson's narration, pictures that complement the contents of the script from start to finish. In this structure the studio anchor is never seen on camera. Producers often employ the video-only format when a newscast includes several VO stories in a row. Not cutting back to the anchorperson at the beginning of each story makes the newscast look less choppy.

The script format for a video-only VO looks like this:

(VISUALS)	(VO FROM THE TOP)
--------------------VIDEO/VO----------------	---------------------Anchor-----------------------
Suspect w/cops at supermarket Locator super: "Downtown"	A SUSPECT IS UNDER ARREST TONIGHT IN THE SO-CALLED LAKEDALE TOMATO BOMBER CASE.
Mug shot of suspect	POLICE APPREHENDED 25-YEAR-OLD SAM WITHERS THIS AFTERNOON IN THE PRODUCE SECTION OF A DOWNTOWN FOOD-MEISTER SUPERMARKET.
Elderly Victim	POLICE SAY HE WAS TACKLED TO THE GROUND BY A 90-YEAR-OLD WOMAN HE HAD HIT IN THE BACK WITH A TOMATO.
	NO TRIAL DATE HAS BEEN SET.

VOICE-OVER/SOUND ON TAPE STORIES

The next level of studio-based news stories adds the important element of sound bites from interviewees. These bites are also called SOTs, for sound on tape. The standard structure for this type of story is the VO/SOT/VO. Think of it as a sound bite sandwich: First the anchorperson reads a voice-over, then there's the sound bite, then another anchor voice-over. VO/SOT/VO stories run in the 20- to 50-second range, depending primarily on the length of the bite.

Role of Sound Bites

By bringing outside voices into the mix, sound bites add depth and interest to TV news stories. Because news programs depend so heavily on the contributions of anchors and reporters, sound bites expand the range of voices heard in the newscast. They focus the storytelling on people other than the journalists who deliver the information.

Sound bites are an excellent way to introduce subjective points of view into stories. When an anchorperson or reporter reads a VO narration, the tone of this information must remain neutral and objective, because it is not the newscaster's place to espouse a point of view. By contrast, sound bites offer the opinions, feelings, experiences, and expertise of interviewees who are not bound by the journalistic restrictions of neutrality and objectivity. Without this first-person perspective, newscasts would be very dull.

"SOTs are effective when they convey emotion regarding a story," says WTTG's Matt Gaffney. "We try to avoid SOTs that tell facts. For example, we discourage reporters and writers from using police sound that merely describes a crime or crime scene. However, if a police officer described a murder scene as the worst investigators have seen in 30 years, and it brought officers to tears, then we would probably use that."

For stories that deal with controversial subject matter, sound bites can help the news writer achieve balance. This doesn't mean that both sides of a story must be given equal time in the sound bites, but it does mean that differing points of view must be properly balanced. If they are not, viewers might perceive the story to be unfair.

Storytelling elements gathered in the field–visuals, interview bites, and natural sound–serve as the building blocks of TV news stories.

Length of Sound Bites

Over the years the average length of a TV news sound bite has gotten shorter and shorter. Today, most bites are in the 10-second range, but this can vary considerably, depending on what is being said and by whom. A quick, "man-on-the-street" sound bite might run only a few seconds, whereas a compelling, complicated statement from an interesting source could last for 20 seconds or more.

Critics charge that sound bites in TV news stories have gotten too short. A common critique of the 10-second sound bite is that it reduces information to a superficial level. Journalists should be on the lookout for instances in which longer, more complex bites are justified, especially in a multilayered story.

The danger of a long sound bite is that it might drag a story down. Short bites, like short VOs and short bits of natural sound, function as pacing devices to keep the material moving along. TV news writers choose sound bites that are informative yet concise, which usually means selecting only the best portion of an interviewee's longer statement. Each situation must be evaluated individually.

Writers should keep several considerations in mind when selecting sound bites for a story. First, there is the way the speaker worded the bite, which might or might not lend itself to excerpting. If the wording is confusing, or if the person has difficulty getting to the point, the bite probably won't work. Second, it is relatively easy to chop off the beginning of a bite or cut out the last few words—this is done all the time. However, taking words out of the middle of someone's statement presents a technical challenge that is best avoided. The final, and most important, consideration in editing a sound bite is to remain true to the interviewee's intended meaning. Each sound bite must accurately reflect the person speaking it.

Structuring a VO/SOT/VO

VO/SOT/VO stories are sometimes referred to as having an A/B structure. This is because news programs generally run the stories as two separate pieces of videotape. The first sequence of video is on the A tape, and accompanies the part of the script that the anchor reads before the sound bite. The B tape begins with the sound bite, followed immediately by another video sequence that plays as the anchor reads the postbite narration. Running the story on two separate tapes like this means the anchor doesn't have to worry that he or she will still be reading when the bite begins, or that there will be a second or two of dead air if the anchor narration ends before the start of the bite.

Script Format for VO/SOT/VO Story

The following script presents a VO/SOT/VO version of the Tomato Bomber story. The story uses many of the same visuals as before, but with the addition of a sound bite from Effie Jones, the bomber's final victim. Note that the bite is clearly marked in both the video and audio columns. The video side tells us what we are seeing—a shot of Effie Jones—along with an indication that her name is appearing on screen as an identifying, or ID, super. The audio side lists the text and the length of the bite. This information helps both the director and the anchor know when to transition from the live read to the sound on tape and back.

	----------------------Anchor----------------------
One-Shot of Anchor Graphic Box: Tomato Bomber Suspect	A SUSPECT IS UNDER ARREST TONIGHT IN THE SO-CALLED LAKEDALE TOMATO BOMBER CASE.
------------------VIDEO/VO------------------	--------------(VO/Natsot Under)--------------
Suspect in custody at supermarket Locator super: "Downtown"	POLICE APPREHENDED 25-YEAR-OLD SAM WITHERS THIS AFTERNOON IN THE PRODUCE SECTION OF A DOWNTOWN FOOD-MEISTER SUPERMARKET.
Old Woman at store	POLICE SAY HE WAS TACKLED TO THE GROUND BY A 90-YEAR-OLD WOMAN HE HAD HIT IN THE BACK WITH A TOMATO.
------------------VIDEO/SOT------------------	----------------------(SOT)----------------------
Shot of Effie Jones ID Super: Effie	Bite: "I felt something smash into me, and it was the Tomato Bomber, so I hit him with my walker." (:09)
------------------VIDEO/VO------------------	--------------(VO/Natsot Under)--------------
Cops w/suspect in police car	AREA SUPERMARKETS HAVE REPORTED SOME TEN INCIDENTS OF TOMATO TOSSING OVER THE PAST MONTH. NO TRIAL DATE HAS BEEN SET FOR WITHERS.

Other VO/SOT Structures

Although the standard VO/SOT/VO structure calls for a single sound bite sandwiched between two live VOs, several alternative structures are also available to the news writer. Let's say you have a strong sound bite you'd like to use, but not much cover video to go with it. In a case like this, one option is to write a VO/SOT, a story that starts with a brief bit of live narration over cover visuals and ends with the sound bite. The reverse—an SOT/VO—might also work, with the sound bite first and the live narration over footage second. It is also possible to cut from the anchor directly to an SOT and then back to the anchor, although this structure is infrequently used, at least in part because going from one talking head to another is visually uninteresting.

For technical reasons, most VO/SOT/VO stories revolve around only a single bite. Sometimes, though, a story works better with more than one SOT; for example, if you are covering a controversial subject you might want to balance the content by including a bite from each side of the issue. In this situation, the simplest structure is to run two back-to-back bites, indicated on the script as follows:

----------------------VIDEO----------------------	------------------------(SOT)------------------------
Shot of defense attorney ID Super: DON DEFENDER	Bite: "My client is not guilty and at the end of the trial we expect him to go free." (:07)
Shot of prosecutor ID Super: PAMELA PROSECUTOR	Bite: "This case is about justice for the victims of a horrible crime. We believe the jury will find the defendant guilty as charged." (:11)

A more complicated structure is the VO/SOT/VO/SOT/VO, which involves a live anchor VO, followed by the first bite, followed by another live VO, then a second bite, and wrapping up with a final live VO. This structure involves three separate pieces of tape, and is therefore more technically daunting both for the director and the anchorperson in the studio. Generally speaking, you should limit yourself to a single-bite VO/SOT/VO. When the story calls for two bites, edit them together back to back to maintain the classic VO/SOT/VO story construction.

SETTING UP A SOUND BITE

When a sound bite appears in a story, viewers need to be able to identify who it is they are looking at and listening to, but a 30- or 40-second VO/SOT/VO doesn't give time for detailed explanations. The news writer has two choices in setting up an interviewee's SOT: a brief VO leading into the bite or a super that identifies the person speaking when he or she is on screen.

If you opt for a VO setup, be careful not to word it too literally. For instance, it is pointless to write a prebite VO that says, "The attorney general had this response today," and then cut to the bite. By going to the attorney general's bite, you accomplish precisely the same result without wasting any words.

Instead of a generic setup like "Professor Linda Johnson explains," it's better to "tee up" a sound bite by adding information: "Half of today's voters don't bother to go to the polls, according to Professor Linda Johnson." Then cut to her with a sound bite that expands on the thought. Take care not to be redundant: What the professor says in her sound bite should add to, rather than duplicate, what you've written in your setup.

If you are setting up two back-to-back sound bites, it often works best to write a single sentence that introduces both. Consider this example: The local school board has made a controversial proposal to lengthen the school year from 9 months to 12 months. At a heated Board of Education meeting, parents speak out on both sides of the issue, and in your story you decide to run two back-to-back bites, one pro and one con. Instead of introducing each bite separately, write a line that offers a generic setup: "Parents on both sides of the issue made their feelings known." This leads you directly into the SOTs without having to interrupt them for a second intro.

The simplest means of identifying the person in an SOT is to run a name super at the bottom of the screen during the bite. Doing so means you might not need any additional setup in the script.

USING NATURAL SOUND FULL

Certain stories call for the use of natural sound played for several seconds at full volume. Examples might include a story involving chanting protestors or a piece about a musical performance. In both of these instances it would be important for the audience to hear the natural sound uninterrupted by anchor narration.

Natural sound full works more or less as a sound bite, and as such it needs to be clearly indicated on your script. Because you're dealing with generic sound and not specific words, all that's needed is a quick description of the audio, along with a running time. This lets both the director and the anchor know how long to pause before the live read resumes.

REFERENCING: THE CHALLENGE OF WRITING TO VIDEO

In TV newswriting, the term *referencing* means the linkage between video and audio. The goal is to match what is being shown with what is being said. Pictures and sound that contradict each other are likely to leave viewers confused.

At the same time, referencing should not be so literal that it creates a sense of redundancy. Pictures and sound should complement each other without becoming repetitive. Let's assume you are showing video with natural sound of a marching band as it parades down the street. It would make no sense as this is happening to have the anchor read narration that says, "The band marches down the street with horns blaring and drums drumming." The images and sound tell us that already.

"Let your visuals frame the story, and don't repeat with words what the visuals are saying," advises longtime television journalist Larry Hatteberg of KAKE-TV in Wichita. "For example, if the camera is shooting a farm scene on a beautiful day do NOT write: 'It was a day where the puffy white clouds stood over Fred Smith's farm like white sentries over a field of green.' You don't write that because the camera has done the writing for you. The viewer can see the white clouds and the green of the pasture—you don't need to write it. You write to the 'edges' of the picture. Write what we can't see."

As Hatteberg's comment indicates, TV news writers should think about visuals first and words second. In practice this means that it's preferable for a writer to screen all available video before beginning to craft a script. Otherwise, the result is what is known in the business as *wallpapering*: the use of generic video to cover the duration of the script. Although this generic video might be visually appropriate, it is unlikely to be as informative and relevant as a script that takes advantage of well-referenced visuals.

Furthermore, the use of generic video could raise legal issues. Let's say you have written a story about a high school homecoming game at which a number of students were arrested for drunk and disorderly conduct. With no actual footage of the arrests, you instead run generic video shot on school grounds the next day. If these images show individual students while the script discusses allegations of underage drinking, the juxtaposition implies that these particular teenagers were the ones involved. Such visual linkage might make your station vulnerable to legal action.

Good TV journalists write *to* the video, creating scripts in which visuals act in concert with narration. As a technique, referencing can be divided into two basic categories.

"Touch and Go" Referencing

A common form of referencing in TV news scripts employs the "touch and go" theory. This means that you first reference what is shown on the screen (touch) and then, as the video continues, offer related details that cannot be visualized or for which you have no specific pictures (go).

Let's take as an example a story about a demonstration outside a prison. The demonstrators are family members of prisoners being held inside, and the point of the protest is to highlight unsafe conditions. TV journalists can easily shoot video of the protest, but it's less likely they could go behind bars to visually document the allegedly unsafe conditions. Therefore, the script would use video of the demonstration to cover the lack of footage from inside the facility. The narration might say something along this line:

> Family members demonstrated outside the County Jail today to protest what they say are unsafe conditions inside. The protestors claim that dozens of prisoners have been assaulted over the past several months, and that prison officials have not responded to their complaints.

Throughout this VO the footage of the demonstrators would continue. Even though the referencing might not be 100 percent literal, it is true to the situation.

Literal Referencing

There might be times when literal referencing is appropriate. Let's say you have video of an outdoor graduation ceremony at which a student collapses from the heat. If the shot is wide and the "action" takes place in one corner of the screen, your script might say something like, "Watch the upper right-hand corner of your screen...." Situations of this sort might require literal referencing to help viewers make sense of what they are seeing. Writers should reserve this language for special occasions, however, lest the referencing become redundant.

CHECKLIST OF KEY POINTS

- Of the four main types of TV news scripts, three are studio-based: anchor readers, voice-overs, and VO/SOT/VOs. Although these stories contain video and recorded sound, they are read live by anchors in a studio.

- TV news scripts are double-spaced and written in all capital letters, with each sentence indented as a new paragraph. Scripts are written in a split-column format, with visual elements listed on the left and sound elements on the right. Because anchor narration qualifies as a sound element, the portion of the script that will be read aloud runs in the right column.

- Anchor readers, or readers, are short stories, 10 to 20 seconds in length, which are read on camera. Producers use readers when no video exists for a story. Sometimes readers are accompanied by over-the-shoulder graphics.

- Voice-overs, or reader/voice-overs, cut away from the anchorperson to add a visual element, usually video, but sometimes other visuals like still pictures or maps. VO stories run between 10 and 30 seconds.

- Some VO stories begin with the anchor on camera and then cut to the visuals for the rest of the script. In other cases video or other pictorial elements run throughout the anchor's narration. Video-only VOs are commonly used when several VO stories appear back to back in the newscast.

- VO/SOT/VO stories, or VO/SOTs, include visuals and also sound bites or natural sound. The inclusion of these audio elements means that at the appropriate point in the story, the anchor stops reading and the recorded sound plays at full volume. VO/SOT/VOs run between 20 and 50 seconds.

- Sound bites are desirable in TV news because they add a first-person perspective to stories that would otherwise be missing. Because bites come from people other than anchors and reporters, they are an effective way to include subjective information like opinions and personal experiences.

- In writing VO/SOT/VO stories, this is the rule of thumb: VO narration for factual information; sound bites for feelings, opinions, and personal experiences.

- Sound bites within VO/SOT/VOs usually run in the neighborhood of 10 seconds, although there may be occasions when longer bites are justified. Man-on-the-street sound bites, for instance, merit less time than a heartfelt reaction from an individual who survived a violent crime.

- VO/SOT/VO stories are structured like a sandwich: two VOs with a sound bite in the middle. First comes the anchor's introductory VO, then the bite, then a closing VO.

- Other versions of this structure include the VO/SOT, which starts with anchor narration and ends on a sound bite without any postbite VO, and the SOT/VO, which reverses that order.

• When stories include sound bites, it must be clear to the audience who is speaking. The script should identify the interviewee either in a VO setup before the bite, or with an on-screen super that gives the person's name and a brief description of who he or she is. In the case of a VO setup, it is a good idea to "tee up" the bite by adding a bit of substantive information.

• Instead of sound bites, some stories call for the use of natural sound full. Natural sound is audio recorded at the scene of a story that adds context: chanting protestors, traffic noise, a musical passage, and so forth. From a scriptwriting standpoint, natural sound works the same way as sound bites.

• Referencing is the linkage between video and audio. For writers this means the two tracks—pictures and sound—need to complement each other without being redundant. In touch and go referencing, writers use the visuals as a jumping-off point for providing related information. Literal referencing draws viewers' attention to something specific on the screen.

ASSIGNMENTS/ANALYSIS

Assignments

The following assignments give you an opportunity to practice writing in each of the different studio-based story formats.

Writing Anchor Readers

Based on the information provided, write four stories in the anchor reader format. These stories will air at 5 p.m. today. Be sure to type your script copy in all caps, double-spaced. Each story should run 10 to 20 seconds long.

STORY #1: WAREHOUSE FIRE

The following information is from a Lakedale Fire Department report.

LOCATION Argus Distributors, 4200 Federal Highway, Lakedale. Argus is a wholesaler of small household appliances. The company employs 25 people.

TIMING Fire reported at 12:23 p.m. today by a passing motorist. First units arrived at 12:27 p.m. Fire under control at 1 p.m., but building and contents were destroyed by the fast-moving fire.

ESTIMATED DAMAGE $1.2 million to building and contents.

PROBABLE CAUSE OF FIRE Electrical short in main building power supply, according to John Arthur, media spokesman for Lakedale Fire Department.

ADDITIONAL DETAILS Argus Distributors was closed for a company-wide vacation, and no one was in the building at the time of the fire. Company owners say they intend to rebuild.

STORY #2: FATAL ACCIDENT

The following information is from a Lakedale Police Department accident report.

VEHICLE #1 Car driven by Charles L. Dayner, 16, Lakedale.

VEHICLE #2 Hotel shuttle bus driven by Lars Johnson, 34, Finchester. The bus was returning to the Union Hotel from an airport run and was empty of passengers.

TIME 9 a.m. today

LOCATION Ruzetta Lane and Lindbergh Avenue, Lakedale.

POLICE RECONSTRUCTION OF EVENT Dayner was driving westbound on Ruzetta Lane at a high rate of speed. He failed to stop at the stop sign before making a left turn onto Lindbergh Avenue into the path of the shuttle bus. Dayner's car was totaled, the bus was seriously damaged. Dayner was transported by ambulance to General Hospital, where he died at 2 p.m. No injuries to bus driver. No charges filed.

STORY #3: HOLD-UP

The following information is from a Lakedale Police Department report.

CRIME SCENE The Party Town Liquor Store, 231 South Bank Avenue, was robbed at gunpoint.

STORE CLERK Bo Bellini, Lakedale. His age: 28.

HOW IT HAPPENED A man with a gold stocking cap over his head entered the store at 3:12 p.m. today. He pulled out a pistol and demanded that Bellini empty the contents of the cash register into a backpack.

POLICE RESPONSE Officer Ana Lopez answered a silent alarm triggered by Bellini at 3:16 p.m. She arrived at the store at 3:20 p.m.

AT THE SCENE When he saw the police car, the suspect fled out the back entrance. Officer Lopez shouted a warning and fired a shot at the man, but she missed. The suspect ran down the alley, escaping from police.

DESCRIPTION OF SUSPECT The clerk said the robber was a Caucasian male with blonde hair and beard, about 6 feet tall and weighing around 150 pounds. He was wearing blue jeans and a dirty white T-shirt with a torn right sleeve.

STORY #4: LOTTERY WINNER

The following information is from the State Lottery Director Melvis Ansonia.

A winner stepped forward this morning to claim a $2 million prize that has gone unclaimed for 29 days. The winning ticket had to be redeemed within 30 days. The ticket belongs to a 78-year-old great-grandmother and widow named Mabel Fisher. She has lived in Lakedale's Greenside area all her life. She worked as a cafeteria cook for the Lakedale Public Schools before retiring 10 years ago. With her winnings Mrs. Fisher plans to buy a house near her daughter, son-in-law, and three grandchildren, who live in the suburb of Rock City. She also plans to send her daughter's family on a Hawaiian cruise and donate $10,000 to her favorite charity, the Lakedale Area Animal Shelter. Mrs. Fisher told lottery officials she wasn't sure she wanted to claim the prize, because she feared people would only appreciate her for her money. This was the first time Mrs. Fisher had played the lottery. She bought her winning ticket at a convenience store in Greenside. She had hidden the winning ticket in a cookie jar for safekeeping.

Writing VOs (Afternoon Newscast)

Based on the following information, write the following VO stories to air at 5 p.m. today. You are writing for a local Lakedale newscast. Be sure to follow proper script format, clearly indicating all visual elements and when they appear. Each story should run 20 to 30 seconds.

STORY #1: INDUSTRIAL EVACUATION

WHAT A small town near Lakedale is evacuated after an explosion and fire at a fertilizer plant.

WHERE Vanderwood Industries, a factory in the town of Vanderwood, population 4,000. The plant employs about 40 people and manufactures agricultural fertilizer products. Vanderwood is 20 miles south of Lakedale.

WHEN The explosion happened about 2:30 p.m. inside the plant, sparking a fire. The fire is still raging at 5 p.m., when your story airs. Firefighters arrived on the scene 10 minutes after the initial explosion.

DETAILS The entire population of Vanderwood has been evacuated. School buses from a number of area school districts were used for this purpose. The evacuees were taken to a holding facility at the National Guard Armory in Lakedale. Further evacuations of residents downwind from the fire may be necessary. No injuries. Cause unknown. Members of the media are being kept a mile away from the Vanderwood Industries plant. Source: Sheriff Fred Wyatt.

AVAILABLE VISUALS

- Map of the area, showing Vanderwood and the plant location
- Aerial footage of town, including black cloud of smoke rising from the factory
- Shots of buses carrying evacuees traveling along the highway outside town
- Shots of evacuees arriving at the National Guard Armory in Lakedale
- Shots inside the armory showing people milling around

STORY #2: EMERGENCY LANDING

WHAT/WHERE/WHEN A commercial airliner makes a safe emergency landing on Runway Two at Lakedale International Airport, which is located several miles south of the city. The plane lands at 3:45 p.m. this afternoon.

DETAILS Transcontinental Airlines Flight 445, carrying 50 passengers and five crew members, was flying en route to Chicago from (a major city near you). Fifty miles west of Lakedale the pilot reported smoke coming from one of the plane's engines and requested permission to land at Lakedale International. As the DC-10 jet was landing, the smoking engine briefly caught fire. Airport firefighters quickly brought the fire under control as soon as the plane came to a stop. The passengers and crew members safely evacuated via emergency slides. After several hours on the ground they were transferred to a charter jet to complete their journey. Source: Sheila Clover, media spokesperson for Lakeport International Airport.

AVAILABLE VISUALS

- Footage of the plane coming in for a landing, with flames visible from the engine
- Shots of the passengers and crew coming down the emergency slides
- Shots of firefighters putting out the engine fire
- Shots of the passengers boarding the charter jet to continue their journey
- Generic exteriors of Lakedale International Airport

STORY #3: VEHICLE CRASHES INTO BUILDING

WHAT/WHERE   A Hummer H2 crashes through the front of the Bubble City Laundromat in northeast Lakedale, causing property damage and injuring the driver, but leaving everyone inside the building unharmed.

WHEN   The incident is reported to the Lakedale Police Department at 1:30 p.m.

DETAILS   Six customers and a laundromat attendant were inside Bubble City at the time of the crash. They told investigators they saw the Hummer enter the parking area in front of the building at an unusually high rate of speed. Instead of stopping, the vehicle crashed through the glass facade of the laundromat, coming to a stop when it hit a row of washers and dryers a few feet inside. All the customers and the attendant escaped harm by scattering to the rear of the building. The driver, who has been identified only as a 25-year-old male, was taken by ambulance to Mercy Hospital, where he remains in serious condition. Charges may be filed against the driver as early as tomorrow. Source: Sgt. Alice Sweeney, media relations officer, Lakedale Police Department.

AVAILABLE VISUALS

- Various building exteriors, showing the damage and the Hummer
- Interiors showing more detailed shots of the vehicle
- Shot of customers milling outside the laundromat after the incident
- Shot of police taping off the accident scene

STORY #4: HECTOR COMES HOME

Write two versions of the following story, using each set of visuals available to you. The facts are the same for both versions.

WHAT/WHERE/WHEN   Around noon on Sunday a boy falls down an elevator shaft in the apartment building where he lives, located at 1001 Freedom Parkway in the South

Bank neighborhood of Lakedale. After spending the night at General Hospital, he is released at 2 p.m. Monday.

DETAILS Hector Reyes, 8, sustained only a broken arm and some minor bruises in the accident, according to police. Police said the accident occurred when Reyes was playing tag with another child in the hall. As he was running, Reyes knocked into a metal grate that blocked the opening to the out-of-service elevator shaft. He crashed through the grate and fell three stories to ground level onto an old mattress that had been dumped into the shaft. Hector's 7-year-old playmate, Louie McMann, ran into his own apartment and dialed 911, and an ambulance arrived a short time later. At the time of the accident both boys' parents were attending a backyard barbecue behind the building. They told police they didn't realize the kids had gone back inside. The incident is still under investigation. Source: Sgt. Alice Sweeney, media relations officer, Lakedale Police Department.

AVAILABLE VISUALS, VERSION ONE

- Still pic (school photo) of Hector Reyes
- Still pic (school photo) of Louis McMann
- Exterior of Hector's apartment building
- Exterior of General Hospital

AVAILABLE VISUALS, VERSION TWO

Same as Version One, plus the following:

- Interior of the apartment building, showing the metal grate and the elevator shaft that Hector crashed through
- Shot of injured Hector being loaded into the ambulance on Sunday, as his parents look on
- Exterior of General Hospital
- Shot of Hector on Monday afternoon emerging from the hospital in a wheelchair. His arm is in a cast, and he is waving to the camera.

Writing VOs (Evening Newscast)

Based on the following information, write the following VO stories to air at 10 p.m. today. You are writing for a local Lakedale newscast. Be sure to follow proper script format, clearly indicating all visual elements and when they appear. Each story should run 20 to 30 seconds.

STORY #1: SKELETAL REMAINS

WHAT Human skeletal remains are found by children playing in the woods.

WHERE The discovery is made along Stony Creek in the suburb of Lakedale Heights. The area is directly behind Carter Park, a favorite playground of neighborhood kids.

WHEN The children found the bones late in the morning and promptly told their parents. Police arrived around noon. After searching the area and carrying out their on-scene investigations, authorities removed the remains around 2:30 p.m.

DETAILS   Three boys, all fifth-grade classmates at Lakedale Heights Elementary School, came across the remains while playing in the woods near their home. The kids were home from school because of teachers' meetings. Police say the bones appear to be the skeletal remains of a woman aged 30 to 40. They say the bones had apparently been dug up by an animal after being buried for an undetermined amount of time. The evidence will be examined by lab specialists for further information. Source: Lakedale Heights P.D.

AVAILABLE VISUALS

- Miscellaneous shots of the wooded area along Stony Creek where the discovery was made
- Graphics map showing where the body was found
- Shot of Lakedale Heights police car at the scene, including close-up of PD logo
- Shots of neighbors, including some children, standing by as the authorities investigate; this footage includes shots of the yellow "do not cross" tape that police have put up.
- Footage of police removing evidence from the site of the discovery (nothing too gruesome)

STORY #2: SCHOOL EVACUATION

WHAT/WHERE   Students are evacuated from South High School in Lakedale after a threatening note is discovered in the cafeteria.

WHEN   The note was discovered at around 1:30 p.m. by a janitor cleaning up after the last lunch shift of the day. School authorities called police, who arrived to assist with the evacuation shortly before 2 p.m.

DETAILS   The janitor, Larry Hill, discovered the note taped to the top of a table in the cafeteria. The words "Important Warning" had been written on the outside. Inside was the message: "A bomb has been placed in this building and will go off before the end of the school day." (The school day ends at 3 p.m.) After police arrived, an announcement was made over the public address system ordering all students to calmly file out of the building and to leave their belongings behind. The evacuation took about 15 minutes. About 500 students, faculty, and staff members took part. Students were first led to a parking lot across the street, then dismissed for the rest of the day. Meanwhile, the LPD bomb squad began going through the building with the assistance of bomb-sniffing dogs. No explosive devices were found. School will reopen as usual tomorrow. Police call the incident an "apparent hoax." The school serves ninth- through 12th-graders. Source: Sgt. Alice Sweeney, media relations officer, Lakedale Police Department.

AVAILABLE VISUALS

- Various exteriors of the school
- Shots of kids leaving the building after the evacuation
- Shots of police and school officials directing kids across the street into the parking lot

- Interior shot of the cafeteria where the note was found
- Graphic showing the text of the threatening note against a background of the school building
- Footage of the bomb squad arriving, including shots of bomb-sniffing dogs entering the building

STORY #3: TENT COLLAPSE

WHAT/WHERE/WHEN   Dozens of people suffer minor injuries when a party tent collapses on the north lawn of the Lakedale Historical Museum in downtown Lakedale. The accident occurred at 8:30 p.m.

DETAILS   About 250 people were attending a fund-raising dinner for the museum when a security vehicle backed into a pole, knocking down the tent. About half the tent immediately collapsed, falling onto an area that included 10 tables, a large buffet table, and a cash bar. Most of the people in the tent managed to get out without any trouble, but several had to be retrieved by rescue workers. Police and emergency medical technician (EMT) personnel were summoned by guests who called 911 on their cell phones. Crews began arriving on the scene within three minutes of the collapse.

About 20 of the injured individuals were transported by ambulance to General Hospital, which is only a few blocks away. Another 20 or so were driven to area hospitals in private cars. The most serious injuries were broken bones, bruises, and concussions. Only two of the injured parties are expected to be kept overnight, one with a broken leg and the other with a possible head injury received from a falling pole. Identities of the victims have not been released. Source: Sgt. Alice Sweeney, media relations officer, Lakedale Police Department.

AVAILABLE VISUALS

- Wide shots showing an overview of the collapsed tent
- Tighter shots showing knocked-over tables, trash cans, and other debris
- Shots of workers attempting to lift the tent back into place
- Shots of some of the injured parties being placed into ambulances
- Shot of one of the EMT vehicles departing the scene with sirens and red lights on
- Shots showing groups of uninjured party guests watching the rescue workers with the tent in the background

STORY #4: CHIMP ATTACK

Write two versions of the following VO story using each set of visuals available to you. The facts are the same for both versions.

WHAT/WHERE/WHEN   A chimpanzee escapes from its cage at the zoo and jumps a zoo visitor. The incident happens around 6:30 p.m. today.

DETAILS   The chimpanzee, a five-year-old male named George, escaped from the Monkey Island area of the zoo during a routine feeding a little after 6 p.m. The animal hid in a tree overlooking the central pedestrian walkway through the zoo.

Unexpectedly, the chimp then pounced on a passerby, a tourist visiting from Argentina. The tourist began screaming, quickly drawing the attention of zoo personnel. After several minutes they managed to lure the animal away with a bunch of bananas. The tourist received a minor scratch on the back of her neck, but other than being shocked, she was not harmed. A doctor who happened to be present treated the scratch in the zoo's first aid area. Zookeepers theorize that the woman's headwear—a bright yellow, floppy hat decorated with a flowing orange scarf—may have attracted the chimp, which has a reputation for being "frisky." The animal was returned to its cage. Zoo officials say they will meet tomorrow morning to discuss security procedures. Source: Wilson Banderas, Zoo Director.

AVAILABLE VISUALS, VERSION ONE

- Shot of the zoo entrance, showing the "Lakedale Zoo Welcomes You" sign
- Shots of Monkey Island, where the chimp lives
- Shot of the tourist who was attacked, seated on a park bench surrounded by zoo officials and the doctor who treated her shortly after the incident
- Close-up of the tourist, who is wearing her bright yellow hat and flowing orange scarf
- File footage of George (shot last year), showing him scampering around Monkey Island

AVAILABLE VISUALS, VERSION TWO

- Same as Version One, but with one additional piece of footage: home video shot by a zoo visitor that shows the blurry figure of the chimpanzee on the screaming woman's back

WRITING VO/SOT STORIES (NOON NEWSCAST)

Write the following stories as VO/SOT/VOs, using the available facts and elements. Make sure to follow proper script format, indicating your choice of visual and sound elements, including identifying supers and graphics. Stories will air at noon today on a local Lakedale newscast.

STORY #1: DOGNAP

WHAT/WHEN   A blind man whose seeing-eye dog was stolen from his home appeals to the public for the animal's return. The theft occurred overnight; the man is interviewed at 11 a.m. today.

WHERE   The man lives in a first-floor apartment in Lakedale's Universityville neighborhood.

DETAILS   The blind man, Jack Hilliard, is 45 years old. He is employed by Liberty Industries for the Blind, a company that manufactures household products made by the visually impaired. The dog, a German shepherd, is named Lucky. The dog had lived with Hilliard for the past four years. Hilliard told police (and repeated during the interview) that when he woke up this morning he noticed a cold draft coming in from an open window. Because he had not opened the window, he went to investigate, and discovered that someone had forced it open. Hilliard began searching for Lucky but could not find him anywhere. Hilliard called his upstairs neighbor, Georgia Anderson, who came down to help look for the animal. Instead, Anderson found a note on the kitchen table that said, "We took your dog—hope you won't miss him." The burglars had also gone through Hilliard's wallet, removing all the cash (about $50). Police came to investigate, but say they have no clues in the case other than the handwritten note. Anderson and other neighbors are circulating a "reward" poster, offering $500 cash to anyone who returns the dog. Sources: Jack Hilliard, Georgia Anderson.

AVAILABLE VISUALS

- Video of Jack Hilliard walking through his house with a cane
- Still photo of Hilliard with Lucky
- Still of the "reward" poster that neighbors are circulating
- Home video of the blind man and his dog
- Shots that show where the burglar(s) broke in through a window
- Exterior of the apartment building where Hilliard lives

AVAILABLE SOTS (ALL ARE BITES FROM HILLIARD)

- "Lucky wasn't a pet—he was a working dog. He was my eyes. I can't believe anyone would want to take him from me."
- "I'm a pretty heavy sleeper, so I probably wouldn't have heard if Lucky started barking. Lucky's got a gentle personality—he wouldn't resist if somebody tried to take him away."
- "To whoever took Lucky, I say please, please, please bring him back—no questions asked."

STORY #2: EMERGENCY LANDING

WHAT/WHERE/WHEN   A small plane makes an emergency landing at Lakedale International Airport at around 9:30 a.m.

DETAILS   The plane, a Cessna 172, comes in for an emergency landing when its engine fails a few minutes after takeoff. The pilot, identified as Jerome Milgrew, is a local dentist with a practice in downtown Lakedale. He was alone in the plane. Milgrew contacted the control tower at Lakedale International to report his trouble. They quickly cleared the runway of other traffic to make way for Milgrew's Cessna. Fire and ambulance crews stood by in case of a crash. Milgrew was able to bring the plane down successfully, although he did skid off the runway into the grass before coming to a stop. Although Milgrew was not injured, he was taken to Mercy Hospital for observation. He was released an hour later. Milgrew had been en route to a conference in Albany. The airport was fully operational a few minutes after the emergency landing. Sources: Milgrew and Lakedale International Airport media spokesperson Sheila Clover.

AVAILABLE VISUALS

- Footage of Milgrew's plane coming in for a landing, including the part where he skids into the grass
- Shot of Milgrew emerging unharmed from the Cessna
- Shots of ambulance and fire vehicles standing by at the scene
- Exterior shot of the control tower

AVAILABLE SOTS (BITES FROM MILGREW AFTER HE EMERGES FROM THE PLANE)

- "Everything was business as usual, then all of a sudden I heard a sputtering sound. Next thing I knew the whole damn engine had crapped out on me."
- "As a pilot you always wonder what you'd do in an emergency. Now that I know, I hope I never have to go through it again."

STORY #3: SOUTH BANK PROTEST

WHAT/WHERE/WHEN   About three dozen residents of the South Bank neighborhood march outside the downtown headquarters of the Lakedale Police Department, 100 Central Avenue. The demonstration takes place around 11 a.m., and lasts for 20 minutes.

DETAILS   The marchers are protesting what they say is poor police protection in the South Bank area. The neighborhood has traditionally had one of the city's highest crime rates. Over the past several weeks a series of 10 muggings occurred in broad daylight, and two days ago an elderly man was murdered by burglars who broke into his home in the early morning hours. South Bank residents have formed a Neighborhood Association in the hope of bringing attention to their cause. After their protest they discussed their grievances with Officer Angela Porroni of the Lakedale Police Department Office of Community Relations. They vow to return to police headquarters every week until they see some improvement in their neighborhood. Sources: Sgt. Alice Sweeney, media relations officer, Lakedale Police Department, and Jeannie Loomis, president of the South Bank Neighborhood Association.

AVAILABLE VISUALS

- Footage with natural sound of the demonstrators: wide shots, mediums, and close-ups that show their homemade signs
- File footage of the South Bank neighborhood
- File footage of the home where the elderly man was murdered, including a shot of his body being removed on a stretcher
- Map of the South Bank neighborhood showing where the mugging incidents have taken place over the past few weeks
- Shot (through a glass window) of the protestors meeting with Officer Porroni after the protest

AVAILABLE SOTS

- Chanting of the protestors (natsot): "Save our streets! Save our streets!"
- Bite from Jeannie Loomis, president of the South Bank Neighborhood Association: "We're sick and tired of being dumped on just because we're not the richest neighborhood in town. We may not have much money in South Bank, but we pay our taxes just like everyone else—and we deserve police protection."
- Bite from Officer Porroni: "We appreciate the people from South Bank expressing their opinions, and we'll work closely with them to make their neighborhood as safe as possible."

STORY #4: CHIMP ATTACK

Write two versions of the following story as a VO/SOT/VO: one using a sound bite from the zoo director, and one using back-to-back bites from the zoo director and the tourist. (Note: Although this is essentially the same story as the one from the VO exercise, some of the timing details have been changed.)

WHAT/WHERE/WHEN A chimpanzee escapes from its cage at the Lakedale Zoo and jumps a tourist at around 10:30 a.m. today.

DETAILS The chimpanzee, a five-year-old male named George, escaped from the Monkey Island area of the zoo during a routine feeding a little after 10 a.m. The animal hid in a tree overlooking the central pedestrian walkway through the zoo. Unexpectedly, the chimp then pounced on a passerby, a tourist visiting from Argentina. The tourist began screaming, quickly drawing the attention of zoo personnel. After several minutes they managed to lure the animal away with a bunch of bananas. The tourist received a minor scratch on the back of her neck, but other than being shocked, she was not harmed. A doctor who happened to be present treated the scratch in the zoo's first aid area. Zoo Director Wilson Banderas theorized that the woman's headwear—a bright yellow, floppy hat decorated with a flowing orange scarf—might have attracted the chimp, which has a reputation for being "frisky" (see quotes that follow). The animal was returned to its cage. Sources: Zoo Director Wilson Banderas and Maria Victoria de Crespo, the Argentine tourist.

AVAILABLE VISUALS

- Shot of the zoo entrance, showing the "Lakedale Zoo Welcomes You" sign
- Various shots of Monkey Island, where the chimp lives
- Wide shot of the tourist who was attacked, seated on a park bench receiving first aid treatment from the doctor
- Close-up of the tourist, who is wearing her bright yellow hat and flowing orange scarf
- File footage of George (shot last year) that shows him scampering around Monkey Island
- Home video shot by a zoo visitor that shows the blurry figure of the chimpanzee on the screaming woman's back
- Shot of Zoo Director Wilson Banderas talking to reporters

AVAILABLE SOTS

- Zoo Director Wilson Banderas: "We think George might have been attracted by the yellow hat. He's a pretty frisky animal. We want the public to know that we take every precaution to protect our visitors. We'll hold a special meeting tomorrow morning to see what we need to do to improve security."
- Maria Victoria de Crespo, victim: "I was watching the monkeys in the cage when suddenly a chimp jumps on me. So I pray to God—and the monkey goes away."

STORY #5: PANCAKE CONTEST

WHAT/WHERE/WHEN   The 20th annual Lakedale Heritage Days event continues for its third day. Today's main activity, held at the Lakedale County Fairgrounds, was a noonday pancake-eating contest, a local tradition that draws great interest.

DETAILS   The pancake-eating contest includes divisions for adult men and women (16 and older) and junior divisions for boys 10–15 and girls 10–15. There's also a unisex "pee wee" division for kids under 10. The contest involves seeing who can eat the most pancakes within a five-minute period. The winners are:

Men's Division: Jimmy Gillespie, 22, of Lakedale—88 pancakes (beating the old record of 86, set one year earlier by the same contestant)

Women's Division: Rosey LaPlante, 30, of Pandora—68 pancakes

Boys' Division: Tubby Jones, 15, of Lakedale—72 pancakes

Girls' Division: Callie Rufo, 14, of Lakedale Heights—55 pancakes

Pee Wee Division: Boris Taloumis, 9, Lakedale—36 pancakes

Each winner receives a $200 gift certificate from the Lakedale Merchants Association. Source: Connie Hookminster, media spokesperson for Lakedale Heritage Days.

AVAILABLE VISUALS

- Shots of the eaters in each of the categories as they chow down
- Shots of people pushing away their plates when they can't take any more
- Shots of all five winners holding their trophies, both individually and as a group
- Pan down the long table where the competition takes place as the contestants eat
- Shots of the pancakes being prepared and delivered to the contestants

AVAILABLE SOTS

- Rosey LaPlante, Women's winner: "If I never eat another pancake in my whole life, it's gonna be too soon."
- Boris Taloumis, Pee Wee winner: "My mom always told me I had a good appetite—I think I could have eaten a couple more."

Writing VO/SOT Stories (Afternoon Newscast)

Write the following stories as VO/SOT/VOs, using the available facts and elements. Make sure to follow proper script format, and include all visual and sound elements, including supers and graphics. Stories will air at 6 p.m. today on a local Lakedale newscast.

STORY #1: DEATH PLUNGE

WHAT/WHERE/WHEN   A Lakedale man plunges to his death in an accident at Scenic Falls Overlook in Victoria State Park around 2 p.m. today. Victoria State Park is about 30 miles west of Lakedale.

DETAILS   Teddy Mulvane, 40, fell 400 feet to his death, apparently while taking photographs from the overlook. Two hikers spotted Mulvane's body shortly after the accident and notified park rangers, who retrieved the body. Mulvane was known to friends and family as an amateur photographer. He was married and the father of 10-year-old twin boys. He worked in Lakedale as a lab technician at General Hospital. Source: State Parks Commissioner Robert Bryan.

AVAILABLE VISUALS

- Still photo of Teddy Mulvane (single shot)
- Still photo of Mulvane (with his wife and sons)
- Various shots of Scenic Falls and the overlook where the accident occurred
- Video of the covered body being loaded onto an ambulance

AVAILABLE SOT

- State Parks Commissioner Robert Bryan: "We believe his camera went over the ledge first. We don't have any witnesses who actually saw him go off the top. We're basically surmising that he slipped."

STORY #2: WANTED FOR QUESTIONING

WHAT/WHERE/WHEN   Police are looking for a local man for questioning in connection with a double murder that happened late last night at an apartment building at 755 Water Street in the South Bank neighborhood of Lakedale.

DETAILS   The bodies of a Lakedale woman, Cathy Langdon, 38, and her daughter, Kallie, 7, were discovered in their home this morning by a neighbor. Each had been shot in the head. Authorities are hoping to question John Gainer, 32, as a "person of interest." Gainer had reportedly been Langdon's boyfriend for the past two months, after his release from the state prison on assault charges. He is believed to be driving a white 1999 Buick Regal with local license plates. The car was seen by neighbors parked in front of Langdon's apartment building last night. Cathy Langdon was a single mother. She worked part-time as a health care aide at a local nursing home. Source: Sgt. Alice Sweeney, media relations officer, Lakedale Police Department, and neighbor Robert Small.

AVAILABLE VISUALS

- Exterior footage of the house where the bodies were found
- Shots of police and police cars at the scene
- Shot of "crime scene" tape sealing off the house

- Still photo of Cathy Langdon with her daughter
- Mug shot of John Gainer

AVAILABLE SOT

- Bite from Robert Small, upstairs neighbor who discovered the bodies: "I was supposed to drive them to Cathy's mother's house this morning. The door was unlocked, so when they didn't answer I went inside. That's when I found them."

STORY #3: LUMBERYARD FIRE

WHAT An overnight fire heavily damages the Jackson Brothers Lumber Company. The investigation into a cause has continued throughout the day.

WHERE Jackson Brothers Lumber Company is about two miles south of downtown Lakedale, at 4500 Federal Boulevard.

WHEN The fire apparently started around 4 a.m. in a storage area behind the main building. The investigation has continued today.

DETAILS No one was injured in the fire, which lit up the night sky. It took firefighters two hours to bring the blaze under control. The owner of the company, Mickey Jackson, says he plans to rebuild. Officials have not determined a cause, but damage is estimated at $1 million. Fire officials say they have not ruled out arson. Jackson Brothers Lumber is one of Lakedale's oldest family-owned businesses. It first opened its doors in 1920, and has been in its current location since 1948. Sources: John Arthur, media spokesman for Lakedale Fire Department, and Mickey Jackson.

AVAILABLE VISUALS

- Night shots of the fire, with plenty of tight shots of firefighters at work
- Daytime shots showing the destruction
- Historical photo showing the original Jackson Brothers Lumber building when it opened in 1920
- A photo from the grand opening of the current lumberyard in 1948

AVAILABLE SOT

- Mickey Jackson, lumberyard owner: "We plan to rebuild as soon as we straighten out the insurance claim. This lumberyard means a lot to the people of Lakedale, and to our family."

STORY #4: PIPE BOMBS

WHAT/WHERE/WHEN Two crude, low-power pipe bombs are found around 2 p.m. along railroad tracks in an industrial park in Lakedale. The bombs are spotted along tracks inside the Eastern Yards Industrial Park, an area of light manufacturing plants just south of downtown Lakedale.

DETAILS A railroad worker spots a suspicious-looking metal box with protruding wires along the side of the track and notifies Lakedale police. Two officers from the Lakedale

Police Department Bomb Squad arrive at the scene about 15 minutes later, along with a bomb-sniffing dog. Within minutes, the dog finds a second bomb nearby, about 20 feet up the tracks. Police detonate the first bomb; the second bomb had already been detonated when the dog found it. Investigators question a number of people in the area, including employees of nearby businesses, but as of airtime no arrests have been made. Trains through the industrial park are briefly delayed. There are no injuries. Source: Captain John DiPraia, head of the Lakedale Police Department Bomb Squad.

AVAILABLE VISUALS

- Footage of the general area of the industrial park
- Various shots of police walking with the bomb-sniffing dog
- Shots of the bomb before it was detonated
- Various close-up shots of the rail line

AVAILABLE SOT

- Captain John DiPraia, head of the Lakedale Police Department Bomb Squad: "We're not sure why these bombs were placed on the tracks. If anyone has seen a suspicious character in the area, we'd sure like to know about it. This isn't the kind of thing we like to see happen in our town."

STORY #5: DOMESTIC SHOOTING

WHAT/WHERE/WHEN   A domestic disturbance results in the shooting of a Lakedale woman. Police have identified her ex-husband as a suspect. The incident took place at a duplex at 859 Lewis Street just south of downtown Lakedale around 8:30 a.m. today.

DETAILS   A woman, Shari Jones, who was living with her mother, is shot and wounded by a man police say was her ex-husband. Husband, Delbert Jones, arrives at the mother's home, barges in with a .38-caliber revolver. Shoots his ex-wife in bedroom where she is sleeping. Shari Jones's mother, Esther Leon, grabs her own gun and shoots the ex-husband as he is fleeing from the house. She wounds him but he escapes into woods behind the house. Mother calls 911, police apprehend the suspect about 15 minutes later. Shari Jones in good condition at General Hospital with gunshot wounds to her leg, Delbert Jones in serious condition at same hospital with wounds to his back and buttocks. Charges of assault with intent to kill filed against him at 3 p.m. in District Court. Source: Sgt. Alice Sweeney, media relations officer, Lakedale Police Department.

AVAILABLE VISUALS

- Exterior of the house where the shooting occurred
- Shot of victim being loaded into an ambulance and driven away
- Shots of police searching in woods
- Still photo of suspect
- Exterior of General Hospital

AVAILABLE SOT

- Rowena Winston, next–door neighbor: "I was asleep in bed when all of a sudden I heard gunshots next door. I knew they'd been having problems, but I never thought things would get this bad."

Analysis: Studio-Based TV News Stories

- Record a local newscast and study the stories that are written as anchor readers. Pay particular attention to sentence structure, length, and whether the story is accompanied by any kind of over-the-shoulder graphics.
- Record a local newscast and study the stories that are written as VOs. Pay particular attention to the lead sentence, the transition from anchor desk to video, and the referencing of text with visuals.
- Record a local newscast and study the stories that are written as VO/SOTs or VO/SOT/VOs. Pay particular attention to the choice of sound bites, the setup for the bite, and whether there is a VO tag after the bite.

WRITING NEWS PACKAGES

TOPICS DISCUSSED IN THIS CHAPTER

ASSIGNMENTS/ANALYSIS

WHAT IS A NEWS PACKAGE?

A *news package* is a fully edited, self-contained story on videotape, complete with visuals, sound bites, reporter narration, reporter stand-ups, and natural sound. Unlike the story formats discussed in Chapter 3—readers, VOs, and VO/SOT/VOs—packages are not read live by an anchor or reporter in a studio. Instead they are written and edited before the newscast begins, with the narration recorded and all other visuals and sound integrated into the final product at that point.

Another key difference is length. Packages have different running times, but for a typical newscast the average length is between one minute, 15 seconds and two minutes. Ninety seconds is standard, hence the newsroom saying, "Down and dirty, a minute-thirty."

Packages are introduced live by either a studio anchor or a reporter in the field. It is not unusual for a package to run as an element within a reporter's live shot. In that instance the studio anchor tosses to the reporter in the field, who then tosses to the package. The package is generally followed by a reporter tag, and perhaps a brief question-and-answer exchange between the reporter and anchor.

Reporter packages are a fundamental component of full-length newscasts. Packages are reserved for the most important and most interesting stories of the day. When properly handled, news packages can compress a great deal of information—visuals, recorded sound, and the reporter's narration—into a brief but reasonably complete story.

HOW A NEWS PACKAGE IS PRODUCED

Packages evolve in several stages. First, after a reporter is assigned a topic, he or she conducts as much preliminary research as possible before heading into the field. This research might involve making phone calls, conducting web searches, reading newspapers and magazines, screening previously aired stories on the topic, talking to colleagues who have covered the issue, and so forth. Good reporters do as much preproduction research as possible to maximize the time they spend in the field.

The exception to this rule would be a breaking news story. In that situation, the priority is getting to the scene as quickly as possible. In the case of breaking news, preliminary research matters less than checking out the circumstances firsthand.

Second, the reporter and photographer (in smaller markets both functions might be handled by a single person) travel to the appropriate location to shoot interviews and other visual elements of the story. Before leaving the location, reporters generally shoot at least one stand-up in the field. If time allows, they might shoot several different stand-ups to increase their editing options. Certain stories involve more than a single location, which entails extra travel. Although each circumstance presents its particular challenges, the common denominators do not change: There is always footage to shoot, sound to record, and a deadline to meet.

Third, after shooting is complete, the reporter prepares to piece together the package. Sometimes this means returning to the newsroom to write and edit. Other times the writing and editing are done at a remote location and fed back to the station for play-back, especially if the journalist will be introducing the material during a live remote. Whatever the location, the reporter's first order of business is to screen everything that has been shot in the field and make note of the video, sound bites, and stand-ups. This process of note taking is called *logging,* and the more video and sound that have been compiled, the more logging there is to be done. "I have learned over the years not to ask unnecessary questions," says Katie Hammer, a reporter at KFSN-TV in Fresno. "It only makes for longer logging."

Logging is facilitated by a feature called time-code—essentially, a time stamp that is automatically embedded onto the videotape as it records in the field. In logging their tapes, reporters note the time-code for the various shots and sound bites so these elements can be quickly accessed during the editing process. To make the process of scriptwriting more efficient, reporters usually transcribe in full any sound bites they plan to include. This information makes it easier to write into and out of the bites.

Fourth, the journalist sits down to write the package in script form. Having screened all the video and logged all the sound bites, the reporter now chooses which elements to include and which to omit. If additional visuals are required—archival footage, still photos, graphics, and so on—those also have to be tracked down.

Except on rare occasions, reporters write formal scripts for their packages. The script serves several purposes. It is used as a guide during the editing process. At stations that offer closed captioning, it provides the necessary information for that service. The script, or a rewritten version of it, can also be posted on the station's website. Before a package is edited, many stations require that a producer or executive producer read and approve the written script, a step that serves as a safeguard against potential problems.

Once the script is complete, the reporter records his or her VO narration in a sound booth or editing room. If the editing is being done at a remote location, these VOs will be recorded in an appropriately quiet setting, such as the news production truck. For on-location recording reporters often use special *lip microphones* that filter out background noise.

Fifth, using the script as a blueprint, the package is edited, either by a video editor or in some cases by the reporter or photographer. If the script has been properly written, the editing stage should go relatively smoothly. If not, the process becomes one of trial and error, a luxury that might not be available when time is of the essence.

Finally, once the package is fully edited the reporter or producer orders any supers the director will need to key during the package. This list must include—in sequence—the correctly spelled names of interviewees, locators, and any other explanatory information to be superimposed during the newscast itself. Unlike graphics, which are preproduced, supers are added live as the package airs.

It should be noted that the process of shooting, writing, and editing a news package can happen very fast. Extra time may be available for producing a feature story or for nonbreaking news, but frequently the package must be turned around in a matter of hours, or even less if the events happen close to airtime.

Reporter Sean Kelly of WCVB-TV in Boston says his record turnaround time for a package is about 20 minutes start to finish. The story involved a late-night fire at a church in which several people were killed. Kelly and his photographer spent 10 minutes shooting cover footage of the fire and conducting brief interviews with survivors and a fire official. The other 10 minutes were devoted to writing and editing the package. "We crash-recorded the (VO narration) tracks while I ad-libbed, laid down three sound bites, and wallpapered the 1:15 piece with long shots of the burned building and victims getting treatment," Kelly recalled. "I doubt the Emmy people will be calling to congratulate us, but viewers got the information, and it looked clean."

STRUCTURING A NEWS PACKAGE

Like other forms of narrative storytelling, packages are structured with a beginning, middle, and end. The beginning establishes the story, the middle develops it, and the end resolves or wraps it up, at least to the extent possible.

Each TV news package really has two beginnings: the live lead-in that is read either by the reporter or anchorperson before the videotape begins, and the first 15 to 20 seconds of the edited videotape. These two beginnings must make sense together, meaning they need to be written so that no information is repeated from one to the next. To draw viewers into the story from the start, both the live lead-in and the opening seconds of the package need to be compelling, which means using interesting language, images, and sound.

The middle section of the package constitutes the bulk of the story. Here is where the main points are communicated, either in sound bites or reporter narration. Because of the brevity of TV news packages, reporters must limit themselves to a few key ideas per package. Too much detail will bog down the package and hamper the pacing.

The end of the package presents an opportunity to leave viewers with a final impression. A package can conclude with a sound bite, reporter VO, or stand-up. Whatever the writer's choice of ending, the goal is to provide the audience a sense of closure, both visually and with sound. Most TV networks and stations employ a standard "out," which means a reporter will sign off with a particular phrase; for example, "Reporting for the Channel Six News, I'm Jennifer Wong."

A standard 90-second package allows for only a few sound bites, a handful of VOs, a natural sound transition or two, and a single reporter stand-up. Structurally speaking, no individual ingredient of a package should be allowed to dominate. Instead the story should create a sense of forward motion, weaving bites, VOs, and natural sound into an effortless whole that guides viewers along naturally.

The objective is to keep each element short and concise. If your script is top-heavy with VOs, restructure it to introduce sound bites and natural sound. If you're long on bites, break them up with short VOs or natural sound transitions. Although each situation presents its own challenges, it's generally a good idea to shift gears every 5 to 10 seconds or so to keep the story flowing.

With complicated subject matter it might also be advantageous during the anchor introduction to set up the story with a quick VO or VO/SOT before going to the reporter's package. This breaks the information into smaller structural segments and thereby helps the pacing. Dividing the material into sections in this way is especially appropriate when the story offers several angles that need to be developed. It is important, however, that the information in the package is different from what has been presented in the anchor setup.

Another suggestion is to use your strongest video as early in the story as possible. The objective is to encourage viewers to stick with the report, and compelling pictures can make the difference between someone watching or changing the channel. To the degree possible, all the visuals in the package should generate interest. Experienced TV journalists make the point that a properly constructed television news story is one that makes sense to the audience even with the sound turned down.

GETTING STARTED AS YOU WRITE A NEWS PACKAGE

Different journalists take different approaches to writing package scripts. Obviously, experience brings confidence, and the process of putting together a news package becomes less intimidating over time. However, each set of circumstances presents particular challenges, and reporters can never get too relaxed about the task at hand. If a journalist is bored with a story, viewers will be, too.

Before anything else, the reporter must first figure out what the package is about. This might seem self-evident, but even the most routine stories should be approached with a fresh eye. Every day brings news of accidents, crimes, and disasters, but no two incidents are exactly alike. A creative journalist will highlight what stands out about each story. What differentiates the situation? What makes it worthy of a viewer's interest? These preliminary questions are always worth asking.

As a general rule, it is a good practice to draw up a brief outline for the package after you have finished shooting and before you begin to write. Keep in mind that time limitations will allow you to concentrate on only a few key ideas. If you try to cover too much ground you will quickly lose focus. Decide which key ideas you want to stress, and include them in the outline.

Before doing any writing, thoroughly acquaint yourself with the available visuals and the sound bites. These are the raw materials from which you will sculpt your story.

The best television journalists "write to the pictures," which means taking your cue from the pictorial possibilities and working from there. Choose your strongest video and let it set the tone for the package.

When beginning a package script, start with the elements that cannot be changed: the sound bites, natural sound, and reporter stand-ups that you have shot in the field. Once you have identified which of these you want to use, your story outline will begin to take shape. Save your VO narration for last, as the VOs are completely under the writer's control and can be easily altered to suit the needs of the story.

Finally, use your lead-in and tag as a place to add supplementary details, or to present material that doesn't make it into the taped package.

WRITING PACKAGE LEAD-INS AND TAGS

Lead-Ins

A *lead-in*, also called a toss, is the live introduction that precedes a package. Lead-ins are read either by an anchorperson in the studio or by the story's reporter from a remote location. Package lead-ins are usually no more than 10 to 20 seconds long. Despite their brevity, however, they are important in laying the groundwork for the story that follows.

Lead-ins help prepare the viewer for the package. Because they are delivered just before the package begins, lead-ins must not be redundant with the opening seconds of the package. For this reason, the reporter who writes the package will probably also write the lead-in. At the very least, whoever writes the introduction needs to have screened the package to avoid duplication of language or content.

A live lead-in should relate organically to the taped package, so that viewers take in the information as a seamless whole. Because it is live, the lead-in offers the chance to update the latest developments in a story. This is particularly useful in the case of breaking news, when events might have changed between the time a package is edited and the time it airs.

The language of lead-ins should be clear, direct, and conversational. Good writing helps the anchorperson make a connection with the audience at home and keeps viewers interested enough to stick with the package.

According to Mike Beaudet, an investigative reporter at WFXT-TV in Boston, "I always write the lead-in first before starting the package. It forces you to boil down the story. Then if I get stuck when I'm writing the package, I go back and read the lead-in and often it refocuses me on the point of the story."

Tags

A *tag* is a short bit of additional information read live by the anchor or reporter at the end of the taped package. These usually run only a sentence or two in length, just enough for another quick fact or two.

Tags provide a sense of closure for the audience and serve as a transition between the taped package and the rest of the newscast that follows. When writing tags, it's a good idea to add information that might not have been known when the package was edited or that the reporter did not have time to include in his or her script. Tags are also a good place to bring the story forward by mentioning what might happen next, especially if the subject matter is of an ongoing nature. For instance, if your package deals with a criminal case, the tag is a perfect opportunity to mention the next step in the legal process.

When a reporter introduces the story from the field, that person also provides the postscript. When this is done live, the reporter and anchor are likely to engage in a brief question-and-answer during the tag. Q-and-A in a live tag is almost always worked out ahead of time to avoid duplicating information that was included in the package or to avoid putting the reporter on the spot by asking something for which he or she lacks a response.

Because these Q-and-A tags are prearranged, it is important that they not come across as phony. Use the tag to add legitimate details about the story, not to promote upcoming newscasts or repeat what has already been said.

SOUND BITES VERSUS NARRATION

In writing a news package, when do you use sound bites and when do you use reporter narration? The same rule that applies to VO/SOT/VO stories also works for packages: Use sound bites for *objective* information (facts), reporter VOs for *subjective* information (emotions).

Use sound bites when they:

• express a strongly held opinion.

• offer a first-person perspective.

Gathering interview sound bites is one of the key functions of the TV journalist. Sound bites bring a first-person perspective to news packages, conveying the interviewee's feelings, experiences, and opinions.

- reflect an individual's personal experience.

- provide insight into the personality of the interviewee.

- offer colorful, conversational language.

Use VO narration when you are reporting:

- facts and figures.

- dates and times.

- complicated sequences of events.

- items on a list, like criminal charges.

- other straightforward, noncontroversial information.

VO narration, unlike recorded sound, is wholly under the writer's control, giving the journalist a good deal of flexibility. A news writer is well positioned to economically summarize impersonal data, so assigning this information to the reporter as a VO makes sense. Objective information also suits the journalist's role as a neutral nonparticipant in the story.

Some packages—features as opposed to hard news—lend themselves especially well to sound bites and natural sound. Veteran television journalist Larry Hatteberg of KAKE-TV in Wichita has gained national prominence for his feature profiles of interesting characters from around the state of Kansas. When he encounters an individual with a powerful personality, Hatteberg makes it a point to let that person tell as much of the story as possible. "In those cases," he says, "I become the subject's producer. I organize their thoughts, put it together visually, and write very little. I find that viewers like that. They like to hear people like themselves and they relate to it better than having a reporter talk to them. Reporters aren't real people, but their friends and neighbors are. By becoming the subject's producer, they sell the story for you to a waiting and receptive audience."

This approach would not work in every situation, but Hatteberg makes an important point: Writing a TV news package means knowing when to step out of the way of the material.

INCORPORATING SOUND BITES

Because virtually all news focuses in some measure on human beings, the majority of TV news packages include sound bites with interviewees. Interview bites have the added advantage of shifting the emphasis of a story away from the reporter. However much of a presence he or she might be, the package is not about the journalist.

When a sound bite appears in a story, it is crucial for viewers to understand who it is they are seeing and hearing. This is accomplished in several ways. One method is to write a brief VO that runs just before the bite, a VO that specifically sets up the speaker. In this approach you would use a cover shot of the person in an appropriate, noninterview context; ideally the person would be doing something visually interesting, something that helps explain who he or she is. During this shot a short VO sentence would explain the person being shown. For example, the shot might show a woman working at her computer as the VO says: "Professor Anita Calderon is an expert on constitutional law." From here you would cut directly to the bite.

A lazy version of this is to dispense with the cover video and start the shot of the interviewee a few seconds before his or her bite kicks in. During this prebite portion of the shot, the reporter offers a VO that identifies the speaker, at the end of which the audio of the bite is brought up full. Generally, this style of setup is unacceptable. In TV news terminology, it's known as *lip flap,* because the interviewee's lips are moving as the reporter or anchor is talking.

In many instances, a VO setup for the sound bite is neither necessary nor possible. Remember that if you lack cover visuals, you can always rely on your lower-third super to identify the speaker of a sound bite. In fact, whether you use a VO setup or not, the interviewees in your package will most likely be identified by a super. With that in mind, a VO setup might not be necessary, and the time it takes could be better devoted to other information.

For a discussion of how to "tee up" a sound bite, see the discussion in Chapter 3. Whether the sound bite runs within a package or a VO/SOT/VO story, the same rules apply.

How long should a sound bite within a package be? This depends, of course, on its content. Generally speaking, most interview bites run 10 seconds or less, although strong content justifies extra length. Short bites are desirable, but they must not be too short. When sound bites fly by too quickly they might not make sense.

Extremely short sound bites (five seconds or less) should be used sparingly. They work as man-on-the-street reactions, where the idea is to cut together a range of opinions, and where it is not necessary to run an identifying super for each speaker. Short bites are also appropriate in packages where the interviewee appears on camera more than one time. Otherwise it might be difficult for viewers to identify who it is they are seeing and hearing.

WRITING VOICE-OVER NARRATION

Reporter VOs work best when they are concise and to the point. Except in rare cases, a piece of VO narration should not exceed 15 seconds in length. If you find yourself going longer than that, divide the information into separate, shorter VOs, broken up with a natural sound transition or bite.

A quick glance at your news script should give you a good indication of whether your VOs are too long. If you see dense blocks of reporter narration on the page, chances are you can improve the script by abbreviating the VOs and finding other ways to convey the information—through sound bites, natural sound, or stronger visual sequences.

As with all TV newswriting, reporter VOs should be structured as simple sentences that are easy to read out loud and easy for viewers to hear and comprehend. Don't try to cram too much information into a VO, or the narration is likely to collapse under its own weight. Remember, too, that VOs should add new information to the story, not replicate what is contained in the sound bites.

Finally, because television is a medium of both pictures and sound, a key objective of VO narration is proper referencing. This means matching the words of the VO narration to the images on the screen. This can be a tricky balancing act. On the one hand, you don't want to be too literal in narrating exactly what the viewer is seeing. It would be ridiculous to show a shot of an ambulance racing down the street against a VO that says, "This ambulance is racing down the street."

At the same time, however, the words of the VO cannot contradict what is being shown on screen. Think of the pictures and the narration as two separate layers of information, complementary but not redundant. The images are communicating one idea to viewers, and the words should be communicating something additional—related, but different. Returning to our ambulance example, as the vehicle races down the street, the script should be adding context: "The victims were rushed to General Hospital." In this way the pictures and sound work hand in hand without duplicating each other.

USING NATURAL SOUND

Well-told news packages make liberal use of natural sound. Natural sound helps viewers feel they are experiencing the event directly, infusing the storytelling with an extra layer of reality. Good reporters devote as much attention to natural sound as they do to sound bites, visuals, and the other building blocks of TV journalism.

Anna Crowley, a reporter at WCNC-TV in Charlotte, considers herself an avid fan of natural sound. "The sound of a burbling brook, a fire crackling, a farmer starting his tractor, a cheering crowd, rain in a storm, the heavy panting of a running back in full sprint—once you start thinking in terms of natural sound, it's everywhere."

Two kinds of natural sound are used during packages: full and under. *Natural sound full* means the audio plays at full volume, with no competition from VOs or other sound sources. This technique is also called a *natural sound break*. *Natural sound under* means the natural sound plays under narration.

Natural sound breaks are often used at the beginning of a package, especially when there is interesting audio to work with. Let's say you're writing a story about a dangerous railroad crossing. You might want to start the package with a shot of the railroad crossing sign accompanied by a few seconds of natural sound full of the warning bells and a train speeding by. From this beginning you then go to either a reporter VO or sound bite that sets up the rest of the story.

Natural sound breaks are also effective as transitions within packages. For instance, in a news package about a protest at city hall, it would make perfect sense to include a few seconds of the protestors chanting at various points during the story. Not only can this help you move from one part of the package to another, it also gives viewers a sense of what it would have been like to witness the event firsthand.

Natural sound breaks can even be integrated into the middle of a sentence. Let's say the story is about a community's preparations for a hurricane. The reporter writes a line that says, "Local supermarkets are running low on basic supplies...and if you haven't bought plywood for your windows yet, it may be too late." Two pieces of video accompany this narration, a shot of customers at the checkout line and a homeowner nailing plywood over the windows of his home. On the audio side, the reporter pauses in his narration after the words "basic supplies" and natural sound of the cash registers plays full for a couple of seconds. At the end of "it may be too late," the reporter again briefly pauses for nat sound full of the hammering.

Some journalists prefer to place natural sound breaks before the narration. In the previous example, this would mean starting with a few seconds of audio of the cash registers, followed by the line, "Local supermarkets are running low on basic supplies..." Then would come a couple of seconds of hammering, and the second half of the VO.

Whether it is used within a sentence or between VOs, natural sound serves as a counterpoint to the narration and makes the storytelling more interesting. Some types of packages lend themselves particularly well to natural sound: coverage of a speech or rally, for example, or stories involving music or dancing. Other packages offer less obvious opportunities for natural sound. Still, it is rare to come across a story totally lacking in natural sound.

Natural sound under is something the writer need not be too concerned with. This type of nat sound is routinely added during the editing process, as a subtle accompaniment to the VO narration. Natural sound full, on the other hand, must be clearly written into the script.

REPORTER STAND-UPS

Reporter stand-ups happen when the journalist speaks directly to the camera. In a live reporting situation, these take the form of story introductions and tags, and are delivered live from the scene. As elements of a news package they are recorded on videotape and edited into the final product.

Package stand-ups come in two basic varieties. The internal stand-up runs in the middle of the package, usually functioning as a transition from one part of the story to another. Let's say you are doing a report on a controversial proposal to build a prison in a small town. The first half of the story might focus on reaction from townspeople who support the idea, and the second half on the plan's opponents. An internal reporter stand-up could serve as a bridge that connects the two sections of the story.

The closing stand-up is designed for use at the end of the package. It typically offers either a summary or a sense of where the story is headed next. Closing stand-ups almost invariably end with the reporter *tagging out,* which means attaching a predetermined phrase to his or her name: "For the Six O'Clock News, I'm Bambi Woods," or "From Capitol Hill, I'm Chip Biffster." If the reporter delivers a live tag

Reporter standups are an important component of TV news packages. Standups work particularly well as bridges within a story or as closers.

from the field immediately after the taped package, the package should not conclude with a closing stand-up, because that would mean cutting from one shot of the reporter to another.

By the same token, it is almost never advisable to begin a package with a stand-up, as this places too much emphasis on the reporter. It is also extremely rare for an average-length package to include more than one stand-up; after all, the story isn't about the reporter. The best policy is to let at least 30 seconds of video and sound go by before you cut to a stand-up, and to limit yourself to one stand-up per package.

Chapter 5, "The On-Camera Journalist," takes a closer look at how reporters use stand-ups in their stories.

SCRIPT FORMAT FOR PACKAGES

Package scripts are written in standard television script format, with video indicated in the left column, audio on the right.

The video column lists all the visual elements in the story: "shot of suspect," "still photo of the mayor," "map of downtown area," and so on. Any supers should also appear in the video column, as these qualify as visual material. If the story cuts to an interviewee giving a sound bite, for example, the video column should include a super to that effect: "Jane Doe, Defense Attorney."

The audio side lists all sound elements: reporter VOs, sound bites, natural sound, music, and so on. The script must indicate whether recorded sound will be used full or under. The audio should correspond to the video throughout the script. Each sound bite needs to be written out in full, along with an accurate running time. VOs, natural sound transitions, and music should also be clearly indicated and timed. Copy for VOs must be double-spaced and in all caps; everything else can go upper- and lowercase, single-spaced. Indent each new sentence.

By timing each of the sound elements in the script, writers are able to calculate a total running time for the complete package.

Sample Package Script

Again, we revisit the Tomato Bomber story, this time in package form.

(VISUALS)	(SOUND)
One-shot of anchor w/graphic	POLICE HAVE A SUSPECT IN THE SO-CALLED LAKEDALE TOMATO BOMBER CASE TONIGHT … AND A 90-YEAR-OLD GREAT GRANDMOTHER IS BEING HAILED AS A HERO. BAMBI WOODS HAS THE STORY.
---------------------Take PKG---------------------	-----------------------PKG-----------------------
VIDEO	**AUDIO**
	----------------VO (natsot under)--------------
Shot of Effie Jones in crowd of reporters Locator super: "Downtown"	WHEN EFFIE JONES LEFT FOR THE SUPERMARKET THIS MORNING, SHE HAD NO IDEA SHE'D END UP A MEDIA SENSATION. (:06)
	------------------------SOT------------------------
CU of Effie ID Super: Effie Jones	Bite: I came in for groceries and left with a notch on my belt. (:03)
	----------------VO (natsot under)--------------
Effie talking with cops	TODAY AUTHORITIES CREDIT THE 90-YEAR-OLD GREAT-GRANDMOTHER WITH SOLVING THE CASE OF THE LAKEDALE TOMATO BOMBER … A MAN POLICE SAY IS RESPONSIBLE FOR A MONTH-LONG SERIES OF ATTACKS ON SHOPPERS AT LOCAL GROCERY STORES. (:12)
	------------------NATSOT FULL------------------
Suspect being led away	Natsot Full for :03, cops clearing a path for the suspect
	----------------VO (natsot under)--------------
Tighter on Suspect	POLICE ARRESTED SAM WITHERS, AN UNEMPLOYED PAINTER, AT A DOWNTOWN FOOD-MEISTER THIS MORNING AFTER A TOMATO BOMBING ON MS. JONES. (:08)

	------------------------SOT------------------------
CU of Effie	Bite: I felt something peculiar as I passed through the produce section, and lo and behold I'd been hit by the Tomato Bomber. Well, the man was standing right there—so I hit him with my walker. (:12)
	----------------VO (natsot under)--------------
Shot sequence in produce section	STORE EMPLOYEES MANAGED TO KEEP THE SUSPECT CONFINED IN THE PRODUCE SECTION UNTIL AUTHORITIES ARRIVED TO MAKE THE ARREST. (:08)
	------------------------SOT------------------------
CU of store manager ID Super: Alvin Poindexter	Bite: Mrs. Jones was amazing. She's been following the story on the news, so she knew right away what happened. And she decided to fight back. (:10)
	------------------------SOT------------------------
CU of Effie	Bite: All I wanted was my groceries, and the next thing I know I'm a victim. Well, no tomato bomber can try to pull that on me! (:10)
	----------------STAND-UP/SOT----------------
Reporter stand-up outside supermarket	POLICE SAY THE SUSPECT WILL BE ARRAIGNED TOMORROW IN COUNTY COURT. NOW, THANKS TO A 90-YEAR-OLD FIGHTER, LAKEDALE SUPERMARKETS ARE ONCE AGAIN SAFE FOR SHOPPING. REPORTING FOR CHANNEL xx
TRT (Total Running Time): 1:22	NEWS, I'M BAMBI WOODS. (:10)

REWRITING A PACKAGE INTO A VO OR VO/SOT/VO

News writers are often asked to shorten, or "bust down," a package into either a VO story or VO/SOT/VO. This happens when a story that first ran as a package is shortened for a later newscast. In this situation, the trick is to boil the package down to its essence by selecting the most significant shots and sound elements. In the case of a VO/SOT/VO this means choosing a single sound bite around which to construct the story. For a VO story the writer must summarize the information without using any sound bites at all.

If we were rewriting the Tomato Bomber package into a VO/SOT/VO, the best single bite in the mix is the second one from Effie Jones, in which she explains how she took on her attacker. Because Effie is the focus of the story, it makes sense to give her the sound bite. If we were rewriting the story as a VO, it would be important to include a shot of Effie as the narration referenced her actions in the supermarket. Both versions of the story should also include a shot of the suspect, as this visual would be of interest to the audience.

Rewriting a package into a VO or VO/SOT/VO is common when the news value of the story has diminished and a full package is no longer warranted. Also, TV newscasts are reluctant to repeat packages from one program to the next. Changing the format from a package to a shorter story allows producers to run the item without subjecting viewers to something they have already seen in an earlier newscast.

TIPS FOR WRITING BETTER PACKAGES

Good writers employ a number of strategies for improving their packages.

Structure

Before you begin to write, lay out a rough structure for the package that organizes the material logically. Structure the story so that each element flows into the next, and make sure you are not repeating any information.

Pacing

Do not use VOs or sound bites that are excessively long. Although no firm rules govern the pacing of package scripts, you should generally be shifting gears about every 5 to 10 seconds.

Referencing

Make sure that your pictures match your narration and bites. Nothing is more confusing in a package than a visual that contradicts the verbal side of the script. By the same token, strong visuals don't always require a great deal of additional description. Remember that in TV news, pictures do much of the storytelling for you.

Language

Use language that is simple, direct, and easy to follow. Write sentences that are short. Avoid passive voice. Don't tell viewers how they are supposed to feel; instead, let the facts speak for themselves.

Time References

Packages that are written for evening or late-night newscasts might also run in programs that air overnight or the next morning. With that in mind, it's best to avoid specific time references like "today," "tonight," or "this morning" to eliminate audience confusion.

QUESTIONS TO ASK YOURSELF AS YOU WRITE

Here are a few questions to ask yourself as you put together a script for a TV news package:

- What is the main point of my story? If this is not clear to you, it won't be clear to viewers.
- Do I have an interesting beginning for my story, something that pulls viewers in?
- Does my anchor lead-in properly integrate with the beginning of the taped package?
- Is the middle section of the story focused on a few key points?
- Does the story have a strong ending, both visually and in content?
- Are the various structural components—bites, VOs, natural sound transitions, and so on—interwoven, or does one particular component overshadow everything else?
- Have I used natural sound effectively?
- Do the sound bites convey what sound bites are supposed to? Are they short?
- Are the VOs tightly written? Do they help move the story forward?
- Have I told the story through people, or is the journalist too dominant a presence?
- Have I left viewers with something they are likely to remember?
- Have I taken full advantage of lead-ins and tags to add supplementary, up-to-the-minute information about the story?

CHECKLIST OF KEY POINTS

- A news package is a fully edited, self-contained story on videotape, complete with visuals, sound bites, reporter narration, stand-ups, and natural sound. The usual running time is between one minute, 15 seconds and two minutes, with an industry standard of 90 seconds.

- Packages begin as ideas. If there is time, the reporter will conduct preliminary research before heading into the field to shoot and conduct interviews. After production is complete, the reporter writes a script and edits the raw video and sound into a package. This phase of the process takes place either back at the station or in a remote production truck.

- News packages are structured with a beginning, middle, and end. The beginning unfolds in two parts: the lead-in, read live by an anchor or reporter, followed by the opening 15 or 20 seconds of the edited story. The beginning section establishes the situation, the middle section develops it, and the ending resolves the story or points toward what is likely to happen next.

- Because of their brevity, news packages give the reporter time for only a handful of sound bites and VOs. Each element must be carefully chosen, and no single ingredient should dominate.

- When putting together a package script, start by selecting the elements that cannot be changed, such as sound bites, natural sound, and stand-ups that have been shot in the field. After that, write the VO narration.

- Use lead-ins and tags to add supplementary information, especially any late-breaking developments that might have occurred since the package was shot and edited. Lead-ins and tags should not duplicate information contained within the package.

- Use sound bites from interviewees for opinion, first-person perspectives, and emotional content. Use reporter narration for factual details or complicated information that needs to be compressed. Keep sound bites and VOs short.

- Well-told news packages use lots of natural sound, either at full volume or under the narration. Natural sound breaks work particularly well as internal transitions.

- Reporter stand-ups are used either as transitions within packages or as closers. It is rarely advisable to begin a package with a stand-up.

- Referencing is an important component of writing news packages. Make sure the video matches the audio, but not in a way that creates redundancy.

- Script formats for TV news packages are the same as for studio-based stories: visual elements in the left column, sound elements in the right column.

- Writers are often asked to shorten TV news packages into VO or VO/SOT/VO stories for later newscasts. This involves choosing the best video and usually a single sound bite, and compressing the text into a 20- or 30-second story.

ASSIGNMENTS/ANALYSIS

Assignment: Writing News Packages
The following five exercises give you an opportunity to practice writing news packages. The first three are hard news stories, and the last two are news features.

Package #1: Triple Homicide on Castleway Drive

You have been assigned to cover a triple homicide in a fashionable residential section of Lakedale. You spend several hours at the scene of the crime shooting video and conducting interviews with police and neighbors. Now you must piece it all together for the 5 p.m. local newscast.

Using the available facts, visual elements, reporter stand-ups, and interview bites listed in the transcripts, construct a TV news story about 1:30 in length, about the Castleway Drive murders. The story should be scripted in TV news style, following the sample script in your textbook. Clearly lay out the desired visuals, VOs, stand-ups, sound bites, supers, graphics, and so on. Time your script to make sure it falls within the allotted length. After you finish the package script, write a separate 10-second anchor intro that will be read immediately before the story and also a short anchor tag to run afterward.

THE BASIC FACTS

John Smith, 45, his wife Mary, also 45, and Mary's 80-year-old mother Tessie Tupelo, were found shot to death in their home at 145 Castleway Drive. The bodies were discovered at 10 a.m. today by John's secretary, Lou Ann Lindermeyer, who came to the house to pick up her boss. Lindermeyer was planning to take Smith to the airport for a business trip to Mexico. Police said when she rang the bell and didn't get a response, she tried the door knob, which had been left open. Inside she found the three bodies bound and gagged on the living room floor. Each had been shot in the head.

Police arrived on the scene and began their investigation. At 3:30 p.m. the chief of police held a news conference for reporters (see transcript).

OTHER PERTINENT FACTS

Castleway Drive is in the city's fashionable River Bluffs district, where homes sell for $1 million and up. John Smith owned a business called International Fasteners, which imports a variety of Velcro products from Korea. Mary and Tessie did not hold jobs.

AVAILABLE VISUALS/NATURAL SOUND

- Exterior of house: several shots, including the yellow police barriers
- Driving shot down Castleway Drive past high-dollar houses
- Shots of body bags being removed from the house and loaded into an ambulance, natural sound of the ambulance door slamming
- Shots of neighbors watching as police work at the scene
- Shots of police putting up barricades and measuring distances
- Shot of investigator talking on a two-way radio, with natural sound
- Still photos of the three victims in happier times
- Shot of a distraught Lou Ann Lindermeyer being led away from the house by police

AVAILABLE VISUALS/NATURAL SOUND

These sound bites are given to you in their entirety. You will need to cut them down to more manageable lengths without making them meaningless.

As for visuals, assume that you have an interview shot of the person delivering each sound bite. This doesn't mean you have to stay on the "talking head" for the duration of your bites, if you would find it appropriate to cut to something else. You can also assume that in addition to the bites themselves you have cover footage of each interviewee. This is footage you can use for setting up the person in question, should you choose to.

Police Chief Al Varden (reads a statement summarizing the information already listed, then takes a few questions):

Q. Any suspects in the case?

A. "At this time we have no suspects in this case. We are hoping to find someone who might have seen suspicious activity around the Smith home this morning. If anyone can help us out, we need to hear from them."

Q. Were fingerprints or weapons found inside the house?

A. "We have no comment on that at this time."

Q. Were there any signs of forced entry into the house?

A. "As far as we have been able to determine, there were no signs of forced entry into the house. We are operating on the assumption that the killer or killers might have been known to the Smith family."

Q. Do you suspect there might have been more than one assailant?

A. "At this point in time we have no comment on that."

Q. Where does the investigation go from here?

A. "Our investigation is continuing. Obviously, we have a number of people to interview here in the neighborhood, to see if they heard or saw anything unusual this morning. We will also be talking to business associates of Mr. Smith and other acquaintances of the victims. Again, I encourage the public to come forward with any information they may have. I'll admit to you candidly, we can use some help in this case. There's evidence, but there's a lot more we could learn. I'm sorry, I have no more time for questions. We'll keep you updated as we learn more."

Lucille Miranda, president of the River Bluffs Neighborhood Association:

• "The senseless killings of John and Mary Smith, and Mary's mother Tessie, are something this neighborhood will never recover from. To think that just yesterday they were so alive … so full of life (breaks down crying)…. What can you say about a world where this kind of thing can happen to people like John, Mary, and Tessie? I can't continue. I just hope somebody fries for this."

Marcia Harrison, another neighbor:

• "It's the kind of thing you always hear about, but you never expect it to happen in your neighborhood. John and Mary were two of the nicest people you'd ever hope to find. Tessie was loved by everybody on this street. It's just devastating. When I heard the sirens this morning, I thought it must be a fire somewhere. I wouldn't have believed in a million years three people could be murdered like that, right here on Castleway Drive."

Billy Tibbets, 12-year-old neighbor boy who mowed the victims' lawn:

- "They seemed like real nice people. I never would have expected anything like this to happen. I mowed their lawn last week, same as I do every Saturday. They always paid me right when I finished. Usually tipped me an extra buck, too."

REPORTER STAND-UPS

You have shot two stand-ups on the scene, which you might or might not choose to use in your package. Both show you standing in front of the Smith house:

- "Residents of this well-to-do section of town expressed surprise that such a grisly crime could be committed against three of their own neighbors." (runs :09)

- "And so, investigators say, the long hours of sifting through the evidence have just begun. Police are asking anyone with information to come forward. For the Five O'Clock News, I'm _____. (runs :13)

Package #2: "A Lion on the Loose"

You have been assigned to cover the story of an escaped lion whose unexpected appearance scares the residents of a rural area 10 miles west of Lakedale. Along the road where the lion was spotted you shoot video and conduct interviews with eyewitnesses. You later shoot video of the lion being brought down with a tranquilizer and captured. And you follow the sheriff to a local home where the lion's owner is questioned. After completing your interviews, you return to the site of the capture to shoot a stand-up. Now you must piece the story together for the noon newscast.

Using the available facts, visual elements, and interview bites, construct a TV news story about 1:30 in length about the lion on the loose. The story should be scripted in TV news style, following the sample script in your textbook. Clearly lay out the desired visuals, VOs, stand-ups, sound bites, supers, graphics, and so on. Time your script to make sure it falls within the allotted length. After you finish the package script, write a separate 10-second anchor intro that will be read immediately before the story and also a short anchor tag to run afterward.

THE BASIC FACTS

At around 9 a.m. today the Lakedale County Sheriff's Office receives a call from Midge Bello, a rural resident who reports a lion in her back yard. After she makes the call, she picks up the family video camera and shoots some footage of the animal through the window. By the time officers arrive 15 minutes later, the animal is gone.

At around 10 a.m. a second report comes in, this from a woman named Lucy Chadwell, who lives about a half-mile west on Sedgwick Road from Mrs. Bello. Lucy Chadwell says that after spotting the lion in her front yard, she hustled her two young children inside—but it was too late to save the family dog, a Pekinese named Pudding, whom the lion attacks and kills. (The Chadwell children are Maria, 4, and Jimmy, 2.)

Sheriff Fred Wyatt and his officers arrive at the Chadwell home at 10:05 a.m., but as they pull into the driveway the cat scampers away out of sight into a nearby area along Liberty Creek. The sheriff calls in animal control officers and a sharpshooter, and after these individuals arrive 20 minutes later, the group heads toward the creek.

Here they find the animal taking a nap. Under the supervision of Animal Control Officer June Harper, a sheriff's sharpshooter fires a tranquilizer dart into the lion. After the drug takes effect, the officers heave the unconscious animal into the back of a panel truck for the trip to the Lakedale Area Animal Shelter.

Meanwhile, the owner of the lion, an area resident named Arnold Childs, has notified the sheriff's office that his animal is missing. After the lion is captured, Sheriff Wyatt drives to the Childs home and visits briefly with Childs, who declines to speak to reporters. Wyatt talks with reporters before he leaves. He says he'll meet with the district attorney in a few hours to discuss possible charges against Childs.

AVAILABLE VISUALS/NATURAL SOUND

- Exteriors along Sedgwick Road, including driving shots that establish the area
- Exteriors of each of the two homes where the lion was spotted
- Shot of Lucy Chadwell playing with her kids in the living room of their home, with natural sound
- Exteriors of the creek area behind the Chadwell home where the lion retreated
- Shots of the lion being tranquilized; you're there for the entire sequence of events, meaning you have shots of the lion sleeping, of the tranquilizer dart being prepared, of the gun being fired, and of the animal being hauled into the van. You also have natural sound of the gun going off.
- Shot of Sheriff Wyatt in conversation with Arnold Childs at the Childs home (no audio of their conversation)

OTHER FOOTAGE (HOME VIDEO)

- About 20 seconds with natural sound of the lion wandering around in Midge Bello's backyard, including a few seconds in which the animal seems to look at the camera and roars

AVAILABLE INTERVIEW SHOTS/SOUND BITES
These sound bites are given to you in their entirety. You will need to cut them down to more manageable lengths without making them meaningless.

As for visuals, assume that you have an interview shot of the person delivering each sound bite. This doesn't mean you have to stay on the "talking head" for the duration of your bites, if you would find it appropriate to cut to something else. You can also assume that in addition to the bites themselves you have cover footage of each interviewee. This is footage you can use for setting up the person in question, should you choose to.

Midge Bello, eyewitness (interviewed in her backyard):

- "I'm taking my dishes out of the dishwasher, and I glance out the window and see a lion wandering around. I tell you, that cat was prowling around back there like he owned the place. I thought to myself, am I nuts? That's why I grabbed the video camera—so the sheriff wouldn't think I'm nuts."
- "Let me tell you, it's not every day you see a lion in your backyard."

Lucy Chadwell, eyewitness (interviewed in her home):

- "I was out in the front yard playing with the babies, and the next thing I know this lion jumped out of the trees into the yard. I grabbed the kids and got inside as fast as I could. When I looked out the window, the lion had our little dog in its mouth, just chewing it like a sandwich. Poor Pudding—we've only had her a week."
- "I don't know if the lion escaped from the circus, or what. I just know you never want to get that close to one. The kids were totally flipped out."

June Harper, Lakedale County Animal Control officer (interviewed at the scene where the lion is captured):

- "We'll take the lion to the county animal shelter until we figure out what to do with him. We may end up sending him to a wild animal park somewhere. A cat this size shouldn't be kept as a pet."
- "We don't like to tranquilize unless we have to—and in this situation we had to."

Fred Wyatt, Lakedale County Sheriff (interviewed outside the Childs home), question-and-answer with peporters:

Q. Do you know how the animal escaped?

A. "Apparently the lion was kept in a barn behind the house. The owner thinks he might have left the barn door unlocked."

Q. Are you filing charges against the owner?

A. "As I understand it, state law prohibits keeping dangerous jungle animals on residential property—but I'm meeting this afternoon with the D.A. to pin down the legalities. We'll let you know if charges are filed."

Q. Is Mr. Childs under arrest?

A. "Mr. Childs is not under arrest. He's cooperating with authorities."

Q. Sheriff, is this the first time you've ever dealt with a situation like this?

A. "Well, we caught a crocodile at the county beach a few years back, but this is my first lion. I always wondered what it'd be like to go on a safari. Now I know."

REPORTER STAND-UPS

Write your own reporter stand-up for this story. Indicate the location for the stand-up, and include the copy in the script.

Package #3: Highway 17 Sniper

You have been assigned to cover the story of a sniper incident along Highway 17 in which a motorist is killed. You shoot video of the scene and interview authorities and an eyewitness, then interview a criminal justice expert. After a suspect is arrested, you get a shot of him and attend a news conference about the case held by the district attorney. Once you've completed your interviews and field production, you return to the scene of the incident to shoot a stand-up. Now you come back to the newsroom to piece the story together for the 4 p.m. newscast.

Using the available facts, visual elements, and interview bites, construct a TV news story about 1:30 in length about the Highway 17 sniper. The story should be scripted in TV news style, following the sample script in your textbook. Clearly lay out the desired visuals, VOs, stand-ups, sound bites, supers, graphics, and so on. Time your script to make sure it falls within the allotted length. After you finish the package script, write a separate 10-second anchor intro that will be read immediately before the story and also a short anchor tag to run afterward.

THE BASIC FACTS

At around 10 a.m. today a motorist driving along Highway 17 about 10 miles east of Lakedale is shot and killed by a sniper perched on a highway overpass. The bullet strikes the driver in the head. He loses control of the vehicle, a blue Buick with Ontario plates, which crashes into a tree. A motorist heading in the other direction, Benny Battaglia, stops to help and is also shot at (but not hit) by the sniper. Battaglia hides behind a tree and summons help on his cell phone. Highway patrol officers arrive a few minutes later, close a mile-long stretch of the road, and pull the first motorist out of his vehicle. He is declared dead at the scene. Authorities do not release his identity pending notification of next of kin.

While investigators case the location, other law enforcement units fan out to hunt for the suspect. Acting on a telephone tip, they locate and arrest 21-year-old Bobby Borth at his home a half-mile from the overpass around noon. Officers also retrieve a .22-caliber rifle from the home. Sheriff's deputies take Borth to Lakedale County Jail. There are unconfirmed reports that the suspect confessed to firing the shots.

At 2:30 p.m. District Attorney Roberta Philpot holds a news conference at which she announces that Borth will be charged with first-degree murder. He is expected to be arraigned tomorrow morning.

Highway 17 was reopened to traffic two hours after the shooting.

AVAILABLE VISUALS/NATURAL SOUND

- Exteriors of the section of Highway 17 where the shooting took place; lots of video to choose from, including static shots of the accident scene and shots taken from inside a moving car
- Exteriors of the vehicle that crashed into a tree after the shooting
- Exteriors of the overpass where the sniper perched, including point-of-view shots taken from the overpass toward the highway
- Exteriors at the scene showing the highway patrolmen investigating the site
- Shots showing the "road closed" signs after the highway is sealed off

- Shots of officers diverting motorists from the accident site
- Shots of Borth being led out of his home into a police vehicle; note that this shot runs only 10 seconds

AVAILABLE INTERVIEW SHOTS/SOUND BITES

These sound bites are given to you in their entirety. You will need to cut them down to more manageable lengths, without making them meaningless.

As for visuals, assume that you have an interview shot of the person delivering each sound bite. This doesn't mean you have to stay on the "talking head" for the duration of your bites, if you would find it appropriate to cut to something else. You can also assume that in addition to the bites themselves you have cover footage of each interviewee. This is footage you can use for setting up the person in question, should you choose to.

Sgt. Jerry Garten, State Highway Patrol Spokesman (interviewed at the scene, before a suspect was taken into custody):

- "It appears that the gunman was firing directly at vehicles as they approached the overpass. Unfortunately, his aim was too good."
- "We can't say for sure if other cars were fired at or not before this vehicle got struck. We did receive several calls from people in the area who had heard gunshots. And we know that the motorist who stopped to help—Mr. Battaglia—was also fired at."
- "We have not yet released the name of the victim. We'll do that after we can get in touch with next of kin."
- "We decided to close the road as a precaution for other motorists. We'll reopen it when we're sure it's safe. This is the kind of thing you don't take a chance on."
- "Fortunately, we don't see this kind of incident too often. It's hard to believe somebody could just take a gun and open fire on people driving down the road, but that sure is what happened."

Benny Battaglia, eyewitness (interviewed at the scene):

- "I was driving along minding my own business when I saw the Buick careen out of control. It went off the road and smashed into the tree. I thought the driver had had a heart attack. I pulled over to help, and as soon as I was out of the car I heard a gunshot. The bullet missed me, but I swear I could see it go by. So I ran behind a tree and called the cops. Boy, am I glad I had my cell phone with me."
- "I wasn't really scared until after the Highway Patrol showed up and told me what was going on. I guess they'd already figured out what was going on. As soon as I realized I could've been hit, I said a silent prayer. A few seconds later, and that could have been me."

District Attorney Roberta Philpot (from her news conference):

HER STATEMENT

"Shortly after noon today, officers from the Lakedale County Sheriff's office arrested a suspect in the sniper homicide of a motorist on Highway 17 earlier today. The suspect is identified as Robert Borth, who goes by the name of Bobby. He is 21 years old and a resident of the area where the shooting took place. Borth was taken into custody and transported to the Lakedale County Jail, where he was booked on charges of first-degree murder. His arraignment will take place tomorrow morning in Lakedale County District Court. The officers also retrieved a .22-caliber rifle from the home, which we're looking at as evidence. I have time for a few quick questions."

Q. What else can you tell us about Borth?

A. "Not much. We do know that he was employed as a dishwasher, and that he lived with his parents. The parents were out of town, but they have been contacted."

Q. How did authorities find the suspect?

A. "After the road was closed, the Sheriff's Office received a telephone tip from a neighborhood resident who had seen the suspect walking along the road with a rifle."

Q. Can you tell us who phoned in the tip?

A. "Not at this time."

Q. We've heard reports that Borth confessed to the shooting.

A. "I can't confirm or deny that."

Q. Does the gun they found match the one that fired the bullets?

A. "It's too early to tell. That's one of the things the forensics lab will be looking at. I'm afraid that's all the time I have for questions."

Professor Lyndon Carthage, criminal justice expert (interviewed at his office at Lakedale University):

- "Sniper incidents of this type are fairly uncommon, thank God. But over the past 10 years something like 50 shootings of this type have taken place around the United States, where the gunman is firing from an overpass. Most of the time no one gets hit. This was a tragic exception."

- "There's no particular profile for someone who would do something like this. About the only thing we can say about highway snipers is that they tend to be young, Caucasian, and male, which fits the pattern in this case."

- "The scary thing for all of us is that there's no way to protect against this kind of thing. All of us assume a certain risk every time we get behind the wheel, but the last thing you'd ever expect is to get shot while you're driving along the highway. The one positive thing is that nobody else got hurt."

REPORTER STAND-UPS

You have shot two stand-ups at the scene, which you might or might not choose to use in your package—but don't use more than one. Both show you standing along the highway, which has now been reopened to traffic. Please note that you cannot edit these down—they must be used in their entirety:

- "Just two hours after the shooting, authorities got a lucky break—an anonymous telephone tip that led to the arrest of young man from the neighborhood." (:10)

- "Borth will be arraigned tomorrow in Lakedale County District Court. Meanwhile, along Route 17, traffic is returning to normal. For the Six O'Clock News, I'm _____." (:12)

Package #4: Farewell to Land-o-Fun

You have been assigned to cover the last day of Land-o-Fun, a local amusement park that has been in operation for more than 50 years. You travel to the park to shoot video and conduct interviews with the owner of Land-o-Fun and with people who have come to enjoy the place one last time. From a position on the merry-go-round, you also shoot several versions of a stand-up. Additionally you shoot an interview with the Lakedale City historian at her office downtown. After completing your production work, you return to the newsroom to search the archives for film footage from the park's past. Now you piece the story together for the 5 p.m. local newscast.

Using the available facts, visual elements, reporter stand-ups, and interview bites as listed in the transcripts, construct a TV news story about 1:30 in length about the closing of Land-o-Fun. The story should be scripted in TV news style, following the sample script in your class-pack. Be sure to clearly lay out the desired visuals, VOs, stand-ups, sound bites, and so on. Remember to time your script so that it meets the 1:30 length. Also write a separate 10-second anchor intro and a brief anchor tag to run afterward.

THE BASIC FACTS

After more than 50 years in operation the local amusement park Land-o-Fun is closing its doors. The decision to shut down came from owner Henry Moon, whose parents, Mack and Clarisse Moon, opened Land-o-Fun in 1955, the same year Walt Disney inaugurated Disneyland in southern California. According to Henry Moon, Land-o-Fun could no longer compete with larger, more sophisticated amusement parks. After losing money for several years, and following a disastrous fire in 2003, Henry Moon decided he had no choice but to cease operation. He sold the land to a real estate developer, who plans to turn the 35-acre park into a housing development.

From the first day Land-o-Fun opened for business on June 3, 1955, the park became an instant success. As one of Lakedale's major attractions Land-o-Fun drew thousands of visitors a week, and a visit to the park was considered an essential part of childhood for every kid in town. Many a Lakedale birthday party took place at Land-o-Fun, and for a number of years any student in the Lakedale public schools with either a straight-A average or a perfect attendance record automatically received a free all-day pass as a reward.

By the late 1980s the park had seen a substantial drop in attendance. A 1989 shootout at Land-o-Fun resulted in the deaths of two teenagers. Police at the time described the episode as gang-related. In July 2003 fire destroyed the wooden roller coaster, which was not rebuilt. According to investigators, the fire was set by a disgruntled employee. He later pleaded guilty to arson.

Land-o-Fun is located in southwestern Lakedale, at the intersection of Congress Road and Starboard Highway.

AVAILABLE VISUALS/NATURAL SOUND

- Exteriors of the entrance to Land-o-Fun, with its trademark sign of a large, smiling clown; natural sound of the park's relentless theme song, played on a calliope
- Shots showing visitors buying tickets at the ticket booth, with natural sound
- Exteriors around the park of the various rides: the train, the merry-go-round, the haunted house, bumper cars, and so on, all with natural sound
- Shots of the concession stands
- Shots of people lined up at the various rides
- Shots from on board the park's miniature railroad, with natural sound of the train whistle
- Map showing the location of Land-o-Fun
- Architectural drawing showing the real estate development planned for the location
- File footage from the park's opening in 1955 (without sound)
- Still photo of Henry and Clarisse Moon, park founders, in 1955
- File footage from the aftermath of the gang shooting in 1989
- File footage of a fire that burned the wooden roller coaster in 2003
- Various still photos from the park taken over the past 50 years

AVAILABLE INTERVIEW SHOTS/SOUND BITES

These sound bites are given to you in their entirety. You will need to cut them down to more manageable lengths, without making them meaningless.

As for visuals, assume that you have an interview shot of the person delivering each sound bite. This doesn't mean you have to stay on the "talking head" for the duration of your bites, if you would find it appropriate to cut to something else. You can also assume that in addition to the bites themselves you have cover footage of each interviewee. This is footage you can use for setting up the person in question.

Henry Moon, park owner (interviewed at the scene):

- "My parents opened Land-o-Fun in 1955, one year before I was born. They both passed away about 10 years ago."
- "Selling the park is the hardest decision I've ever had to make. Land-o-Fun is the only job I've had during my entire life, and I know I'll miss it. When you run a business like this, you make a lot of friends, and it won't be easy to tell them goodbye."
- "Unfortunately, keeping the park open became out of the question financially. It's pretty tough for a mom-and-pop operation in these economic times."
- "The fire that destroyed the roller coaster was the final nail in our coffin. We just couldn't afford to rebuild it, and frankly, the park was never the same without that attraction."
- "We've heard from hundreds of people in the community who have fond memories of Land-o-Fun. That's been the one gratifying thing in all this."

Abby Mantz, Lakedale city historian (interviewed at her office):

- "From the day it opened, Land-o-Fun was a runaway success. It became a Lakedale landmark almost instantly."
- "It's no accident that Land-o-Fun opened right in the middle of the baby boom. Parents in the 1950s and 60s needed a place to bring their kids for special occasions."
- "Times change, and there was a feeling that Land-o-Fun didn't keep up with the times. After the gang shootout in 1989, a lot of parents felt the park wasn't a safe place to send their kids any more."
- "The closing of Land-o-Fun marks the end of an era in Lakedale. It's doubtful there will ever be another local amusement park on this scale."

Rogene Pinto, park visitor (interviewed at the scene with her children):

- "My parents brought me here on my 10th birthday, and I never forgot it. I wanted my kids to be here on closing day."
- "It's sad to think this place will become just another housing development. I wish there was some way it could always stay what it was."

LaSalle James, park visitor (interviewed at the scene with his children):

- "I've been riding these rides since I was old enough to walk. I guess all good things must end someday, but I never expected they'd tear down Land-o-Fun."

Flavia Gilberto, 8-year-old park visitor (interviewed at the scene):

- "I like Land-o-Fun. I was sad when my mom told me they were closing it, cause we come here all the time."

Billy Kingston, 10-year-old park visitor (interviewed at the scene):

- "I didn't really want to come today but my parents made me. The rides are okay if you're a baby, but to me they're kind of stupid."

REPORTER STAND-UPS

Write your own reporter stand-up for this story, and include the copy in the script. Assume that you have shot the stand-up on board the merry-go-round as it is in operation.

Package #5: The Pink Lady of Coronet Lane

You have been assigned to cover a neighborhood controversy involving a homeowner's decision to paint all the structures on her property a shocking pink. At the scene you shoot video and conduct interviews with the homeowner and her neighbors. You also interview attorneys from both sides and an art expert from Lakedale University. Now you return to your station to piece it all together for the 5 p.m. newscast.

Using the available facts, visual elements, reporter stand-ups, and interview bites as listed in the transcripts, construct a TV news package about 1:30 in length about the "Pink Lady" controversy. The story should be scripted in TV news style, following the sample script in your textbook. Clearly lay out the desired visuals, VOs, stand-ups, sound bites, supers, graphics, and so on. Time your script to make sure it falls within the allotted length. After you finish the package script, write a separate 10-second anchor intro that will be read immediately before the story and also a short anchor tag to run afterward.

THE BASIC FACTS

Isabel Peterson, a 62-year-old resident of the Blueside neighborhood of Lakedale, finds herself at the center of a neighborhood feud. About six weeks ago she began radically redecorating her small, Cape Cod-style home at 112 Coronet Lane. Mrs. Peterson, a retired telephone operator and widow, has owned the house since 1971. She says the idea to "go pink" came to her in a dream. The next morning she woke up and began to paint everything on her property—the house, a detached garage, and a wooden fence that runs along the front of the lot—in a series of bright pink shades. The home had previously been painted white with green trim, a far more standard color scheme in this quiet neighborhood of mostly working-class residents.

Neighbors began complaining the day the painting began, and they haven't stopped since. Occupants of the two houses on either side of Mrs. Peterson pleaded with her to reconsider, as did the homeowner directly across the street. But Mrs. Peterson has held firm, insisting that it is her right to paint the property whatever color she wishes. Mrs. Peterson handled most of the paint job herself, with help from one professional painter whom she hired to deal with the higher reaches of the one-story house.

After their pleas were ignored, neighbors on Coronet Lane formed a group called Sink the Pink, hired a lawyer to represent them, and filed suit in county court demanding that she choose a more reasonable color scheme. Mrs. Peterson responded by hiring a lawyer of her own. The case is expected to go before a judge in county court next week. Meanwhile, the house is attracting dozens of visitors every day, most of whom drive by on the narrow street and gawk.

AVAILABLE VISUALS/NATURAL SOUND

- Exteriors of the house—extensive footage shot on the ground showing various angles of the house, garage, and fence
- Driving shot down Coronet Lane, showing the contrast between Mrs. Peterson's house and the others on the street
- Other shots of the neighborhood
- Footage shot a couple of weeks earlier of Mrs. Peterson and the painter she hired applying pink coats of paint, with natural sound of them talking
- Interior shots of Mrs. Peterson's home, which she has also begun to paint in shades of pink
- Interior shots of Mrs. Peterson at her clothes closet, modeling the new pink outfits she has bought for herself
- Still photo showing the house with its previous color scheme
- Still photo of Mrs. Peterson working as a telephone operator in 1972
- Shots of sightseers walking by the house, with natural sound of the sightseers talking about what they see

AVAILABLE INTERVIEW SHOTS/SOUND BITES

These sound bites are given to you in their entirety. You will need to cut them down to more manageable lengths, without making them meaningless.

As for visuals, assume that you have an interview shot of the person delivering each sound bite. This doesn't mean you have to stay on the "talking head" for the duration of your bites, if you would find it appropriate to cut to something else. You can also assume that in addition to the bites themselves you have cover footage of each interviewee. This is footage you can use for setting up the person in question, should you choose to.

Isabel Peterson, "The Pink Lady":

- "It all came to me in a dream. I had a vision that I was supposed to paint everything on the property pink, and to start wearing pink myself. I don't really understand why. I just know I'm supposed to."

- "I realize the neighbors don't like it, but last time I checked, this was still America. And in America property owners have the right to express themselves."

- "I never used to even like pink. It always seemed like kind of a silly color. But now I can't get enough of it."

- "If people want to call me eccentric, that's their business. My business is to follow my dream."

- "If I lose this case in court, I guess I'll just have to move to Florida. Sure would be a shame, though."

- "This project has cost me a lot of money, let me tell you. Between the cost of the paint, the labor, the new clothes, and the lawyer I imagine I've spent about 15,000."

Phil Agard, next-door-neighbor and head of Sink the Pink:

- "Look, nobody denies that Mrs. Peterson has rights. But she's a member of a community, and that community has rights too."

- "I think if maybe she had compromised a little, this wouldn't have gotten so out of hand. I mean, she could have painted the shutters pink and nobody would've said a word."

- "I'm concerned about our property values in this neighborhood. Who wants to live next to all that pinkness?"

- "This is a quiet neighborhood. We don't really like all the publicity. And we're getting tired of all the sightseers coming through on the narrow streets."

Britta D'Amato, next-door neighbor on the other side:

- "Everything was fine around here until Isabel had that dream. That dream's become our nightmare. I mean, if she's sick let's help her, but just because she's lost it—that shouldn't be our problem."

Belinda Choy, Mrs. Peterson's attorney:

- "Mrs. Peterson is violating no laws. Maybe the color isn't everybody's cup of tea, but it's her choice to make. If the people next door don't care to look at it, I'd suggest they install a hedge or a fence."

Melvin O'Malley, attorney for Sink the Pink:

- "The house has become an eyesore. The city wouldn't let somebody turn their front yard into a garbage dump, or an elephant pen, or anything else that was bad for the neighborhood. Why should one person's desires be placed above the good of the community?"

Professor Andy Snyder, professor of art at Lakedale University (and specialist in the area of folk art):

- "Mrs. Peterson isn't the first person in America to get a little carried away with her decorating scheme. Compared to what's out there, this house is actually pretty tame."

- "It doesn't really go with the rest of the neighborhood, but that's what's unique about it. Maybe the neighbors should take a deep breath and relax."

REPORTER STAND-UPS

You have shot three stand-ups on the scene, which you might or might not choose to use in your package—but don't use more than one. All three show you standing in front of the pink house. Please note that you cannot edit these down. They must be used in their entirety:

(1) "What turned a plain white cottage into a palace of pink? Mrs. Peterson says the idea came to her one night in a dream." (:07)

(2) "The question now goes to the courts, where a decision could come as early as next week. If she loses, Isabel Peterson says she's moving out of state. For the Five O'Clock News, I'm _____." (:11)

(3) "Adding up the cost of the paint, the labor, the new wardrobe, and the lawyers, Mrs. Peterson estimates she's spent $15,000 on her new look. The cost to the neighborhood cannot be calculated. For the Five O'Clock News, I'm _____." (:12)

Analysis: TV News Packages

- Record a news package from a local newscast and study its structure. Pay particular attention to how the reporter begins and ends the story, and count the number of sound bites, reporter VOs, and natural sound breaks.

- Compare how two different TV news outlets cover the same story in package form. Determine which version works better, and analyze why.

- Watch a local newscast and study the use of package lead-ins and tags. Do the lead-ins and tags add supplementary information? Do they repeat information from the packages? Are there seamless transitions between the live material and the edited packages?

- Record a news package from a network newscast and study its structure. Pay particular attention to how the reporter begins and ends the story, and count the number of sound bites, reporter VOs, and natural sound breaks.

THE ON-CAMERA JOURNALIST

TOPICS DISCUSSED IN THIS CHAPTER

- The Role of an On-Camera Journalist • Live Remotes
- The Hazards of Reporting Live on Camera • Reporter Stand-Ups on Tape
- Working as a TV News Reporter • Anchoring the News
- Interviewing on Camera • Techniques of TV News Interviewing
- Finding Work as an On-Camera Journalist • Checklist of Key Points

ASSIGNMENTS/ANALYSIS

- Assignment: Reporting Live From the Field
- Assignment: Reporter Stand-Ups • Assignment: Anchoring
- Assignment: Live Interviewing • Analysis: On-Camera Journalism

THE ROLE OF AN ON-CAMERA JOURNALIST

The most visible part of the TV journalism process is also the most fundamental: an anchorperson or reporter talking to the audience via the lens of a camera. On-camera journalists, also referred to as *talent,* are the public face of the news operation, and as such they have a particularly crucial and difficult role to play. Talent is more than a label; it's also a job requirement.

To work as an on-camera journalist means being able to stand comfortably in front of a camera and provide reliable information to a mass audience in a coherent and interesting way. No one is born knowing how to do this, and indeed most TV journalists receive little or no real training in the mechanics of appearing on television. Direct experience is not only the best teacher; more often than not it is the only teacher.

TV journalists function on camera in a variety of capacities: as anchors and reporters, obviously, but also as interviewers, interpreters, analysts, comforters, and guides. They must be equally at home in live, breaking news situations and in the more controlled circumstances of television studios and videotaped segments. And they must do so while subjecting themselves to the scrutiny of thousands of viewers. Being an anchorperson or reporter means putting yourself on the line day after day in a highly personal way, and anyone who chooses this path must be prepared to face brutal criticism. The best defense is developing a thick skin.

Although a large percentage of those who toil in television newsrooms never appear on camera, the challenge of working as talent should be familiar to all TV journalists, no matter their job title. Because television news is a collaborative process, its participants have an obligation to understand each other's jobs.

On-camera journalism happens in two primary modes: live—originating either from the studio, the newsroom, or the field—and recorded, as in the stories that reporters shoot on location and edit for the newscasts. Working live is generally considered the more difficult task because there is no safety net. Working on videotape at least provides the opportunity for do-overs.

LIVE REMOTES

Television journalists are expected to report live from the field on a regular basis. These reports are called *live remotes* or *live shots,* and the vast majority of them originate

On-camera journalists work around the clock to cover the news. Reporters and crews get used to operating at unusual hours and in unusual locations.

at locations around the viewing area. Live, on-camera reporting also takes place at various sites within the TV station: the studio, the newsroom, the weather center, and so forth. Whatever the setting, all TV reporters need to be comfortable handling live shots. Telling a story live on camera is a skill every bit as vital as writing and interviewing.

Remotes can involve live, breaking news, or they can merely serve as backdrops against which preproduced stories are introduced. Reporters routinely operate in both situations, and although the skills required are similar, major differences exist between these two kinds of remotes.

Live shots that introduce taped stories can be done from any location where news occurs. Crime scenes, courthouses, city halls, legislative buildings, police stations, jails, airports, schools, and hotels: These are the mainstays of TV news remotes. Most stories introduced from the field are packages, but sometimes VO and VO/SOT stories run instead, especially when a reporter hasn't had time to turn around a package.

TV news stations follow a standard structure for live remotes with internal video-tape: The anchorperson reads a brief setup, then tosses to the reporter, who introduces the taped story from the field. At the end of the tape the reporter reappears from the remote location for a brief tag and perhaps a quick question-and-answer session with the anchor. These *outros* generally end in a standard *tag out* with the reporter saying something like, "Reporting live from Lakedale City Hall, I'm Bambi Woods."

In setting up an internal story on tape, whether it's a package, a VO, or a VO/SOT, the reporter delivers a line called the *roll cue*. The roll cue is a signal to the director in the control room that it's time to start playing the video. Even in the most chaotic live remotes, when there hasn't been time to put together a formal script, the control room needs a roll cue to properly synchronize the various visual and sound elements.

Although journalists in the field might sometimes have occasion to use a teleprompter, the reporter normally delivers his or her material either from notes or from memory. This calls for advance planning on the reporter's part, not just in coordinating a roll cue with the control room, but also in organizing the introduction and tag. Well-conceived live remotes have a clear beginning and end, and the content of the live report must not duplicate what's contained in the taped story.

Doing live remotes requires a good deal of dexterity on the reporter's part. Going live means talking directly to viewers, so the reporter's basic communication skills come into play. Experts advise anchors and reporters to think of the camera lens as a person, and tell the story as though they are talking face to face to another human being. This also means using language that is clear, concise, and conversational.

Above all, reporters must maintain a sense of calm during live remotes. Technical glitches occur constantly—videotapes that don't play, microphones or picture signals that go dead, interruptions from weather, traffic, or aircraft buzzing overhead. Live on-camera journalists soon master the art of rolling with the punches. In the final analysis, there's really no alternative.

THE HAZARDS OF REPORTING LIVE ON CAMERA

Reporting live breaking news can be fraught with peril. In the competitive arena of breaking news, the biggest danger is getting a story wrong. Experienced TV journalists warn against reporting any information you cannot confirm. Stick to what you know, and don't go out on a limb with something you might later have to retract.

Veteran journalist Beth Parker describes the pressure of going live on a big breaking story, in this case the announcement of a verdict in the trial of Washington, D.C. sniper John Muhammad. Parker recalls the event as one of her greatest breaking news challenges:

> I had spent six weeks living away from home covering the trial, and it all culminated in that verdict. I had to be outside the courthouse in front of the camera. We had to fill a lot of time ad-libbing as we waited for the verdict live on the air. We also had to devise a foolproof way of conveying the verdict from a colleague in the courtroom to a producer outside to me standing in front of the camera ad-libbing. We decided to make cue cards for each of the criminal counts Muhammad faced. That's a situation where you want to get the information on the air first, but caution must prevail. Obviously, we didn't want to risk reporting the wrong information. The system we devised worked flawlessly.

Parker's anecdote says a great deal about the realities of working as a TV journalist. First, the fact that she spent six weeks covering the John Muhammad trial shows the degree to which big stories can dominate a reporter's professional life. Second, in situations like a trial or an impending live press conference, reporters are often asked to "hurry up and wait" for events to happen. Third, a lack of concrete developments does not obviate the newsroom's desire for live reports from the field, which means the journalist must be able to ad lib and fill time even when there is little new to say. Finally, the need to get the story on the air as quickly and accurately as possible requires forethought by the reporter—in this instance, the prearranged system of cue cards.

For young journalists just beginning their television careers, live remotes can induce a feeling of panic. Over time, after negotiating dozens of live shots, reporters develop nerves of steel. A case of the jitters is not necessarily a bad thing. Experienced on-camera journalists learn to channel that energy into their delivery, using the moments before airtime to take a deep breath and focus on what they want to say.

Beyond nerves, the most difficult thing about reporting from the field might be the unpleasant conditions under which live remotes often take place: hurricanes, blizzards, ice storms, heat waves, floods, wildfires, drunken crowds, and police stand-offs, to name a few. Reporters have been known to sneeze during live shots, or be attacked by insects. Whatever the circumstance, the journalist must remain unflustered and in control.

Doing a live remote can also mean coping with mischievous onlookers who are determined to insinuate themselves into the process. Like all TV reporters, Anna Crowley of WCNC-TV in Charlotte has developed a few tricks to deal with disruptive members of the public during live shots. "I usually try to fake them out by rehearsing so realistically that they aren't quite sure when I'm on," she says. "I also recruit bystanders to help me out with crowd control if necessary. Sometimes I will confront the people before the live shot and ask, 'Do you really want your face associated with this sex offender story I am doing?,' or whatever story I'm covering. I will also shut down my monitor so they can't see themselves on the air. If that fails, I warn the producer to pay close attention and kill the live shot if it gets out of control."

As always in a live reporting situation, the wisest policy is to be prepared for anything.

REPORTER STAND-UPS ON TAPE

In addition to live shots, TV journalists regularly appear on camera in videotaped stand-ups. Stand-ups, which are a regular feature of television news packages, are short passages within the story in which the reporter speaks directly into the camera. Coming up with effective stand-ups is a constant challenge for on-camera journalists, because this part of the story can easily backfire if not done properly. When stand-ups succeed, they can be highly effective storytelling tools. When they don't, the reporter can come across as foolish.

As we saw in Chapter 4, stand-ups typically serve as either bridges within stories or as closers. It is rare to begin a package with a stand-up. This is particularly true when the reporter introduces his or her package from the field, because it would mean cutting directly from the reporter live to the reporter on tape. Some TV journalists avoid internal stand-ups altogether when they are introducing and tagging from the field, on the theory that the reporter is already a strong enough presence in the story. Because packages rarely run longer than 90 seconds, an internal stand-up takes time that might be better devoted to sound bites, natural sound, and narration.

Effective stand-ups function as more than structural devices. Clever reporters take advantage of stand-ups to point out specific locations or to visually explain aspects of the story that are otherwise difficult to convey. For instance, let's say you are doing a package about a neighborhood church whose members are seeking to close down an adult bookstore that has opened next door. The reporter could do a walking stand-up that starts at the church and ends at the bookstore as a way of physically illustrating just how close the two buildings are.

A stand-up might involve an on-camera demonstration of some kind, as in the following example: A consumer products agency releases a list of toys that have been declared unsafe for preschool children because the toys contain small pieces that could break off and be ingested. A reporter stand-up might visualize this problem by showing how easily a broken toy could become a dangerous object in a child's hands.

Stand-ups can also be useful in plugging visual gaps in TV news packages. A reporter doing a story about the proliferation of muggings in a particular section of town would probably not have access to video of any of the actual crimes. An on-camera stand-up with the journalist walking down a neighborhood street where the muggings occurred could help compensate for the absence of footage.

Recent years have brought a trend toward stand-ups that involve motion. On its face this is not a bad idea; television is, after all, a medium of moving images. However, motion for the sake of motion can backfire when it merely calls attention to itself. TV journalists need a reason for any unusual movement in their stand-ups. Otherwise, the action might come across as gimmicky. Reporter Anna Crowley applies a simple test to her stand-ups: "I ask myself, would my brothers make fun of me for this?" When she still isn't sure, she goes ahead and shoots the stand-up, then solicits opinions from trusted advisers in the newsroom before editing it into the story.

In producing stand-ups, reporters must plan ahead and give careful thought to how the information they are delivering on camera will integrate into the rest of the package. If not, the stand-up that has been shot in the field could prove worthless in the editing room. "I know I've been burned when I don't plot out the full story," says reporter Mike Beaudet of Boston's WFXT-TV. "You get back to the station thinking you have the perfect stand-up, only to realize the information you said in your stand-up really needs to come earlier in the package." Beaudet offers this piece of advice: "Don't make the mistake of putting the lead in your stand-up."

When time allows, reporters typically shoot more than one version of a stand-up in the field to give themselves maximum flexibility during the editing process. It might be useful, for instance, to shoot one stand-up that could be used as a bridge within the package, and another that could work as an ending, then make the choice while writing the script. It might help to shoot two versions of the same stand-up, one short and one a bit longer. Just because a stand-up has been shot in the field doesn't mean it has to be included in the edited version of the story.

One suggestion for doing stand-ups is for the reporter to think of him- or herself as a tour guide, pointing things out in the scene. Whatever the situation, effective stand-ups should have a clear reason for being. If not, they probably aren't necessary. In the words of Tim Tunison, assistant news director at WBAL-TV in Baltimore, "You should be standing where you are for a reason. Make sure you communicate that to the audience."

WORKING AS A TV NEWS REPORTER

According to Tim Tunison, "TV reporters have to be fearless. They have to be willing, at any time, to engage everyone and anyone in conversation. If you're not willing to pick up the phone and call a mother whose son was found murdered in the street, find another career. At some point every TV reporter will be asked to do the uncomfortable—and it will happen more than you'd like."

The work is exciting, demanding, and full of pressure. There's no better job for someone who thrives on variety, because each day brings something different. You might interview a presidential candidate on Monday, a serial killer on Tuesday, and a Nobel Prize–winning scientist on Wednesday. Versatility is one job requirement, but TV journalists must also be articulate, focused, and able to turn around a story fast.

What is the average workload for a television news reporter? Much depends on the size of the market and the amount of news that breaks during a given cycle. Reporters typically generate one or two packages a day, or perhaps one package and a shorter story like a VO/SOT. In addition to interviewing and writing their stories, most reporters are also responsible for at least one live shot per day, sometimes more. The exception to this pattern would be investigative journalists, who work at a slower pace than reporters assigned to breaking news stories.

Being a television reporter involves more than just interviewing and writing. A considerable portion of the TV journalist's job is devoted to planning stories, both before and after they have been shot in the field. In the case of breaking news, there could be little time to prepare, but for the vast majority of stories, much of the work takes place before the reporter and photographer ever leave the station.

Once an assignment has been made, journalists begin making phone calls and conducting other preliminary research to track down as much relevant information as possible. They preinterview potential sources by phone to find the best people they can include in the story. They think about the visual material they will need to make the piece work for television. Being organized saves the reporter precious time once in the field, and also facilitates editing.

Let's take a look at the principal categories of reporting that on-camera journalists routinely deal with: spot news, investigative stories, beat reporting, and features.

Spot News

Spot news is another term for breaking news: unscheduled events that the journalist gets sent out to report, often while the story is still unfolding. General assignment reporters can expect to cover a great deal of spot news in their careers. For many it is a particularly rewarding challenge.

"If you're a news junkie, spot news is a rush," says Sean Kelly of WCVB-TV in Boston. "You're seeing a news story develop right in front of you. No one knows anything about it except you, because you're there and you get to report it firsthand. The negative side of that is it's often difficult to confirm information that flows to you

Television journalism is an extremely competitive field. When covering a big story, reporters and their crews may find themselves part of a "media scrum."

furiously and from all kinds of sources. Your news judgment, ethics, and quick, coherent thinking are never more important than in spot news."

As Kelly's comment suggests, covering spot news means making quick assessments against looming deadlines. As with all journalism, it is important to stick to the facts at hand, attribute information to sources, and use language that does not sensationalize the situation. Spot news also requires reporters to steel themselves against unpleasant conditions, because the reality of these stories can be gruesome.

Investigative Reporting

Unlike spot news, investigative journalism gives reporters and producers time to track down information and file stories of a more complex nature. Whereas a typical spot news package rarely exceeds 90 seconds in length, investigative reports can warrant several minutes of airtime, or perhaps run in multiple installments. In investigative work the frantic pace of breaking news gives way to a slower, more deliberate style of television journalism.

Like many experienced reporters, WTTG-TV's Beth Parker mixes general assignment reporting with investigative journalism. "I enjoy investigative work because it allows me to dig into a topic," she says. "Most daily stories leave me itching for more time, both to research and write."

The process of putting together an investigative story involves the laborious accumulation of details that eventually add up to something larger. Long before the cameras and microphones are brought in, investigative journalists gather their facts by phone or computer, in public records offices and libraries. The goal is to turn up some shred of information that leads to more information, and so on.

According to Sean Kelly, a member of the I-team at Boston's WCVB-TV:

Investigative reporting takes patience and lots of it. A two-minute story could easily take six months to put together. Actually, a five-second piece of video could take two months to get. Let's say you're looking to prove that a government official has done something illegal. Generally that person isn't dumb enough to be obvious, so it could take a very long time to see it and record it. Good investigative pieces require you to have dogged persistence. You might not find the information you need immediately. But if you know it's there you must keep looking.

Although it is slow and labor-intensive, investigative work offers its practitioners a sense of accomplishment. As Beth Parker puts it:

> Investigative pieces can be much more challenging because those involved in the story often have much to lose or gain by being featured in a TV news story. I've been threatened by gun-toting white supremacists, followed, yelled at, shoved—all in the name of investigative reporting. I've also been lucky enough to help uncover some wrongs and corner a few bad guys. Those are the stories that keep me going.

Investigative journalism produces another benefit: Because good investigative stories stem from original ideas, they almost always result in a scoop for the stations that air them.

Beat Reporting

Beat reporters are specialty journalists, assigned to a topic area that they cover regularly. Depending on the market and the TV station, beats can include such fields as politics, crime, entertainment, health, consumer news, and sports. Some journalists who concentrate in these areas have personal experience in their areas of specialty, for example, medical reporters who are practicing physicians. Others learn the ins and outs of the beat only after they've been assigned to it.

Beat reporters might make daily contributions to the newscasts, or they might appear less frequently, when events warrant. Many beat reporters have regularly scheduled segments within the station's news programs. Certain beats heat up at specific times of the year—political reporters covering elections, entertainment reporters covering the Oscars or the new television season, sports reporters covering playoffs—whereas others are reliably busy year-round, like the crime beat in a big-city newsroom.

According to Glenn Counts, crime reporter for WCNC-TV in Charlotte, the word that best sums up beat reporting is "routine":

> You talk to the same people and cover the same territory most days. It helps you to build trust and to generate stories. Of course, all of this depends on your people skills: how well you communicate, and whether you respect the people you talk to. Having a beat also allows you to develop expertise in one area, and it gives you the luxury of knowing what you'll be doing most days.

"General assignment can be like a stick in the wind," Counts says. "That can be a lot of fun: You could get the story of the day or the stinker of the day. Personally, I'll take a beat any day, assuming it's a beat you like."

Features

Feature stories are an integral part of television newscasts, providing relief from the intensity of breaking news and investigative reports. A light touch is required of journalists

Live shots are a standard feature of television newscasts and a challenge that all TV reporters must master.

who write and report these kinds of stories, because features give the writer a good deal of creative latitude. Where spot news stories tend to follow a standard formula, each feature story creates its own mood, structure, and rhythm.

Larger television stations might have reporters who are assigned exclusively to features, but general assignment reporters in small-to-medium markets can expect to cover a mixture of hard news and lighter stories. Depending on the circumstances, it might even be appropriate to take a feature approach to a straight news story. The package assignment at the end of Chapter 4, "The Pink Lady of Coronet Lane," offers a good example. The story deals with a serious neighborhood controversy, but it also offers feature elements that make it less predictable than the run-of-the-mill crime or accident.

Larry Hatteberg of KAKE-TV in Wichita is one of the country's most respected feature reporters, with more than 40 years of experience as a television journalist. According to Hatteberg, the first requirement of feature reporting is a love for people. "If you don't like people," he advises, "stay as far away from the television news business as possible." Another trait he encourages: curiosity. "You must want to know what makes people do what they do," he says.

TV journalists who specialize in features soon develop a knack for recognizing offbeat characters and situations. Because features tend to be people-centered, strong interview skills are also necessary. "Be a good listener," Hatteberg says. "Some of the most powerful pieces of television journalism are when the reporter isn't talking."

Last but not least, the best feature writers in TV news share an ability to deploy the language of pictures and sound with cleverness and originality. "Understand that the camera is the most important writing tool you have," Larry Hatteberg suggests. This advice applies across the board, whether the subject matter is features or hard news.

ANCHORING THE NEWS

An anchorperson serves as the network or station's lead journalist, and as such that person bears an important responsibility, both to the public and to the rest of the news staff. As the face of the operation—literally—anchors must consistently project an air of authority and credibility. No matter how chaotic the circumstances, they must maintain control. The job is more difficult than it appears.

Mary Bubala, an anchor and reporter at WJZ-TV in Baltimore, describes the position this way: "You have to be able to process information quickly and concisely, stay cool, calm and collected, and have a great depth of knowledge about every topic you are talking about. Lots of people can read a teleprompter well, but few can ad lib well when forced off the prompter by breaking news. It helps to be outgoing, engaging, and smart, too."

News anchors are not actors. Their role is not to deliver information in an emotionally persuasive way, but rather to present the news as objectively and neutrally as possible. This does not mean anchors are robots; obviously, if you've been hired to anchor the news, your personality is an inescapable factor. However, professional distance is desirable.

Live, breaking news gives anchorpeople an opportunity to put their skills to the test. In a breaking news situation an anchor functions somewhat like an air traffic controller, assimilating and reporting information as it becomes available, coordinating updates from producers in the control room and reporters on the scene, and relying on his or her own knowledge to add depth to the reporting. If it's a big enough story, the anchor may remain on camera for hours at a time without any break, even for commercials. It's a difficult task, especially when all of this improvising takes place before thousands of viewers.

"When I sit down on the set to anchor a newscast I expect the unexpected to happen," says Mary Bubala, and that's a good rule of thumb for anyone who works in this capacity. All sorts of things can and do go wrong on live television: teleprompters that stop working, tapes that don't play, live shots that go dead, studio lights that suddenly explode during the middle of a newscast. One of the worst fates that can befall an anchorperson is getting the giggles on the air—but it happens.

Most anchors make their way into the position from a reporting background, and many of the same skills that serve a reporter in a live shot apply to the anchor desk, too. Still, anchoring the news is fundamentally different from reporting from the field, and the job of anchoring entails different responsibilities from market to market. In addition to reading the news, small-market anchors might also be expected to produce their newscasts, lining up the stories, preparing the rundown, and writing the scripts. In medium-to-large markets, anchors play less of a role in producing, but they do get involved in writing the newscast, and in addition to their duties at the anchor desk many of them continue to report from the field.

News anchors must be flexible enough to work either individually or as part of an anchor team. "Solo anchoring is much, much harder," says WJZ's Mary Bubala. "I have anchored for 15 years and split my time between solo and co-anchoring. When you are alone on the desk there is no time to catch your breath, read ahead, or make sure you know how to pronounce a difficult name two scripts away. However, when you solo anchor it is 'your' show and it feels great to be in charge of the pacing, personality, and feel of the newscast."

The responsibilities of a news anchor do not stop at the end of the workday. As the most visible components of a TV station's news operations, anchors play an important public relations role. Bubala describes community service as the news anchor's "second job." Like all anchors, she is expected to make frequent appearances at local community events. "I really enjoy it," she says, "because it allows me to connect with viewers in a positive way. Today TV news is filled with so many negative stories. Community service is my outlet to talk about positive things."

INTERVIEWING ON CAMERA

All on-camera journalists, be they studio anchors or reporters in the field, must be able to conduct successful interviews. Television interviews happen in two principal modes: live and on tape. Live interviews give anchors and reporters a chance to show their chops in a highly constricted format that offers no second chances. Taped interviews are generally looser, requiring a slightly different set of skills.

Live interviews can be conducted on camera or, in some instances, by telephone. Because airtime is precious, most live interviews are extremely short—sometimes less than one or two minutes, if the interview occurs within the context of a fast-moving newscast. With time at such a premium, the anchor or reporter must have a clear objective of what he or she wants to ask. A live interview allows for little in the way of wind-up. It's more like a sprint than a marathon, with the action beginning the moment the starting gun goes off. Each question must count to the maximum possible degree, and if the interviewee veers off topic, it's up to the questioner to either steer the conversation back on track or wrap things up.

Taped interviews are a completely different animal than their live counterparts. Where live interviews are brief and compressed, videotape offers the luxury of conducting an interview at a more leisurely clip. A reporter's mission during a taped interview is to generate usable sound bites for the story, and that becomes somewhat easier at

Interviewing skills are essential to anchors and field reporters. Live interviews call for different techniques than interviews conducted on tape for later editing.

the comparatively relaxed pace. Furthermore, when the question-and-answer exchange occurs on tape, there are more opportunities to follow up or revisit points that need further clarification.

Nonetheless, TV news interviews on tape are also subject to deadline pressures. This gives the journalist an incentive to be well organized going into the interview. For each interviewee the objective is to know what kinds of sound bites you are looking for, and to elicit them in a form that will work in the edit room. If an interviewee gives a garbled response, or an answer that is either too long or not entirely coherent, the reporter must reask the question to get a more TV-friendly version of the statement.

At the local level, most television journalists function as field producers for the stories they go out on. This makes the reporter responsible for various production aspects of the shoot, from selecting interview locations to suggesting camera angles to the photographer. In choosing a location for the interview, both technical and aesthetic factors enter the equation. On the technical side, questions of lighting and sound might dictate where an interview can be shot. It is generally easier to shoot interviews outdoors, for instance, where the light tends to be more favorable. On the other hand, noise levels outdoors are difficult to control. Depending on weather conditions—if it's raining or snowing, for example—an indoor shoot might be the only option.

On the aesthetic side, the location should provide visual interest, ideally in a way that reinforces the content of the story. For example, if you are interviewing a farmer, it would make sense to position him next to his tractor. Visually this works better than plastering the interviewee against a living room wall. Each situation presents its own possibilities, and attentive reporters know to seek out locations that underscore context.

Different types of interviews call for different production setups. Man-on-the-street interviews are conducted on the fly, with both the interviewee and the reporter standing informally, and the reporter using a handheld microphone. These interviews tend to be done in clusters, and the shorter the response, the better. In an in-depth interview the subject is generally seated and is outfitted with a separate mic. The feel is more deliberate and more formal, and the reporter spends more time drawing out sound bites that can be used in the edited story.

The circumstances of the interview also determine how it will be produced. An interview that takes place at the scene of an accident or natural disaster will probably not be a formal, sit-down exchange between reporter and source. An interview with a reluctant participant—while the person is getting into a car, for instance—might have to be done quickly, under less than optimum production conditions. On the other hand, an interview with an expert source is likely to involve a formal setup and more time for questions.

TECHNIQUES OF TV NEWS INTERVIEWING

A TV interview is a human interaction, and like all forms of interpersonal communication it requires sensitivity and respect on the interviewer's part. Putting the subject at ease can produce better responses. Listening can be as important as speaking. The framing of a question can make the difference between a first-rate sound bite and useless verbiage.

Many sources are quite accustomed to being interviewed for television, and these individuals require little in the way of advance prepping when it comes time to shoot the Q-and-A. Others, those who do not regularly deal with the media, might need help getting over their nervousness. Many reporters make a point of explaining the process to uninitiated interviewees, reminding them not to worry about mistakes because the piece will be edited. It might also be beneficial to briefly mention a few of the production mechanics, such as the need for the interviewee to speak at normal conversational volume and to look at the reporter, not into the lens of the camera.

By the same token, the reporter should avoid asking substantive questions before the camera rolls. People often give their best version of a sound bite the first time they articulate it, and the words might not come out as naturally the second time around. It works better to engage the subject by chatting about topics other than the story—anything from how the person is handling the media spotlight to idle banter about the weather.

According to WCVB's Sean Kelly:

> If you're interviewing someone who is painfully shy or seems uncomfortable, do your best to put that person in a position where he feels at ease. For example, I was attempting to interview a dog trainer who had a great personality when teaching his classes or being around dogs. When we sat him down for a face-to-face interview, he shut down completely. After the third question we quit and asked him to get a dog that he'd been training. We did the interview while he was handling a dog and suddenly his personality returned. We put him back in an element he was used to and it worked.

Kelly cites a valuable piece of advice he got from an experienced network news photographer: Treat sensitive interviews like a date. "You wouldn't rush right in and kiss her. So try to have a conversation with the interviewee without the camera and lights so the person can get to know you and feel comfortable with you."

"Step out of your role as a journalist and talk to your subjects as a real person," advises reporter Katie Hammer of KFSN-TV in Fresno. "Ask them about their family, where they're from—it eases the tension they may feel."

Anna Crowley of WCNC-TV agrees:

> Connect with the people you are interviewing. People can relate to any basic human emotion, so get busy feeling it. Remember that you're not above the people you are interviewing. If you are arrogant or smug and don't take the emotions of the story seriously, it will come across in the story and you will not be able to get the best possible sound. People must know that you are there because you are actually interested in what happened to them. Don't forget that. Listen to what they are saying and connect with it.

Experienced journalists invariably make the point that effective interviewing hinges as much on listening as on asking questions. Reporters keep an ear to the ground for various things in an interview: deliberate obfuscations, avoidance of the questions, new information, and matters that need following up. On a more technical level, TV reporters also listen for how well a subject's response will work in the editing. If it doesn't make a sound bite, it can't be incorporated into the story. Television journalists get good at hearing *edit points*, those moments in an interview when the response seems bracketed by an invisible set of quotation marks.

One of the first things TV reporters learn is to recognize a usable sound bite when they hear one. Usable bites are those that add a first-person perspective to the information by offering an interviewee's opinions, feelings, and expertise. Strong interview bites amplify the information within a story and bring it to life.

Different interviews call for a different style of questioning. Closed-ended questions—those that can be answered simply "yes" or "no"—are desirable when a narrow response is sought: Will you run for office? Are you guilty of the charges? Do you support same-sex marriage? Have you changed your position on capital punishment?

In general, however, open-ended questions work better for television, because they require interviewees to express themselves in longer phrases and sentences. "Yes" and "no" don't function very effectively as sound bites, except when paired with a pointed question. By contrast, a response that reveals a person's feelings or describes a situation provides the necessary ingredients for putting together a story. To get these longer responses, the reporter must phrase the question properly: "What advice would you have for someone going through what you went through?" "Tell me what you saw that night." "Describe what went through your mind when you heard the news."

Experienced journalists think about the structure of their interviews and the order in which they will pose their questions. In cases involving sensitive subject matter, it might work best to start off with factual questions to put the subject at ease before moving to more delicate topics. When interviewing family members of accident and crime victims, Anna Crowley says she deliberately avoids asking details about the incident or the police investigation. "My approach with the family is always this: Let's talk about who was lost here. Who was this person you loved so much? What special quality did he or she have? What should we all know about this person?"

Because TV reporters so often interview vulnerable people, the approach must always be respectful. This means shying away from questions that take advantage of the situation, like asking the mother whose child has been kidnapped to look into the camera and speak directly to the kidnapper. Good interviewers do not exploit the emotions of the interviewee. They ask the questions viewers would want to ask, questions that fill in the blanks of the story.

One final interview technique is important: Remain open to the unexpected. Like many good reporters, WTTG's Beth Parker makes it a point at the end of each interview to ask if there's anything else the person would like to add. "Occasionally people give me a rather perplexed look, but for each person who does that there are five others who were just itching to say something in particular. Some of the best sound bites I get have come from just letting people spout off about what on their minds. Odds are, it's something I didn't even think to ask."

FINDING WORK AS AN ON-CAMERA JOURNALIST

On-camera journalism is a highly competitive field, and anyone hoping to pursue a career as a television reporter or anchor must have realistic expectations. The usual path is to begin in a small- or medium-sized market, gain experience, and work one's way up the ladder to larger markets in bigger cities. News anchors generally start as reporters, moving to the anchor desk only after they have proven themselves in the field.

Beginners in TV news must be prepared to pay their dues. WJZ's Mary Bubala, who started her career in small markets in upstate New York before advancing to Baltimore, offers this suggestion: "If you get a job on-air out of college, start small and work your way up. Reporting and anchoring skills require lots of on-the-job training, so start in a small market, get better, and move on."

Mike Beaudet of WFXT got his first network affiliate job at WLBZ-TV in Bangor, Maine. "A small market is a great place to work out the kinks and get the experience you need," he advises. "You don't want to seriously flub a live shot in a major market. It could cost you your job. You can get away with it in a smaller market."

Whatever the career path, all on-camera journalists apply for jobs using something called a résumé tape or audition tape (also known as a résumé reel or audition reel). Although the terms differ, they all describe the same thing: a videotape compilation designed to showcase an applicant's best work. Résumé reels are short—five to 10 minutes is about the maximum for reporter and anchor tapes—and they are structured according to a standard format.

For reporters, the tape should consist of three to five stand-ups in the field, followed by no more than three news packages. The first package should be a hard news story that shows off the journalist's ability to handle challenging subject matter. After that the tone can lighten, although it's best to err on the side of substantive stories rather than fluff. Some reporters suggest including a run-of-the-mill assignment that you have turned into a creative story; this way the boss can see your ability to tell an ordinary story in an unusual way.

For anchors, the reel should begin with a montage of the person at the anchor desk, with the newscast's taped packages edited out. Résumé reels for anchors might also include an example or two of anchoring from the field or a recent news package that shows off the applicant's reporting skills. WBAL's Tim Tunison cautions anchor candidates, especially females, to maintain a consistent look in their audition tapes. "We see a lot of tapes where the hair changes color and lengths repeatedly," he says. "All this does is tell your potential boss that you haven't found a look that works yet. Pick a look (preferably a good one) and stick to it."

Here are a few other things to bear in mind about the presentational side of your résumé tape: Don't be too casual in your appearance. Men should wear a tie, although jackets might not be necessary unless you are anchoring. Women should wear business dress. Avoid flashy colors or accessories that distract from what you're saying. Keep your hair out of your face. Remember that news directors will probably not watch your entire tape, so make sure the beginning is particularly strong.

What if you don't have a reel of professionally produced stories or newscasts to put on a résumé tape? For beginners, especially new college graduates, this is a common problem. The best solution is to use material you have produced for classroom assignments or as part of a student television operation. The production quality might be imperfect, but a news director will look past the technical flaws to see how you present yourself on camera and to judge your skills as a reporter and writer. If you do an internship at a television station, make friends with a cameraman and ask that person to shoot location stand-ups with you. If that's not possible, have a friend videotape you on camera as professionally as possible, perhaps with equipment from your school. Use an external mic so that the sound quality is good, and pay attention to lighting. Choose locations that are appropriate for a television newscast.

Finally, be aggressive in your search. The level of competition is intense in TV news, and newcomers to the profession face a particularly difficult chore in selling themselves. However, the job search presents an opportunity to show a news director you are persistent, and persistence is a quality every journalist must possess.

"I sent out more than a hundred résumé tapes before I landed my first job at an affiliate," says Mike Beaudet. "I had a stack of rejection letters. But I didn't give up. If you really want a job, you'll get one."

CHECKLIST OF KEY POINTS

- On-camera journalists work both live and on videotape. Different skills are required for each type of situation.

- TV journalists report many of their stories from the field, regularly appearing in live remotes during newscasts. These remotes can include videotaped stories or live interviews, and they require an attitude of calmness and control on the part of the reporter.

- Live remotes can be particularly challenging when they involve breaking news. It is essential that the journalist provide accurate information, even when details are still evolving. Live reports often originate amid unpleasant circumstances: blizzards, floods, wildfires, police stand-offs, and hecklers.

- Reporter stand-ups involve the journalist speaking directly to the camera in videotaped stories, and they must be handled intelligently and with restraint. Stand-ups can be useful in filling visual voids or allowing reporters to do on-camera demonstrations. As structural elements within stories, stand-ups need to be well thought out to integrate logically into the script.

- Most television news reporters cover spot news, breaking stories that crop up at the last minute. Other reporters are assigned to investigative teams that do more in-depth stories or beats that involve a specialized area of coverage like politics, crime, entertainment, health, sports, and so on. Some reporters concentrate on feature stories, in which creative writing is a crucial skill.

- Anchors serve as the face of a news operation. They must be cool under pressure, conversant with the major stories of the day, and able to roll with the punches when unexpected events come along. Although most anchorpeople begin their TV careers as reporters, the two jobs are fundamentally different.

- Television news interviews take place either live or on tape. In a live interview time is of the essence, and there are no second chances. On tape, interviews can be more leisurely, because only short snippets of the information will actually be used in the edited version of the story.

- A TV news interview is a human interaction, requiring sensitivity and respect. The reporter's goal is to generate usable sound bites. Some situations call for aggressive questioning, whereas others require a more conversational approach. Interviewers should be good listeners and keep themselves open to the unexpected.

- Reporters and anchors land jobs by showcasing themselves in résumé tapes. These are short reels that include a mixture of stories in a range of styles. In the competitive world of television news, most on-camera journalists start out in smaller markets and work their way up the ladder.

ASSIGNMENTS/ANALYSIS

Assignment: Reporting Live From the Field

For each of the following stories prepare a 60-second summary and deliver it on camera. Don't write a script that you read word for word. Instead put together an outline that allows you to present the key points in a conversational style. You will not have time to include all the available information.

New Year's Crash

WHAT

During a New Year's Eve celebration in downtown Lakedale, a car plows into a crowd of revelers, injuring at least five people.

WHERE

Along the waterfront in downtown Lakedale, just outside the Lakedale Tower Hotel and across the street from the Blueside Aquarium.

WHEN

Shortly after midnight. You are reporting just minutes after the incident, from an area police have set up as their command post, where eyewitnesses are giving statements.

DETAILS

A maroon Volkswagen Jetta began driving through a knot of people gathered along the waterfront to watch a harbor fireworks show that was seeing in the new year. Several people were trapped under the wheels of the vehicle, according to eyewitnesses.

One eyewitness said as many as 20 people in the crowd threw themselves on top of the car, trying to stop the vehicle and smashing the windshield in the process. The car was estimated to be going about 20 miles per hour. Once the car stopped a number of police officers fought through the crowd and pulled the driver out. Some among the crowd began assaulting the driver, police said. Onlookers in the crowd said the driver had been heard screaming at people to get out of his way as he accelerated into the throng.

According to eyewitnesses, those injured were mostly just knocked over by the force of the moving vehicle. One woman appeared to have a broken leg. Witnesses said people in the crowd began screaming when it became clear the Jetta was aiming directly at them. This is when the crowd began pounding on the vehicle to try to stop it from proceeding.

The driver of the vehicle was quickly arrested. He is charged with assault and battery with a deadly weapon. His name has not been released. A female passenger was also inside the Jetta. Witnesses reported that the two had been fighting over who was going to drive home just before they both jumped into the car and tried to drive off.

At least five victims, as well as the female passenger, were taken to area hospitals, according to police spokesman Sgt. Alice Sweeney. Sgt. Sweeney said their injuries were minor. No one is expected to be kept overnight.

The New Year's Eve celebration drew an estimated 10,000 people into downtown Lakedale. Warm, dry weather made the crowds for this annual event larger than ever. No other problems were reported beyond a few routine incidents, Lakedale police said.

Bridge Collapse

WHAT

The two-lane Waterside Avenue Bridge collapsed early this morning near downtown Lakedale.

WHERE

The Waterside Avenue Bridge crosses the Blue River about a mile east of downtown Lakedale.

WHEN

The collapse was reported around 5:15 a.m. Police barricades blocked the bridge to traffic by about five minutes later. You are reporting this story on the 6:30 a.m. local newscast.

DETAILS

According to police, only two vehicles were on the bridge at the time of the collapse, because of the early hour. One of these, a southbound Chevrolet Lumina, managed to get across just as the middle section of the structure began to give way. The second car, a yellow taxi, was caught right atop the section that broke apart. The taxi dangled from the bridge for several minutes before sliding into the river. This delay gave the driver—Chin Wing, 46, of Lakedale—a chance to escape and crawl to safety. Wing has been taken to General Hospital, where he is under observation for minor scrapes and bruises, police say.

According to police, the driver of the Chevrolet—Maria Blitzen, 27, of Rock City—called 911 from a nearby convenience store to report the collapse. She was on her way home from working the overnight shift at Denny's. Officers arrived on the scene within minutes, and the bridge was closed to traffic in both directions.

The bridge carries about 6,000 vehicles a day, according to the City Transportation Department. This means there will undoubtedly be tie-ups, especially this morning, because many commuters still haven't heard about the collapse. The Waterside Avenue Bridge is one of the city's oldest, built in 1917. It was slated for major repairs next summer. No cause is known for the collapse at this time. A thorough investigation is promised.

The collapse of the Waterside Avenue Bridge means commuters from the area of Lakedale called South Bank will need to find alternate routes to downtown. Police are recommending either the Interstate 33 bridge to the east or the John F. Kennedy bridge to the west. The City Transportation Department says it's too early to say when the Waterside Avenue Bridge will return to service.

Industrial Evacuation
WHAT
A small town near Lakedale is being evacuated after an explosion at a fertilizer plant.

WHERE
Vanderwood Industries, a factory in the town of Vanderwood, population 4,000. The plant employs about 40 people and manufactures agricultural fertilizer products. Vanderwood is 20 miles south of Lakedale.

WHEN
The explosion happened about 2:30 p.m. inside the plant, sparking a fire. The fire is still raging at 5 p.m., which is when you do your live report for the local (Lakedale) news. Firefighters arrived on the scene 10 minutes after the initial explosion. They are still there at airtime.

DETAILS
The entire population of Vanderwood is being evacuated. School buses from a number of area school districts are being used for this purpose. The evacuees are being taken to a holding facility at the National Guard Armory in Lakedale. Members of the media are being kept about a mile from the site, but the smoke is still visible.

The explosion's cause is unknown, but officials confirm the presence of a number of 55-gallon drums of sulfuric acid inside the plant. Also in the plant were undetermined amounts of other potentially harmful chemicals. The fire is causing large, billowing, black clouds of smoke to pour over the town. Potential danger from toxic fumes is the reason residents have been evacuated.

No serious injuries have been reported so far, according to Vanderwood Mayor John Winborn. The cloud of smoke is drifting toward the southwest, away from the town of Vanderwood. Residents in the small towns downwind of the fire have been warned of possible evacuations. The state environmental agency is on the scene to take air samples. Law enforcement officials from the surrounding area, including officers from the Lakedale County Sheriff's Department, have also been summoned to prevent incidents of looting while the evacuees are out of their homes.

Vanderwood Industries has been in business in the town of Vanderwood for about 20 years. There have been no previous problems, according to Mayor Winborn. Company officials and plant employees have been unavailable for comment. Most of them were evacuated along with the residents of the town.

Church Fire

WHAT

The historic Church of St. Anselm, a well-known local landmark, burns to the ground in an overnight fire.

WHERE

The Church of St. Anselm is in the Greenside neighborhood of Lakedale. This is just north of downtown on Central Avenue across from the main entrance to Prospect Park.

WHEN

The fire apparently began sometime after midnight, according to fire officials. The first report of the fire came in at 1:10 a.m. By the time the first truck arrived about five minutes later, the entire roof of the building was on fire. Additional units were called, and firefighters continued their efforts for more than an hour. By the time the fire was brought under control at around 3 a.m., the building was in ruins. You are reporting this story on the 6 a.m. local newscast. Behind you, the fire is still smoldering.

DETAILS

According to fire officials, the fire appears to have started in the main sanctuary area of the church. Arson is not being ruled out as a possible cause, although investigators say it is too early to pinpoint a reason for the fire at this time. They promise a full investigation to determine what happened.

About three dozen firefighters were at the scene during the height of the episode. Six trucks were used in the operation. No one was in the building at the time of the incident. A caretaker who lives on the grounds in a separate building first phoned in the information to the fire department. The caretaker's home was not affected by the fire, nor were any other nearby structures.

The Church of St. Anselm is a Roman Catholic church, with a membership of around 700 parishioners. The wooden structure was built in 1856, making it one of the oldest churches in Lakedale. The building was well known as a local architectural landmark, earning a listing on the National Registry of Historic Places. The church was particularly famous for its stained glass windows, which were imported from France.

Church officials say they have not made a decision about whether to rebuild. Fire officials estimated the amount of damage at over $2 million and said that none of the building's contents could be saved.

Assignment: Reporter Stand-Ups

For these exercises you will need access to a video camera and someone to shoot for you.

- Go to the package scripts at the end of Chapter 4. Some include written stand-ups and others ask you to put together your own stand-ups. Choose several of these, memorize them, then have someone record you delivering them on camera to see how you come across.

- Go to a local landmark in your area that serves as a backdrop for reporter stand-ups—city hall, the courthouse, a busy downtown intersection, and so on—and shoot stand-ups for a story that might conceivably take place there. For the sake of variety, do several versions so you can see what works and what doesn't.

Assignment: Anchoring

- Take the "Reporting Live From the Field" assignments in this chapter and deliver them on camera from behind a desk, as though you were reporting the stories as breaking news. To approximate the feel of going live, work from notes rather than a script.

- Take the reader, VO, and VO/SOT/VO scripts you wrote in Chapter 3 and practice delivering them. Then have someone record you reading them on camera from behind a desk.

Assignment: Live Interviewing

- Find someone to interview about a subject that person knows something about. Conduct a five-minute live interview and record it for later critiquing. You will also need someone to serve as a floor director. That person's job is to count you down as you begin the interview, then keep time and cue you to finish when your five minutes are up. Because you have only five minutes, make sure to structure your questions in a concise and logical way.

Analysis: On-Camera Journalism

- Record five live remote reports from local and network newscasts and critically analyze them. How well does the reporter tell the story? Is the information presented factually and authoritatively? How well do the live portions of the report integrate with the videotaped portions?

- Record a live TV news interview from a local or network newscast and critically analyze it. How well does the interviewer ask questions? How much information is elicited? Are there things the interviewer could have done better?
- Arrange to follow a local TV reporter on a story and write a description of the experience.
- Study the on-camera delivery of the major TV anchors in your market, and write a comparative analysis that examines the strengths and weaknesses of the various players.

PART TWO

PRODUCING

CHAPTER SIX

NEWS JUDGMENTS

TOPICS DISCUSSED IN THIS CHAPTER

- What Makes a Story Newsworthy? • The Seven News Judgment Criteria
- Applying the News Judgment Criteria • Problems of News Judgment Decision Making
- Covering Diverse Communities • News Judgment and Sensitive Subject Matter
- Other Influences on News Judgment Decision Making • Enterprise Reporting
- Investigative Journalism • Feature Stories • Checklist of Key Points

ASSIGNMENTS/ANALYSIS

- Assignment: News Judgment Decision Making
- Assignment: Turning Nonvisual Stories Into TV Stories
- Assignment: Dealing With Breaking News
- Assignment: Developing Enterprise and Investigative Stories
- Assignment: Developing Feature Stories
- Analysis: News Judgment Decision Making

WHAT MAKES A STORY NEWSWORTHY?

What makes a story worth covering in a television newscast? Producers, reporters, assignment editors, and other newsroom decision makers make constant judgments about the journalistic value of the numerous events that unfold on a daily basis. Because of limited personnel resources and the constraints of time, only a small fraction of potential stories can be covered. Therefore, a key challenge facing news personnel is selecting the important items and bypassing the less important.

Some stories are no-brainers. If a plane crashes at the local airport and kills everybody on board, that's clearly an event worth covering. Still, even a situation this obvious calls for news judgments: How much coverage does the accident merit? Which angles are most newsworthy? Are there aspects of the story that call for a different approach to the material—say, investigative journalism as opposed to straight reporting, or feature storytelling versus a hard-news angle? How might the story play in different time slots? In the days following the accident, how much attention should the story continue to generate?

Most events covered by TV news operations are less dramatic, and in some ways that makes them more difficult to gauge. Decision makers must rely on a combination of instinct, experience, and—most significant—a keen sense of the viewers and their needs. A story that functions as the lead item on a noon newscast might not rate similar placement at 6 p.m., when the composition of the audience is different. A story that receives front-page play in the newspaper could be of less consequence on television, where information must be conveyed visually. Certain stories, or certain material within stories, might be more suitable for the station website than an on-air newscast.

Newsworthiness is a fluid exercise, subject to endless reevaluation. The plane crash at the local airport might look like the day's obvious lead, but 30 minutes later something bigger could come along to supplant it. Stories that are assigned to reporters in the morning planning meeting might be abandoned in favor of unexpected news that breaks in the afternoon. News producers are always readjusting the day's menu, as facts on the ground overtake theoretical plans. The value of news stories, like stocks on the stock market, remains in constant flux, rising and falling as competing factors alter the equation. As is always the case in television news, journalistic decision makers must be able to roll with the punches.

THE SEVEN NEWS JUDGMENT CRITERIA

Although news judgments are inevitably subjective, TV journalism operates according to a set of unwritten rules. Let us consider the seven criteria producers use to assess the newsworthiness of potential stories for the newscasts: impact, timeliness, proximity, conflict, prominence, novelty, and visuals. All these considerations must be weighed against each other in deciding what to include in a given newscast, and some carry more relevance than others. Let's take a closer look at each of these criteria.

Impact

How much of the audience is affected? How direct is the effect? How immediate is the effect? These are the questions journalists ask as they evaluate a story's newsworthiness. One reason weather accounts for so much coverage on television newscasts is that it applies to virtually everyone in the local viewing audience on a more or less equal basis. Other examples of topics with wide-ranging viewer interest include the cost of food, housing, and transportation; proposed tax increases; the closing of major roadways for repairs; and anything else of general concern to the community.

Not all stories will speak to the audience so directly. If the bank president in a local suburb is arrested in an embezzlement scandal, that's interesting to citizens in that particular jurisdiction, but less so to people who live in a different part of the metropolitan area. Impact varies, depending on how broadly a story affects the viewers who tune into a newscast or visit a TV station's website.

Timeliness

In television news, fresher is better. As Tim Tunison, assistant news director at Baltimore's WBAL-TV, put it, "Breaking news is king." Viewers have come to expect timely information from TV news outlets, which are uniquely positioned to cover news as it unfolds.

In evaluating newsworthiness, TV news producers look for subject matter that offers strong visuals, as in this brushfire story.

A story that's big enough might warrant live coverage that interrupts regular programming, although this applies only to the most momentous events. At the very least a breaking story is likely to make an early appearance on the news organization's website, even if viewers must wait until the scheduled newscast to receive a more thorough account. It is worth noting, by the way, that stations are sometimes reluctant to break exclusive stories on their websites, for fear they will tip off their competitors.

Timeliness remains a key consideration in sequencing the stories in a newscast. A story that has broken just before a newscast goes on the air is likely to receive greater play than something that happened four hours earlier, even if it fails to develop into anything major. By the same token, an item that leads the early-morning newscast might not run in a news program that airs that same evening. Here's an example: A major traffic tie-up during the morning commute might be a top story in an early-morning newscast, but later in the day such an incident would be unlikely to merit inclusion in the lineup. By then the story is over and done with, and unless there are ongoing implications, the now-concluded morning traffic jam is of little consequence to the evening audience.

When viewers watch television news they expect to see information that is fresh. That means news producers are constantly revising their judgments about a story's immediacy. Because each set of circumstances is different, the shelf life for news stories can vary greatly. Stories frequently play out over the course of several days, or even longer, depending on the situation.

Coverage of a high-profile crime, for example, unfolds in stages: There is the initial incident, the apprehension of the suspect and early court appearances, the trial phase, the sentencing, and so forth. A year after the original event there might be an anniversary update. Each shift in the story line requires its own evaluation of newsworthiness.

Proximity

Local television news places great emphasis on hometown stories. This means decision makers give priority to anything happening in their own backyards. Conversely, a story of interest to viewers in another state might not be included at all, unless it is too noteworthy to be ignored. By and large, local newscasts report local news. National and international stories may appear as part of a national and international roundup segment, but the usual procedure is to leave national and international stories to the networks.

However, national and international stories often lend themselves to localization. News of an overseas war is not typically something local TV news organizations are equipped to cover, but if a serviceman or servicewoman from your area is injured or killed, that information becomes relevant to a hometown audience. Smart producers will look for ways to find a local angle on the big stories of the day, even when the events do not take place directly in their community.

Among stories of roughly equal importance, the one nearest your audience is the more newsworthy. Thus, if the mayor of your hometown gets arrested for drunk driving, that's a big story to your local audience. If the mayor of a town in the next state over gets arrested for the same offense, the story would probably not make your newscast.

Remember that it pays to know the geography of your local viewing area to understand what matters to the audience.

Certain types of stories might reflect geographical biases, and should be evaluated accordingly. In Southern California, for instance, freeway chases receive extensive coverage. Hurricane warnings are big news in the Gulf Coast states, and blizzards inspire a flurry of stories in the snowbelt. Local events like annual parades, state fairs, or winter carnivals will also garner attention in individual markets. Again, the key is being familiar with your local audience and its traditions and priorities.

Conflict

Conflict is the essence of journalism, just as it is the essence of novels, movies, and plays. That explains the presence in TV newscasts of so many stories about crime, court cases, politics, sports, neighborhood disputes, and the like. Conflict plays well into the dramatic values of the medium. The presence of two or more forces in opposition to one another creates a more interesting story than a situation in which all the players are in total harmony.

Stories involving conflict require the reporter to strike a balanced tone. This means seeking out opposing points of view and making sure that all sides receive a fair hearing. Journalists must also exercise caution in not oversimplifying complex issues that demand nuanced and varied perspectives.

Prominence

By prominence we mean names in the news. Many viewers are interested in the offstage doings of well-known public figures, be they politicians, entertainers, or athletes. To some extent, this interest can be considered frivolous, and newscast producers should take care not to overemphasize celebrity coverage at the expense of serious content.

Within reason, however, it is reasonable to expect that TV newscasts will cover stories involving famous people, both local and national. Celebrities are an inescapable force of contemporary life, and many members of the viewing audience take pleasure in keeping up with the ups and downs of big names. The trick is to present these stories in moderation.

Stories involving local officials—the governor, mayor, police chief, district attorney, and so on—have the benefit of focusing on prominent figures who execute serious functions in the community. As such, these individuals are likely to be regular "cast members" of local newscasts. In the words of an old journalistic saying, "Names make news."

Novelty

Since the dawn of mass media, journalists have shown a weakness for novelty stories, meaning tales of the unusual. One of the oldest clichés in the news business is that dog-bites-man isn't a headline, but man-bites-dog is. Stories about unusual aspects of life capture the imagination and provide a counterpoint to the serious, sometimes depressing material that tends to dominate a newscast. The challenge for producers is to keep novelty stories in perspective.

As a criterion for news judgment, novelty takes a number of forms. A novelty story might deal with a record being set: the oldest pilot to fly across the country, the youngest performer with the symphony orchestra, the world's largest apple pie. It might involve something out of the ordinary that does not involve record-breaking: a fourth-grade class that "adopts" a group of senior citizens at a nursing home, or a dog that raises a stray kitten along with her own pups.

These types of novelty stories, like celebrity news, should be viewed not as the main course, but as dessert. As such, you do not want to overload on high-calorie, low-nutrition content at the expense of news with a more meaningful connection to the audience. Still, a reasonable amount of novelty in a newscast is both acceptable and interesting to viewers. Sometimes those offbeat stories are the ones viewers remember best.

There are also serious stories that take on added news value due to the novelty of their circumstances. A school shooting in the Amish country of Pennsylvania received widespread media coverage in 2006, at least in part because of the unusual nature of the situation, which juxtaposed modern gun violence against the peaceful setting of an old-fashioned one-room schoolhouse. It is natural for TV news producers to play up any event that offers such a jarring twist.

Visuals

Pictures are the lifeblood of television. A story that contains strong video will almost always be more newsworthy for television than a story for which no visuals exist. This is a major difference between television and print journalism.

Stories about fires offer a classic example of the emphasis TV news places on pictures. Unless the fire is particularly large or takes an unusually heavy toll, it is likely to receive only cursory coverage in print. Television, by contrast, will play the story more prominently if there is dramatic video to go with it, even when the incident is otherwise routine.

Because weather affects everyone in the viewing audience, stories about storms are a favorite of TV news producers.

Some stories, of course, are purely visual: the implosion of a high-rise building, a million dominoes falling in perfect choreography, a contest for people who look like their pets, and so forth. Such events serve as catnip to reporters and producers, who are constantly on the lookout for stories with strong pictures.

Other topics, those utterly lacking in pictorial elements, pose greater difficulty for television journalists. The release of a new set of statewide unemployment statistics, for example, might be a newsworthy story, but TV producers will need to find creative visual ways to deliver this information. Too often television journalists take the easy way out, ignoring subject matter that lacks obvious visuals and overemphasizing news items that are pictorially stimulating but otherwise deficient in content. The objective is to cover the important stories in a way that takes full advantage of TV's visual possibilities.

APPLYING THE NEWS JUDGMENT CRITERIA

Let's take a few theoretical stories and see how the seven news judgment criteria apply. For the sake of this discussion, assume you are considering these items for a 5 p.m. local newscast in Lakedale.

Story #1: Traffic

At 4 p.m. a tractor-trailer jackknifes on Lakedale's much-traveled Downtown Loop. The accident causes authorities to close all but one lane of southbound traffic, creating a major traffic jam. An hour later, when you go on the air, only the single southbound lane is still open, and downtown commuters who use the highway to get home are now stuck in extremely slow-moving traffic.

Which news judgment criteria apply to this story? Obviously, the most significant factors are timeliness and proximity: timeliness because the traffic congestion is at its height just as you go on the air, and proximity because the incident is happening in downtown Lakedale. Impact is also applicable here, because of the thousands of commuters who use the highway, not to mention the ripple effect created by all those people arriving home later than expected. Another potential aspect of newsworthiness is the visual image of the cars creeping along the highway, especially if it's possible to get an overview shot from either a helicopter or a tall building along the route.

By these measures, the partial closing of the highway ranks as an important local story, perhaps even a lead if nothing more momentous supersedes it.

Story #2: Teacher Fire

A 37-year-old grade school teacher is formally charged in court at 10 this morning for allegedly setting a fire at Barbara Bush Elementary School the previous afternoon. Authorities say she started the fire in a supply room after being terminated from her position because of absenteeism and complaints from parents. No students were in the building at the time. There were no injuries, and the fire caused only minor smoke damage to the supply room. The suspect had been a third-grade teacher at the school.

The main event in the "Teacher Fire" story happened the previous afternoon, and newscasts from that evening undoubtedly gave this incident a good deal of attention.

Depending on the rest of the day's news, it might even have been a lead. As a news story, this event offers a range of attractions: proximity, timeliness, conflict, visuals, and, perhaps most important, novelty. It isn't every day that an elementary school teacher sets her workplace on fire.

By the next day, the story has lost some of its newsworthiness. However, the fact that the teacher was formally charged in court keeps this item alive and gives news producers an updated angle with which to work. Presumably there are visuals of the teacher at her court appearance, which would be of interest to the audience. After today, the story is likely to subside in importance, at least until the criminal justice process moves into its next phase.

Story #3: Scandal

A congressman from the next state over resigns from office after admitting he accepted bribes in exchange for drafting legislation favorable to lobbyists. The resignation is announced in a written press release that is e-mailed to reporters at noon.

In this instance, the story carries definite news value, but a number of factors weigh against it for a local audience. First, the congressman is not from your state. If he were, this would be a huge story. The lack of direct proximity reduces the impact of this story on viewers in Lakedale. The absence of visuals also works against the news-worthiness of this resignation. If the congressman had delivered his announcement on camera, providing usable video and sound bites, you would have more to work with than a written release. On the plus side, the story is relatively fresh, the announcement having been made only a few hours earlier. Prominence is also a factor, because any member of Congress is an important public figure. There is even a degree of novelty here, because congressional representatives do not step down from office every day of the week, especially amid bribery scandals.

Story #4: Big-Box Store

A Lakedale neighborhood has been split over the proposed construction of a "big-box" discount store on the site of a former hospital. Today at noon opponents of the project held a march at the location, promoting the idea that a park should be built on the land instead. Several hundred people attended the demonstration. According to police, the protesters were spirited but law-abiding.

Proximity is important here, as the controversy is based in Lakedale. Timeliness is also a given, considering that the protest happened today. (The story would be even more timely if the demonstration were occurring live during the newscast, in which case it would make an excellent live remote.) Visuals are potentially interesting, although there's a tendency for all demonstrations to look alike, and in this case there doesn't appear to be anything special about the event from a pictorial standpoint. What the story has going for it is conflict: strongly held opinions on two sides of a contentious issue. If you were the journalist assigned to cover this protest, you would want to balance your report by talking to supporters of the project as well as the demonstrators, thus giving your piece built-in dramatic tension. This is also a good sound bite story because of the intense feelings on both sides.

Story #5: Tattoo Convention
An international convention of tattoo artists is taking place at the Union Hotel in downtown Lakedale. The convention began this afternoon with a "Body Art Fashion Show" in which models displayed their tattoos for an enthusiastic audience. The convention will run for three days.

The story has proximity and timeliness, not to mention excellent visuals. Novelty is the real attraction here, however, because this type of gathering does not occur on a regular basis. Clearly this event qualifies as a feature story, something to be aired toward the end of the newscast, but it's the sort of thing audiences are likely to watch and remember. The tattoo convention is also a highly promotable story, giving producers something to highlight in their news teases and viewers something to stick around for.

PROBLEMS OF NEWS JUDGMENT DECISION MAKING

Because journalism is an inexact science, the seven news judgment criteria occasionally lead producers astray. This happens when the criteria are misapplied, or applied in the wrong proportion. Evaluating stories according to their impact, timeliness, proximity, conflict, prominence, novelty, and visuals might seem reasonable on the surface, but as standards by which to assess newsworthiness, there are limits to their effectiveness.

Impact

As the most important of the news judgment criteria, impact is also the least controversial. Television newscasts seek to serve a wide range of viewers, making impact an obvious priority. This does not mean, however, that every story will affect every member of the audience. By definition, stories with broad impact are relatively rare. Just because a story has a limited focus does not mean it should be overlooked; after all, some portion of the audience is likely to be interested.

Some stories that have a widespread effect might not be all that interesting. Many viewers legitimately complain that TV news stations overhype natural phenomena like blizzards, heat waves, and heavy rainstorms, just because they have broad audience impact. A foot of snow is certainly newsworthy, but unless you're in Florida, it might not warrant the first 15 minutes of a newscast.

Timeliness

Providing timely information is something television news is particularly well positioned to do. Nonetheless, the ability to report stories as they happen poses significant challenges to TV journalists. The desire to get the story first, before the competition, might backfire if the reporter has not had time to gather and confirm the facts.

Live television can be especially dangerous in this regard. In 1981, after the assassination attempt on President Ronald Reagan in Washington, D.C., ABC News erroneously reported the president's death. In 2005 Fox News Channel announced the passing of

Pope John Paul II 24 hours before he actually died. These kinds of mistakes, made under competitive pressure, do a disservice to the audience and erode the public's trust in television news. They bring embarrassment to the journalists involved, especially the on-camera personalities who deliver the information. This is the bottom line: It is better to be right and late than wrong and first.

The impulse to go live must be tempered with common sense. When word of a major breaking story comes over assignment desk scanners, newsroom personnel might be tempted to report the information before they have confirmed it. This is never a good idea, because facts can rapidly evolve. Responsible journalists never report stories without first checking their veracity.

Proximity

Overemphasis on local coverage could mean that important national and international stories get shortchanged. American TV networks are justly criticized for their limited international coverage, and for paying more attention to certain parts of the world (Europe, the Middle East, Japan) than others (Latin America, the Caribbean, Africa, most of Asia). Although it is not the mission of local news to offer extensive national and international reporting, even local newscasts can find ways to broaden their horizons. Local stations should not hesitate to come up with their own angles on national and international stories of the day, especially when the news is big. Keep in mind that the world is more interconnected than ever.

Conflict

Conflict and journalism go hand in hand, but as a criterion for making news judgments, conflict has its limitations. Complicated issues can seldom be reduced to black and white, yet the time constraints of television news make it difficult to present a nuanced picture of a multilayered situation. The goal for journalists covering complex stories is to ensure that differing points of view are fairly represented.

At the same time, the quest for balance could lead reporters to give undue weight to individuals, groups, and opinions that are extreme in nature. Consider this scenario: You are a journalist covering a rally against racism that is attended by several hundred people. Across the street three white supremacists show up to stage a counter-rally. Should both groups get equal time in your story? Absolutely not. Although it's likely you would include at least a shot of the supremacists—like it or not, they are part of the event—balance in no way implies equal time.

In making editorial judgments about complicated social issues, journalists must exercise common sense. Every issue might appear to have two sides, but in some cases that sense of pro and con might reflect a media construct, not reality.

Prominence

The downside of prominence as a news judgment criterion is an overemphasis on celebrities and their doings. Journalists should draw a distinction between well-known figures who play a substantive role in public life, such as elected officials, policymakers, opinion leaders, and so on, and celebrities from the worlds of show business, sports, and fashion. Of course entertainers, athletes, supermodels, and debutantes will inevitably be included in newscasts, but to what degree? Perhaps the best way to handle celebrity news is to group the stories together in a segment that deals with lighter material, like the kicker segment at the end of the newscast.

Novelty

If a newscast is top-heavy with novelty stories, viewers might not get enough protein in their news diets. Novelty, like all things, must be enjoyed in moderation. Some novelty stories might simply be too silly for a serious newscast. Again, the goal should be to choose novelty stories judiciously and not to overplay them by running them too high in the newscast. Novelty stories are perfect for the feature slot at the end of the newscast. Outside of that context, they could come off as frivolous.

Visuals

When the hunger for pictures overtakes the principles of sound journalism, trouble can arise. A high-speed freeway chase might supply dramatic visuals, but unless there is something more to the story than cars zipping down a highway, it could deserve only minimal attention. Visuals alone do not necessarily justify a story.

The primacy of visuals manifests itself in another troubling way for TV journalists when they rely too heavily on *video news releases (VNRs)*. VNRs are, in effect, press releases in the form of edited television packages with video and sound. Corporations, government agencies, and other organizations send these tapes to producers, reporters, and assignment editors in hopes of generating favorable news coverage.

VNRs should never be used as a substitute for original reporting, although there might be legitimate occasions for including isolated elements from VNRs in journalistic stories. For instance, it might be difficult for TV journalists to illustrate a story about a new pill on the market that has just won Food and Drug Administration approval. A corporate VNR that includes footage of the pills coming off the assembly line provides a visual element useful to the storytelling. In a situation like this, there is no problem excerpting video from the VNR, as long as the source of the visuals is clearly labeled. When journalists try to pass off VNRs as original reporting, on the other hand, they violate the ethical standards of their profession.

COVERING DIVERSE COMMUNITIES

One of the key challenges of contemporary television journalism is reporting the news in a way that accurately reflects the viewing audience. In making judgments about which stories to cover and which sources to talk to, newsroom decision makers must take into account the diversity of the communities in which they operate. According to the code of ethics of the Radio and Television News Directors Association (RTNDA), electronic journalists should "seek to understand the diversity of their community and

Newsworthiness hinges largely on what is important in a local community. A small-town news operation is likely to cover local civic events like parades, fairs, and festivals.

inform the public without bias or stereotype" and "present a diversity of expressions, opinions, and ideas in context."

A relatively simple way of reflecting diversity in TV newscasts is to seek out expert sources from varied backgrounds to include in stories. Local professional associations are a good place to track down such individuals. Of course, the quest for diversity among interviewees extends beyond the use of expert sources. Journalists should constantly be on the lookout for opportunities to incorporate minority voices into all of their stories. The possibilities are wide-ranging, from person-on-the-street sound bites to pieces that focus on a "typical" viewer.

By the same token, producers and reporters need to think creatively in choosing stories to ensure that the full spectrum of community members and activities is being fairly represented. In the words of Scott Libin, former news director of KSTP in Minneapolis, "We're making sure we don't cover certain neighborhoods only when something terrible happens there, that we don't show up only when the emergency lights are flashing and the crime scene tape is flapping in the wind."

In an article in RTNDA's *Communicator* magazine, Libin pointed out the journalistic advantages of maintaining regular contact with communities the news media have traditionally underserved: "We're making sure we know people there so we can report on the good things that are happening there. It helps us do better coverage there when there are bad things. But more important, it helps us present a more accurate image of what really is happening out there."

Some TV stations have been at the forefront in covering diverse communities. KRON-TV in San Francisco has been a national leader in producing stories about race, ethnicity, and civil rights. The station assembled a multiethnic group of staffers and managers for an ongoing series called "About Race," with topics that included interracial marriage, relations between different ethnic communities, and the way KRON's own reporters cover minorities. The newsroom's efforts were honored with a number of prestigious awards.

As the world becomes increasingly interlinked, television journalists must be prepared to report stories that span cultures and communities. On one level, diverse coverage is smart marketing, because of its potential to expand the viewing audience. However, diversity in storytelling also produces sound journalism.

NEWS JUDGMENT AND SENSITIVE SUBJECT MATTER

Daily journalism inevitably deals with difficult subjects, many of which raise questions of taste. News judgments are routinely affected by a desire on the part of journalists to display sensitivity toward the audience. Matters of taste apply not only to the choice of stories, but also to how stories are presented on the air.

A number of topic areas can be classified as sensitive: Death, illness, violence, sex, religion, social class, and children all call for a tasteful storytelling approach. Producers must bear in mind that TV news is watched by a broad viewership. As such, it is probably wise to err on the side of caution when dealing with potentially troublesome subject matter.

TV newscasts do not generally cover suicides, for instance, unless there is a compelling reason to do so. If a well-known individual kills himself or herself, that person's prominence might justify an exception to the policy, as might a suicide that takes place in a highly visible public setting. Even in those circumstances, however, such stories are likely to be downplayed.

At the same time, news is news, and unpleasant stories cannot and should not be avoided. The clergy abuse stories that rocked the Roman Catholic Church in the early 2000s combined several potentially controversial themes, yet the importance of the information required that it be fully reported. In such situations, where audience sensitivities are a factor, the collaborative nature of TV news can be a blessing. Producers and reporters should weigh the pros and cons collectively, and reach consensus about what is acceptable and what is not.

Dealing with children calls for a high degree of sensitivity on the part of reporters and producers. According to the RTNDA code of ethics, journalists should "exercise special care when children are involved in a story and give children greater privacy protection than adults." The ethics code also singles out victims of crime or tragedy, urging sensitive and compassionate treatment by reporters and photographers. The process of newsgathering brings journalists into regular contact with vulnerable individuals, who must always be approached with dignity and respect.

TV news personnel operate within the ethical guidelines of their profession. This means handling delicate subject matter as objectively as possible, using language and images that do not inflame the story, and balancing controversial information with opposing points of view. Remember, sensationalism is easy. Journalism is hard.

OTHER INFLUENCES ON NEWS JUDGMENT DECISION MAKING

Beyond the standard news judgment criteria, other factors influence the journalistic process of deciding what to cover. Let's briefly consider the most important of these institutional influences: time constraints and the competition for ratings.

Time Constraints

Television news operates under the tyranny of the clock. This holds true on several levels. Operating against the clock means journalists must gather, write, and produce their material incredibly fast, often in real time as stories are breaking. Working under tight deadlines gives little opportunity for reporters to explore a topic in depth. Racing against the clock also increases the likelihood of getting something wrong.

Furthermore, the tyranny of time dictates storytelling that is compressed. On television, time is money. This means that stories tend to be short, sometimes too short. When a news item runs only 20 or 30 seconds, viewers might barely be able to process what they have seen and heard before the anchor moves on to something new.

A legitimate grievance against TV journalism is that it does not do a good job penetrating the surface. Particularly in the context of fast-moving commercial newscasts, information too often flies by quickly and superficially. To compensate for this structural brevity, TV news writers need to take advantage of all the storytelling tools in their toolbox: images, graphics, location sound, narration—whatever applies. When all cylinders are firing, the layers of information work hand in hand to create depth.

The expansion of TV news websites gives reporters another venue for relaying information, one that is unencumbered by the strict time limits of on-air programming. A 90-second story about a complicated court case, for instance, might not allow for many details. As an adjunct to that story, though, the reporter can post relevant documents online for anyone interested in learning more. As online news outlets expand, TV journalists will increasingly use both platforms—telecasts and the website—to deliver more thorough coverage.

Competition for Ratings

The tyranny of time is one problem for television news. The tyranny of ratings is another. TV is a highly competitive business, and inevitably the quest for larger audiences affects the thinking and planning of newsroom decision makers. Pick the wrong stories and viewers might tune you out. Pick the right stories and ratings could go up. When ratings go up, advertisers pay a higher premium for commercial airtime, and that keeps the bosses happy.

This is not to suggest that producers should choose stories with only ratings in mind. TV news executives realize that viewers tune in to newscasts in the expectation of receiving a range of information, serious as well as not so serious. If the product becomes too fluffy, it can easily lose credibility with the audience.

Still, competitive pressures exert their pull. There is always competition to get stories first, to get them exclusively, and to get the best pictures and sound bites. There is always the temptation on the part of viewers to change the channel. In the final analysis, news judgments are a combination of what's good for the viewers and what's interesting, goals that need not be mutually exclusive.

ENTERPRISE REPORTING

Although day-to-day events account for the vast majority of stories in a television newscast, other ideas are developed and produced by newsroom personnel. These nonbreaking news stories come from a variety of sources: individual reporters and producers, the assignment desk, viewer suggestions, articles in newspapers and magazines, blogs, press releases, and so forth.

The term *enterprise reporting* refers to stories that are developed by reporters, as opposed to stories handed to them by an assignment editor. Enterprise reporting is a proactive exercise, in contrast to breaking news, which by definition involves reacting to events. Because breaking stories so often fall into predictable categories—accidents, crime, disasters, and the like—enterprise journalism offers the opportunity to delve into important topics that go beyond the day-to-day routine of spot news.

Enterprise reporting begins with a good idea, usually backed up by some preliminary research. If the story looks promising—if it offers visual possibilities, potential interviewees, and enough substance to warrant the effort—then the reporter sets out to shape the material into a television report. Enterprise journalism is particularly common among beat reporters, whose job it is to specialize in a specific topic area. With the exception of the police beat, where breaking news is the coin of the realm, beat reporting requires journalists to generate original ideas.

"Far too many reporters come to work each day expecting handouts from the assignment desk or the morning meeting," says WBAL-TV's Tim Tunison. "Our best reporters come to the morning meeting with at least three story ideas—every day. The most successful reporters set the agenda for their day rather than allowing management to set the agenda for them."

According to reporter Anna Crowley of WCNC-TV in Charlotte, enterprise stories have the added benefit of being journalistically rewarding. "There is so much ownership in breaking a story," she says. "And the longer I do this for a living, the more that kind of satisfaction is important to me—actually digging for and reporting on real stories instead of something faxed to us in a press release."

Reporter Sean Kelly of WCVB-TV in Boston makes the point that small-market newsrooms tend to rely more heavily on reporter-generated story ideas than big-city newsrooms. "When you're reporting in a major market the news often changes dramatically by the hour," Kelly says. "You're still expected to enterprise stories, but there's less of a demand for them since news is constantly breaking. But don't sit back waiting for it, because when the producers or EPs (executive producers) say they need a story, you'd better be ready with an idea." Kelly adds that the longer a reporter works in a particular city and develops local contacts, the easier it becomes to formulate enterprise stories.

INVESTIGATIVE JOURNALISM

Especially in larger urban markets, many TV stations also have investigative units whose mission is to produce nonbreaking news stories of an in-depth nature. Sometimes these stories take the form of multipart series or longer than average news packages, and sometimes they are standard-length reports. The work of an investigative unit is "to uncover information as opposed to just reporting the news," according to Jennifer Berryman, executive producer of the Team 5 Investigates unit at WCVB-TV in Boston.

Investigative stories cover a broad swath of subject matter: consumer fraud and rip-offs, government inefficiency and corruption, criminal activity, and the like. "My goal is always to uncover something new," says Berryman:

> That may be a relevant detail about a suspect's or company's past that the average reporter might not have thought to ask, or shedding light on something viewers thought they knew all about. On the surface, all of our competitors have the same tools we do—AP wires, CNN, video feeds, and newspapers. But what our investigative stories must do differently is to ask, and then answer, questions our viewers might never have thought about. Ultimately, we hope that all the stories we do reveal the truth.

Ideas for investigative stories come from a wide range of sources. Mike Beaudet, investigative reporter with the Undercover Unit at WFXT-TV in Boston, says his station receives dozens of tips each week from viewers. Many of these turn into legitimate stories, and others are discarded immediately, like the man who left a voice mail expressing frustration because he couldn't get women to date him.

Leads that sound promising often fail to pan out. Beaudet recalls one such instance: a tip from a viewer about a manager at a state agency who allegedly reported for work only a few hours a day. "It sounded like a perfect example of government waste," he said. "Our investigative unit jumped on the tip, and began surveillance of this state worker. After days of watching her, we quickly realized that this manager worked odd hours. Her co-workers thought she was a no-show manager, but it turned out she was putting in time at night as well. This is just one of many examples of investigative stories that are killed."

According to Beaudet, "We put in almost as much time on stories that never see air as investigations that do. But it's that one memorable story that comes along every so often that makes you pay attention to every tip you get. You never know when the great tip will become an unbelievable story."

FEATURE STORIES

Interesting and offbeat feature stories are highly prized commodities in television newsrooms because they are popular with viewers. Unlike breaking news, however, features tend not to fall into a reporter's lap. They must be discovered and cultivated.

"The best ideas come from the viewers," according to longtime feature reporter Larry Hatteberg of KAKE-TV in Wichita. "When you have a reputation for telling video stories, the suggestions begin to flow across your desk. When you showcase someone, another viewer will be reminded that there is a person in his town that would make a great story." Hatteberg says about one out of every eight ideas he receives from members of the audience gets produced as a video piece for the newscast. He also regularly combs small-town newspapers in his viewing area looking for potential subjects.

What makes a good feature? According to Hatteberg, "The stories I believe make the best television stories are those that are like an onion. When you slice an onion in half, you find layer after layer. The same is true with a good TV story. When you research it, you find layer after layer of video possibilities. Good television news features must contain those layers of visual elements." Hatteberg offers the following example:

> You receive a call telling you about someone who is about to turn 100 years old. It's a common newsroom call. In most cases, it's not a story. So many people are living to be 100 that it has become common and therefore not news. But, if that 100-year-old is still working as a reporter for the local newspaper, lives in the house she was born in, and takes care of her livestock...that's a story! Those are the video layers I'm talking about. It is those layers that permit you to visually move the story from one element to another without boring the viewer.

CHECKLIST OF KEY POINTS

- Judging the newsworthiness of stories is an ongoing process. Some news items are easy to evaluate, whereas others are less clear. As events change throughout the day, news judgments must be constantly revised.

- Newsroom decision makers apply seven criteria in evaluating newsworthiness: impact (how much of the audience is affected?), timeliness (how fresh is the story?), proximity (how close to home is the story?), conflict (does the story have built-in tension?), prominence (are noteworthy people involved?), novelty (is there something unusual about the story?), and visuals (does the story offer pictorial possibilities?).

- The seven criteria must be applied carefully. In the quest to be timely, for instance, journalists who cover breaking news must not report more than they know. Getting a story first is less crucial than getting it right.

- In covering stories with built-in conflict, it is important to keep the various points of view in proportion. The objective is to present all relevant sides of the story, not literally to provide equal time.

- TV journalists should not overdo stories about famous people, or stories that offer novelty value but little substance. Although interesting, these items are more like the dessert after the meal rather than a source of nutrition.

- TV journalists should make careful use of VNRs provided by outside sources. Any footage used from a VNR must be clearly labeled as such.

- Good TV journalism is inclusive of the entire viewing audience. This means producers and reporters should strive to ensure that diverse communities are not left out of the coverage and that they are represented fairly.

- Producers should be cautious in their approach to sensitive material involving death, illness, violence, sex, religion, social class, and children. TV newscasts do not generally cover suicides unless a prominent individual is involved.

- With time at a premium, TV newscasts might not be able to give complex subject matter a full hearing. In these cases, it is best to provide supplementary information on the station website.

- News judgments are subject to competitive pressures. Although stories are not selected exclusively for their audience appeal, the material in a newscast needs to be both interesting and edifying to the viewers.

- Beyond breaking news, TV journalists also cover other types of stories. Enterprise stories are ideas originated and researched by reporters. Investigative journalism involves in-depth reporting that unfolds over a longer period of time than daily news stories. Features are lighter stories with a human-interest emphasis. Like enterprise stories, these are usually developed by individual reporters, often from suggestions by viewers.

ASSIGNMENTS/ANALYSIS

Assignment: News Judgment Decision Making

Evaluate the newsworthiness of the following stories for a 5 p.m. local newscast, then see if you can come up with new angles for a 10 p.m. or 11 p.m. newscast.

Resignation

In a 4 p.m. news conference the Lakedale Superintendent of Schools, a popular community leader who has held the job for the past 10 years, makes a surprise announcement: She is resigning her office because of poor health.

Prom Ban

The principal of Lakedale Heights High School (LHHS) in suburban Lakedale bans nonstudents from attending the LHHS prom. LHHS students must attend with other LHHS students. The principal says he is trying to prevent a repeat of last year, when a nonstudent at the prom got into a fistfight with several LHHS students. Students quickly organize a protest at the end of the school day.

Drowning

A 36-year-old man drowns in a waterskiing accident around 2 p.m. at a recreational lake outside of town. Police have identified the victim as the founder and president of the city's largest real estate development company. The victim's father, also from Lakedale, is a former U.S. senator.

Overpass Accident

A flatbed trailer illegally loaded with an oversized road-grading vehicle knocks into a highway overpass on the outskirts of Lakedale, causing serious damage to the bridge and closing the busy roadway. The accident happens at 4 p.m., and the highway remains closed to traffic for five hours. Traffic backs up several miles in either direction. Authorities reopen the highway at 9 p.m., but the overpass bridge will not be reopened for at least several days. The driver of the trailer has been charged with reckless driving and leaving the scene of an accident.

Diner Closing

A Lakedale landmark, the Town'n'Country Diner, serves its last meal after 75 years in the same location. The Town'n'Country was a classic stainless steel diner with seating for only 16 customers at a time. The owner said he could no longer compete with the fast-food franchises that have recently sprung up on the same street.

Playground Evacuation

Officials at an elementary school in a small town 30 miles north of Lakedale hastily evacuate the playground after a black bear wanders onto the grounds. About 60 children are outdoors for recess when the bear is spotted at around 10:30 a.m. Animal control officers tranquilize the animal and remove it from the area without incident.

Manhunt

Local and state law enforcement authorities are conducting a manhunt for a convict who escaped from the Lakedale City Jail sometime before nine this morning. Police officials say the 28-year-old man, who was nearing the end of a three-year sentence for armed robbery, managed to get away by hiding in a delivery vehicle. Residents of a semirural area north of Lakedale reported several sightings of a man matching the convict's description early this afternoon.

Food Poisoning

Department of Public Health officials announce in an 11 a.m. news conference that 20 persons who ate corned beef at a local restaurant are under treatment for food poisoning. All of the affected individuals dined at the Cozy Corner Restaurant yesterday. The Director of Public Health is urging anyone else who ate at the Cozy Corner to get in touch with the department as soon as possible.

Excavation

Archaeologists from Lakedale University lead reporters on a tour of a dig at a location 35 miles west of town believed to be an ancient Native American burial ground.

The site has been under excavation for a year, but this is the first time media representatives have been invited to see it.

Angry Parent

The father of a second-grade student at Barbara Bush Elementary School says he will sue the school district if it does not remove a children's book that he claims promotes "a homosexual agenda." The school principal says she has no intention of removing the book, because it is not part of any required curriculum. A reporter from your station interviews both the father and the principal.

Assignment: Turning Nonvisual Stories Into TV Stories

Because they lack obvious visuals, the following stories are particularly well suited for print journalism. How could you make them work for television? Give some thought to how you might make the subject matter more visual, and come up with a list of potential interviewees for each item.

Immigration

Census data released today shows that the percentage of immigrants in Lakedale has reached an all-time high. Most of the new residents have roots in a particular region of north central Mexico.

Sales Tax

Local officials are studying the possibility of a one-cent increase in the sales tax as a means of paying for a new stadium downtown. The current stadium is slated for demolition at the end of next year.

Dropouts

Over the past five years the number of high school dropouts in Lakedale and its suburbs has been steadily rising, leaving school officials uncertain how to deal with the problem.

Construction

The local real estate board reports that new home construction in the Lakedale area has reached a record high. At the same time, so have housing prices.

Judicial Ruling

The State Supreme Court rules today that local cities and towns cannot prohibit sex offenders from living within their borders. The decision followed a lawsuit brought by residents in a suburban Lakedale community where a halfway house for sex offenders had been proposed.

Traffic

A new engineering study shows that average commuting times have doubled in Lakedale in the past 20 years, although the population has increased by only 20 percent. The amount of traffic on the streets has also shown a dramatic increase. The report suggests that two new bypasses will have to be built, one on the west side and one on the east side, through two rapidly growing neighborhoods.

Assignment: Dealing With Breaking News

This next set of stories falls under the category of breaking news. Assess the newsworthiness of each item, and determine how you will handle it for a 6 p.m. newscast.

Hostage

A man is holding a woman hostage on the balcony of the Empire Hotel in downtown Lakedale, with a gun to her head. A police SWAT team has been on the scene since 3:45 p.m., the area has been sealed, and the hotel has evacuated its guests. The police have begun communicating with the man via bullhorn, but so far he refuses to release his hostage. A police source tells your station off the record that the man and woman are believed to be a married couple.

Discovered

Just before you go on the air, a 75-year-old retiree from Lakedale, missing for a week, turns up unharmed in a neighboring state. The man, an Alzheimer's patient, had walked out of an elder care facility and had not been seen since. Police discovered him wandering around a shopping mall in a town about 200 miles from Lakedale. The man's family had appealed to the public for help in finding him, and his disappearance received widespread coverage over the past week.

Tollbooth Crash

Three people are seriously injured when a moving van loses its brakes and slams into a turnpike tollbooth on the edge of town around 5:30 p.m. Two of the injured were in the van; the third worked in the tollbooth. All remain hospitalized. The turnpike on-ramp is about to reopen as your newscast goes on the air.

Airport Evacuation

Lakedale International Airport is evacuated for two hours after a passenger runs through the security checkpoint and gets lost in the crowd. The incident occurs around 2:45 p.m. The incident postpones flights and causes everyone inside the gate area to have to pass through security again. The search for the suspect continues. As you go on the air, operations at the airport are getting back to normal.

Building Collapse

A three-story brick warehouse on the edge of downtown Lakedale collapses around 4 p.m. Several people are believed to have been inside the building at the time of the collapse, but so far rescuers have found only one body, a male whose identity has not been released. The rescue operation is continuing with both human and canine teams at work.

Assignment: Developing Enterprise and Investigative Stories

Create a list of five nonbreaking enterprise or investigative stories for a local TV newscast. For each idea prepare a one-page outline that includes background on the topic, a list of potential interviewees, suggested shooting locations, promotional angles, and a justification for what makes the subject worth pursuing. Your ideas should be more in-depth than standard daily news stories.

Assignment: Developing Feature Stories

Create a list of five nonbreaking feature stories for a local TV newscast. These can be personality profiles, reports about unusual activities or organizations, or anything else that qualifies as an interesting and offbeat story. For each idea prepare a one-page outline that includes background on the topic, a list of potential interviewees, suggested shooting locations, promotional angles, and a justification for what makes the subject worth pursuing.

Analysis: News Judgment Decision Making

- Watch the first couple of segments of a local TV newscast and apply the seven news judgment criteria to the lineup of stories.

- Over the course of a week, track the first few stories on the major local news stations in your area to see how different the story lineup is from one station to the next.

- Watch a day's worth of newscasts on a local TV station—early morning, noon, early evening, and late night—to see how the story lineup changes from one program to the next.

- Choose a story that has some staying power and track how it is played on local TV newscasts over a period of several days.

- Find three examples in local newscasts of enterprise stories, stories that are not covered by every news outlet in town. Analyze the news judgment behind the stories, and see whether you agree with the decision to pursue them.

- Find three examples in local newscasts of investigative stories, stories that dig beneath the surface to uncover unknown details about community issues. Analyze how well the stories are handled journalistically.

- Find three examples in local newscasts of feature stories, stories about unusual characters or activities. Analyze how creatively the stories are written, shot, and edited.

CHAPTER SEVEN

NEWSCAST PRODUCING

TOPICS DISCUSSED IN THIS CHAPTER

- Theories of Newscast Producing • The Content of TV Newscasts
- The Form of TV Newscasts • The Timing of TV Newscasts
- Producing a Short Newscast • Producing a Medium-Length Newscast
- Producing a Long-Form Newscast • Checklist of Key Points

ASSIGNMENTS/ANALYSIS

- Assignment: Producing a Short Newscast
- Assignment: Producing a Medium-Length Newscast
- Assignment: Producing a Long-Form Newscast
- Analysis: TV Newscast Producing

THEORIES OF NEWSCAST PRODUCING

Television newscasts are a combination of content, form, and timing. Stories account for the content, form refers to the architecture of newscasts, and timing is the overriding principle that governs the rhythm and pace of the program.

Producing a newscast presents a specific set of challenges: choosing the right lead, building a logical order to the stories, pacing the material in a way that holds the audience's attention, and fitting the various components into the allotted time and structure.

Each newscast follows a regular format, but these formats can vary from program to program, even when they air on a single station. An early-morning newscast is likely to devote a greater number of segments to traffic and weather than a newscast that airs at noon. Afternoon newscasts can include more features and special segments than a 10 p.m. or 11 p.m. news program, which delivers a more traditional lineup of news, weather, and sports. Late local newscasts carry more national and international stories than newscasts earlier in the day. Webcasts are short and contain only a handful of stories. The specific requirements of each format dictate content as well as structure and timing.

Despite the emphasis on format and structure, experienced newscast producers know that their best-laid plans often get tossed aside in favor of breaking news. Newscasts are inevitably a work in progress, with changes occurring even as the program is on the air.

THE CONTENT OF TV NEWSCASTS

Let's start with the content of newscasts and how producers arrive at their decisions.

Choosing a Lead

The first order of business for anyone in charge of producing a newscast is to select the first story of the telecast: the lead, which is the program's signature piece.

As we saw in the previous chapter, producers apply a set of news judgment criteria to the range of stories available to them: impact, proximity, timeliness, prominence, novelty, conflict, and visuals. These criteria are particularly relevant in choosing a lead. Producers make their determination by asking a series of questions: Which story affects the greatest number of people in my audience? What is the story's timeliness? Is there a local connection? Does the story offer conflict or an unusual angle? Are any well-known players involved? Are there compelling visuals?

Most of the time the day's lead is fairly obvious; after all, it's the biggest thing in the lineup and therefore easily spotted. On a slow news day, however, identifying an appropriate lead might not be so easy. In that situation, choosing a lead can require more creativity on the producer's part. "When the lead is up for grabs, we consider the number of viewers a story will affect or appeal to," says executive producer Matt Gaffney of WTTG-TV in Washington, D.C. "If a crime story is a contender, we consider whether the crime is unusual and whether there is a threat to the public."

If there's no obvious lead, producers might look for a cluster of related items that could constitute a lead. Let's say the day generates several crime stories: a homicide, an armed robbery, and a carjacking. For one reason or another, none of these is strong enough on its own to hold up as a lead. Taken together, though, they could lead off the newscast under the umbrella of a single day's crime in the city.

Alternately, a slow news day might be a good opportunity to lead with an investigative story, something without a specific time link that's just plain interesting. If there's not much going on locally, but a big national or international story develops, it might work to lead with that and cover the material from a local angle.

When a station runs several newscasts back to back, newsroom decision makers try as much as possible to differentiate the lead story from program to program. "We make a conscious effort to have different leads for our different newscasts," says Tim White, former managing editor of WBZ-TV news in Boston. "And if it's the same story we do it in a different way."

In the case of a story that's the obvious lead for all the day's newscasts, it is up to the producer and reporter to find new ways to deliver the information from one newscast to the next. Thus, a reporter might produce several versions of his or her report with different sound bites, different VO tracks, and different visuals to give viewers of the individual programs a chance to learn new information about the story.

The choice of lead story is also affected by time of day. An early-afternoon newscast is likely to lead with something lighter. A newscast at 10 p.m. or 11 p.m. might choose to highlight a national or international story, especially if there hasn't been much happening on the local front. Tim Tunison, assistant news director at WBAL-TV in Baltimore, says at his station the lead at 5 p.m. is usually the best Baltimore city story of the day, because more city residents watch that newscast. "We'll save stories from the suburbs for our 6 p.m. news, when more commuters have arrived home," Tunison adds.

Sequencing the Stories in a Newscast

Sequencing a newscast's lineup of stories—sometimes referred to as *stacking* a program—is one of the producer's most interesting challenges. The process is best thought of as a puzzle to be solved. The goal is to fit together the puzzle pieces, in this case the stories, in a way that makes the most sense while serving the needs of the audience. Unlike some puzzles, newscasts do not have a single solution. There are multiple ways to put the pieces together, and no two producers are likely to arrive at the same outcome, even with the same building blocks.

A common strategy for sequencing a rundown is to look for thematic connections among the items. If the day's events include a number of crime stories, it makes sense to run them back to back. Sometimes the connection might be geographic. Let's say that on a given afternoon both a bank heist and a water main break occur in the downtown area. It might work to run these two stories consecutively. In a local newscast all the national and international items could be grouped together.

There are a number of advantages to running related stories in a cluster. Newscasts include so many unrelated items that they can easily feel disjointed and choppy. Thematic or geographic connections lessen the feeling viewers might have of being whipped around from one story to the next. Connecting the stories also makes it easier on the anchors, providing them with natural transitions. Often these transitions are written directly into the script. Taking our example of the two downtown stories, the transition from the downtown bank holdup to the water main break might read something like this: "While police were investigating the robbery, a different kind of problem kept authorities busy a few blocks away."

Although it is desirable to group related stories together, such connections are not always possible. Sometimes the items are simply too varied to weave into a coherent tapestry. In that case, producers should be mindful of sharp turns in the content. It's not easy for an anchor to make the transition from a murder story to an item about baby elephants at the local zoo, and any attempt to soften the turn with a written transition is likely to sound convoluted.

One solution to difficult transitions is to make an anchor change. Of course this is not possible if the newscast has only a single anchor, but with two people sharing the duties, anchor changes give the producer a useful tool for overcoming sharp turns.

Other Considerations in Stacking a Newscast

Here are a few other things to think about in preparing a newscast rundown.

• The last story in a given segment tends not to be as heavy as the stories at the beginning. This is not a hard and fast rule, just something that usually happens. The philosophy is that a somewhat less intense story serves as a better transition into the news tease going into the commercial break.

• Feature stories and kickers are often saved for the end of the newscast, where they function as the dessert at the end of the meal. Because TV news programs offer a mix of material, producers look for lighter fare to include as a counterpoint to the serious, sometimes depressing stories that dominate. Features and kickers also give producers something other than hard news to highlight in their news teases.

• Teases are a standard feature of every newscast, and are included in the rundown by the producer. Each newsroom has its own policy on teases, but the usual practice is to open the program with a set of headline stories that serve as a tease for upcoming stories. There are also teases at the end of segments just before going into a commercial break. These prebreak news teases generally highlight three or so stories, and can include weather and sports. See Chapter 8, "News Teases," for a detailed discussion.

• Weather and sports occupy standard segments in most newscasts. Although the news producer includes these segments in the rundown, their content is usually not the producer's responsibility. Still, it is important for news producers to work closely with weather and sports staffs, because on many occasions these topics cross over into the regular news.

• Beyond weather and sports, newscasts might feature other standard segments, from consumer and entertainment news to special series. Like everything else in the program, these need to be factored into the rundown.

• Local newscasts might also include regular roundups of national and international news. Newscasts that air in late-afternoon or early-evening time slots usually downplay national and international stories, in recognition of the network news programming that airs on most affiliates around the dinner hour. Later newscasts, those that go on the air between 9 p.m. and 11 p.m., do tend to include at least a few stories from outside the local area. Producers must choose whether to cluster their national and international stories together, or whether the nonlocal stories are more logically distributed throughout the program.

• Depending on the format of the newscast, producers work with either a single anchor or a two-person team. Single anchors make it easy for the producer, who assigns all the live story reads to that person. With double anchors the producer needs to decide who reads which story.

THE FORM OF TV NEWSCASTS

Several factors determine a newscast's structure: the length of the program, how many commercial breaks it includes, how much emphasis it places on nonnews segments like weather and sports, and what sort of standard opens and closes it includes.

Creating a Rundown

A key responsibility of any newscast producer is the preparation of a daily rundown. This document serves as a blueprint for the newscast, laying out the lineup of stories, what form each story takes, graphic elements, timing, talent assignments, and other information relevant to producing the program. This rundown is distributed to the key personnel involved in getting the newscast on the air. It serves as the architecture of the program and gives the various members of the crew a common reference point.

The rundown serves several purposes. For the producer, it is the ultimate guide, both as a planning document and while the program is on the air. Because TV newscasts often undergo last-minute revisions, even while they are in progress, it is important that the producer operate from a clearly developed plan. For the program's director,

The key planning document for any newscast is the rundown, which is prepared by the program's producer and distributed to everyone involved with the production.

the rundown acts as a guide to the technical needs of the newscast. Others involved in the production use the rundown for their own purposes: audio, graphics, live remotes, and so forth.

Rundown formats can differ from newsroom to newsroom, but typically they include the same basic details. A rundown should contain the following information:

Date and Time of the Newscast. Because most stations produce several newscasts in a given day, it is important that each rundown be clearly identified by date and time.

Producer's Name. The producer's name needs to be on the rundown so that all parties who use the document know who is in charge.

Talent. The name of the anchorperson or persons appears on the rundown to clarify who is reading which stories. This is particularly relevant if there is more than one anchor, because the director will need to know when to make camera changes. Additionally, if the newscast contains live remotes in which reporters introduce their own packages, those are also noted on the rundown.

Story Slug and Number. The slug is the name given to a story; each item in the newscast will have its own slug. Each story is also assigned a number. Different newsrooms have different systems for assigning numbers, but a typical way of handling this is to assign numbers by blocks. In other words, every story in the first block will be assigned an A number: A-1 for the first story, A-2 for the second, and so on. The second block is the B block, the third block is the C block, and so forth.

Story Structures. The rundown should make clear which structural form each story is taking: reader, VO, VO/SOT/VO, package, or live remote.

Story Elements. The rundown also includes information about production elements for each story. Does the story use videotape, graphics, or titles? These kinds of details should appear on the rundown.

Timing. One of the most critical pieces of information on any newscast rundown is the timing. Rundowns typically contain two columns of timing: the time for each individual story and a running time that indicates overall length. The running time lets producers know where they stand at any given point in the newscast, so that adjustments can be made if the program is coming up either long or short (producers also call this running "heavy" or "light"). Because newscasts are clock-driven, timing is of the utmost importance during the live telecast.

Assigning Story Structures. In addition to sequencing all the stories in a newscast, producers also decide what structural form each item will assume. This takes us back to our earlier discussion of the various story types:

- The anchor reader, also called simply a reader, is read by an anchorperson who remains on camera for the duration of the script. Average running time is 10 to 20 seconds.

- VO stories, sometimes called R/VOs, add a visual layer to the storytelling by incorporating video, full-screen graphics, or other illustrations to the anchorperson's words. Average running time is 10 to 30 seconds.

- A VO/SOT/VO is a sound bite sandwich: The anchorperson reads a VO, then there's the sound bite, then another anchor VO. Average running time is 20 to 50 seconds.

- A package is a fully edited, self-contained story in which only the introduction is read live. This is the longest, most content-oriented story format. Average running time is one to two minutes, although most packages fall into the 75- to 90-second range.

- A live remote is a story delivered by a reporter or anchor from a location in the field. These usually include video stories—packages mostly, but occasionally a VO or VO/SOT/VO—and are structured as a live introduction, followed by the taped story, then a live tag, often with a follow-up question from the studio anchorperson. In some remotes the reporter is on camera the entire time, perhaps with a live interview. The average running time of a live remote varies, depending on its content.

In deciding which structure to assign to the various stories, producers are also judging how much time and attention each deserves. Does a particular item merit a package or a 15-second VO? Does it include sound bites and visuals that increase its value? Should it be introduced from the field in a remote live shot, or delivered by the anchor in the studio? A producer must be able to justify the structure and length of every story in the rundown.

An especially significant news event might call for more than one report. On air this is usually referred to as *team coverage*. Consider as an example a fatal crash involving an airliner at the local airport. For a story of this magnitude one reporter might be assigned to provide a general summary of the accident, a second to conduct interviews with survivors, and a third to compile a package about previous fatal accidents at the airport. As always, much depends on competing events that are happening within the same news cycle.

THE TIMING OF TV NEWSCASTS

Rapid pacing is one of the hallmarks of modern television newscasts. Producers rely on several techniques to imbue their programs with a sense of forward motion: high story counts, short story lengths, mixed story formats, multiple anchors, shifts from the studio to the field, commercial breaks, and frequent news teases. All of these contribute to keep the newscast moving at a steady clip.

The fast pace of TV newscasts reflects the desire of producers to keep the audience watching. In the competitive world of television, viewers face the constant temptation to change channels. Newscasts are structured with that reality in mind.

The overall length of a newscast is a key determinant of its structure. Obviously, the longer the program, the higher the story count. Length affects newscasts in other ways as well. An hour-long program might include several weather updates, or a reintroduction of the headline stories halfway through. Longer newscasts often incorporate regular segments such as consumer news, entertainment features, traffic updates, and the like.

Although the 30-minute newscast remains the industry standard, news programs can run virtually any length. It is typical on the 24-hour cable networks to have a brief set of headlines at the top and bottom of each hour. These are not newscasts per se, but they function the same way, with producers making judgments and organizing the productions. Webcasts also tend to be considerably shorter than the standard half-hour news program.

Even the 30-minute newscast is not really 30 minutes long. After subtracting for commercials, teases, weather, and sports, the half-hour block can contain only 10 or 12 minutes of actual news stories. Whatever the length, each program's producer will be keenly aware of how much time is available. However frustrating these constraints may be, they must be respected.

Newscast producers concern themselves with two kinds of timing: the timing of the individual stories and the timing of the overall newscast. Producers inevitably learn to develop a head for timing, because anyone who works in live television lives and dies by the clock. While the newscast is in progress the producer pays close attention to how much time has elapsed and how much is left, closely adhering to the schedule laid out on the rundown. If the program is running either long or short, adjustments must be made on the spot.

Producers use commercial breaks and full-length packages as an opportunity to get organized and, if necessary, regroup. Any changes made in the newscast while it is on the air must be communicated to all the individuals involved in the production, and the changes need to be relayed quickly and clearly.

Most news organizations make use of software programs that automatically handle the mathematical calculations involved in producing a newscast. However, program producers must also develop the ability to handle the math manually. During the live newscast the producer is responsible for the timing, and this is usually done the old-fashioned way, using a system called *back-timing*. Back-timing means keeping track of the time that remains, rather than the time that has elapsed. By knowing how much time a program has left, and the length of the elements that are slated to run, the producer can determine if the newscast is running according to schedule.

Because it is easier to cut than add stories while a newscast is on the air, producers tend to have a few extra items on standby for use in the final segment just in case they are needed. A more likely scenario is cutting stories because the newscast is running long. For TV news producers, flexibility is the key.

PRODUCING A SHORT NEWSCAST

Here is a sample rundown for a short, three-minute newscast:

DATE: 10 MAY 20XX
CAST: 7:25 AM
PRODUCER: SCHROEDER
TALENT: BAMBI WOODS

SLUG	TALENT	TIME	RUN TIME
OPEN/WIDE SHOT (of news set)		:05	:00
A-1 MURDER—VO/SOT/VO	BW	:45	:05
A-2 CARJACKING—VO	BW	:30	:50
A-3 TRAFFIC TIE-UP—VO	BW	:25	1:20
A-4 COMMUTER RAIL—VO/SOT	BW	:40	1:45
A-5 AIR SAFETY—VO	BW	:20	2:25
A-6 WX FORECAST—Reader	BW	:10	2:45
CLOSE/WIDE SHOT		:05	2:55
		TRT	3:00

At the top of the rundown we find the date, time of the newscast, and the names of the producer and anchor. From there the rundown lists the individual elements of the newscast and their times, along with a running time. Again, the purpose of two timing columns is to indicate the story times one by one and also the collective running time of the newscast. TRT stands for total running time, in this case three minutes.

The program opens on a wide shot of the news set for five seconds, presumably with music and a title graphic. The lead story, A-1, is a VO/SOT/VO about a local murder, running 45 seconds. A-2 is another crime story about a carjacking, this time a 30-second VO. The next three stories, A-3 through A-5, all relate in some way to transportation. Finally, the anchorperson reads a 10-second weather forecast before the program ends on a wide shot. Note that "weather" is usually abbreviated on newscast rundowns as "WX."

This sample rundown achieves two key objectives of good producing. First, the stories are grouped together thematically, with two crime stories followed by three stories about transportation. Second, the rundown mixes up story formats: two VO/SOT/VOs, three VOs, and a reader. Because the newscast is so short, there is no time for packages or live remotes.

Step by Step: Producing a Short Newscast

Now it's your turn to produce a short newscast.

From the following menu of stories, structure a three-minute, single-anchor local newscast that airs at 7:25 a.m. Wednesday. Because of the brevity of the newscast, do not use any packages or live shots; limit yourself to readers, VOs, and VO/SOT/VOs. You do not need to include all the stories.

Things to remember: In choosing a lead, consider the news judgment criteria. Look for connections among the stories and sequence accordingly. To the extent possible, vary your story formats, keeping in mind the average running time for each.

Story Menu

Governor. Gov. Chet Smith announces at 8 p.m. Tuesday that he will not be a candidate for reelection. This announcement had been expected. The governor has been ordered by his doctors to slow down.

Available elements:

- Footage and bite of the announcement (made at a news conference)
- Exterior shot of the governor's mansion
- File video of the governor at a recent rally

Gas Line. A gas line explosion at 4 a.m. Wednesday closes a two-block stretch of street in an industrial park on the west side. The street is not a major thoroughfare, and there are no injuries or fatalities.

Available elements:

- Footage of the street showing debris
- Shots of firemen putting out a small fire
- Interview bites from the fire chief indicating the cause of the explosion

Taco Teens. A station wagon carrying five teenage employees of Taco Mucho home from work is totaled when the vehicle careens out of control on the Downtown Loop shortly after 11 p.m. Tuesday. The teens are in good condition at St. Mary's Hospital.

Available elements:

- Footage of the wrecked vehicle
- Exterior of the Taco Mucho

Sentencing. Sentencing is scheduled at 9 a.m. today in a high-profile local case involving the kidnap and murder of a convenience store employee. The crime occurred six months ago, and the trial ended last month with a surprise confession by the suspect, who was a former roommate of the victim.

Available elements:

- Courtroom footage and sound bite of the suspect's confession
- Exterior of the courthouse
- Still photo of the victim
- Bite from the victim's brother
- File footage of the rural roadside where the victim's body was discovered

Waterslide. A giant waterslide has its official grand opening Tuesday night in suburban Lakedale Heights. The first 100 customers received free admission.

Available elements:

- Footage of ribbon cutting
- Exteriors of the slide
- Bite from the first customer in line

Traffic. The closing of the heavily traveled Downtown Loop for one week of repairs begins at 6 a.m. today.

Available elements:

- Footage of the freeway showing damage to the roadbed
- Map showing alternate routes
- Bite from project supervisor about how long the road will be closed
- Man-on-the-street bites from motorists who use the freeway

Protest. About two dozen residents of the South Bank neighborhood march through the downtown streets at 9 p.m. Tuesday to protest what they say is poor police protection. The neighborhood has one of the city's highest crime rates.

Available elements:

- Shots with natural sound of residents marching
- File footage of the South Bank neighborhood
- Angry bites from marchers

Pros and Cons of the Stories. As you think about how to put together a three-minute newscast from this menu of stories, let's consider the pros and cons of each item.

Governor. The fact that it's the governor gives this story prominence, but the announcement had been expected, so the information is not exactly a bombshell. The news conference took place the previous night, so by the time you go on the air this story is 11 hours old. The visuals are not terribly fascinating.

Gas Line. The story is timely, and could conceivably affect some morning commuters. However, the street is not a major thoroughfare, and there were no injuries or fatalities. The footage of the explosion's aftermath could potentially be interesting.

Taco Teens. This is one of those "every parent's nightmare" kind of stories, and is interesting to the audience in that sense. Still, the injuries were minor. The visuals are OK, but nothing the viewers haven't seen a million times. The timeliness and proximity of the story are strong.

Sentencing. The high-profile nature of the case makes this an interesting local story, and with sentencing just hours away, the timeliness of the story is obvious. The visuals and sound bites aren't bad, but at this point they offer nothing new. The story offers limited audience impact.

Waterslide. Some portion of the audience might find this story worth watching, and it does have timeliness and proximity. It feels more like a commercial than a news story, though, and the visuals and sound bites are of limited interest.

Traffic. The strength of this story is its impact: Commuters will have to deal with the closing of a major downtown thoroughfare. Timeliness is also strong, because the road closes just one hour before you go on the air. Visuals are limited, but the map showing alternative routes would be helpful to viewers. The sound bites have potential, especially the man-on-the-street bites from motorists who use the freeway.

Protest. The story is strong on proximity, but less strong on timeliness, as the march took place the previous night. It also offers conflict and solid emotional content. With feelings running high on the issue, the sound bites are likely to be powerful. Impact is somewhat limited. The problem is of great concern to those who live in South Bank, but less relevant to the vast majority of viewers who don't, and only 25 or so people turned out for the march. Visuals are average.

After you complete the exercise, take a look at the following rundown and read the rationale for it that follows:

DATE: 10 MAY 20XX
CAST: 7:25 AM
PRODUCER: SCHROEDER
TALENT: BAMBI WOODS

SLUG	TALENT	TIME	RUN TIME
OPEN/WIDE SHOT		:05	:00
A-1 TRAFFIC—VO/SOT/VO	BW	:45	:05
A-2 GAS LINE—VO	BW	:30	:50
A-3 TACO TEENS—VO	BW	:25	1:20
A-4 PROTEST—VO/SOT/VO	BW	:45	1:45
A-5 SENTENCING—VO	BW	:15	2:30
A-5 GOVERNOR—Reader w/graphic	BW	:10	2:45
CLOSE/WIDE SHOT		:05	2:55
		TRT	3:00

Rationale. In piecing together this newscast, the first order of business is choosing a lead. Traffic was chosen for two reasons: because it has the greatest potential impact on the audience, and because of its timeliness. No other story on the menu offers this combination. As a lead story, Traffic merits a bit of extra time, so in this rundown it is structured as a VO/SOT/VO. The best sound bites are probably those from commuters, because the bite from the project manager is merely a factual summary of something the anchorperson could just as easily deliver. The bites from motorists, on the other hand, are likely to add emotional content to an otherwise routine story.

Gas Line works as the second story because it flows logically out of Traffic: Both involve transportation, and both have implications for the morning commute. Taco Teens fits into the third slot because it, too, deals with traffic, although it lacks the audience impact of the previous stories. Both of these items work as short VOs because of the available video footage.

Protest would probably have merited a more prominent spot in the lineup had it not occurred the night before. Still, the issue is solid, and the strong sound bites from the neighborhood residents make this story worth running as a VO/SOT/VO. Because Protest deals with crime, it makes sense to go next to Sentencing. Sentencing is timely, but the story has not yet taken place, reducing its newsworthiness somewhat. With so much file footage available, this story works well as a VO.

Finally, Governor wraps up the sequence. It's a somewhat lighter story than some of the other items on the menu, but its relative lack of timeliness means it shouldn't run much earlier. Governor could run as a VO/SOT/VO if there were time, or even as a VO, but the footage is pretty generic, and the newscast already contains lots of VO stories, so on this rundown it has been designated as an anchor reader with an over-the-shoulder graphic of Gov. Smith.

PRODUCING A MEDIUM-LENGTH NEWSCAST

Now let's try a slightly longer newscast that expands beyond readers, VOs, and VO/ SOTs. This time you are in charge of putting together a seven-minute local news segment that airs at 5 p.m. today. You have a single anchorperson and the technical capability for one live remote. The menu of stories represents your choice of subject matter, with video and audio elements listed for each item.

Your completed newscast rundown should follow the sample in this chapter, clearly showing the order of your stories, segment structure, how long each story will run, and what form it will take. Use the slugs that have been designated for each story. Of the seven minutes you have for the entire newscast, subtract five seconds for your open and five seconds for your goodbye and closing credits. This newscast contains no teases.

Step by Step: Producing a Medium-Length Newscast
Story Menu
Grand Opening. Grand opening at 2 p.m. of a large office building downtown. This high-tech facility is housed in a renovated, 100-year-old local landmark that used to be a pharmaceutical factory. The building, which takes up a city block, has been

retrofitted with the latest technological advances. Twenty companies and 350 employees will work there.

Available elements:

- Video of the opening ceremonies
- Bites from Gov. Smith and building developer
- Footage inside the facility showing some of the high-tech gadgets

Queen of Spain. The reigning Queen of Spain arrives at Lakedale International Airport at noon. She is met by the mayor and governor, among other dignitaries. The queen will open an exhibition of Spanish art at the Lakedale Art Museum later this evening.

Available elements:

- Shot of the plane landing
- Video of the queen emerging and being met by the dignitaries
- Bites from the queen and the mayor
- Natural sound of band music being played to welcome the visitor

Teacher Fire. A 37-year-old grade school teacher is charged in court at 11 a.m. with setting a fire at Barbara Bush Elementary School earlier this week. Police say she started the fire in a supply room after being fired from her job at the school because of absenteeism and complaints from parents. No students were in the building at the time. There was minor damage to the building, but no injuries.

Available elements:

- Video of teacher in court
- File footage of the fire at the school
- Bites from the suspect's lawyer, the school principal, and the district attorney

Doctor Arrest. A local physician is arrested at his office at 4 p.m., allegedly for writing illegal prescriptions for painkillers. The doctor's arrest came as part of a police sting.

Available elements:

- Exterior shot of office
- Shot of the doctor being led into a police car
- Bite from a patient supportive of the doctor
- Bite from the district attorney

Employment. A new employment report is released at noon showing Lakedale County has the highest rate of job growth in the state, thanks to the growth of internet-related industries. Employment now stands at an all-time high.

Available elements:

- File footage of local businesses
- Shot of city skyline

- Shot of the employment report
- Bite from Mayor Norma Lyons about the booming economy

Doggie Day Care. A new business in town offers day care services to canines, including home pickup and delivery. (Note: There's no time element involved in this story; it can run at any time.)
Available elements:

- Video and natural sound of the dogs
- Bites from owner of facility and some of her customers

Police Chief. Lakedale Police Chief Al Varden is found dead in his home at 3 p.m. by his wife. He had been shot through the head in an apparent suicide. Varden had been suffering from health problems. A 20-year veteran of the department, Varden had been chief for the past three years. Friends and supporters have gathered at the home.
Available elements:

- File footage of Varden at work
- Still photos of Varden and his wife
- Exteriors of house
- Bites from police department spokesman, Mayor Norma Lyons, neighbors

Pileup. A section of interstate highway about 10 miles north of town is briefly closed following an accident involving several cars and a semi trailer. Injuries were minor. The truck apparently jackknifed after its driver fell asleep, causing the other cars to collide. The accident occurred at 6 a.m., closing the highway for half an hour.
Available elements:

- Video of the aftermath
- Bites from police and eyewitnesses

Wings. A 4-year-old boy who had been missing for several hours is rescued from a tree by the fire department around 2 p.m. The boy is fine. He told firefighters he had run away from home and climbed the tree because he wanted to see if he could fly. He brought a pair of homemade cardboard wings with him. Too scared to jump, he finally called out for help and was discovered by a pedestrian.
Available elements:

- Video of the rescue
- Shot of the boy and his parents being reunited
- Bites from the mother, the rescuer, and a quick bite from the boy
- Natural sound of onlookers applauding the rescue

Vandalism. School officials at Ben Franklin Elementary report that all the building's south-facing windows had been shattered by vandals overnight. Classes began two hours late to allow clean-up. There are no suspects.

Available elements:

- Video of the aftermath
- Interior shots of janitors cleaning up
- Shots of kids arriving late at school
- Bite from principal

Pros and Cons of the Stories. As before, let's consider the pros and cons of each item on this menu of stories:

Grand Opening. The story is both timely and local, with positive implications for the community and its economic well-being. The appearance of Gov. Smith lends prominence. Visually this isn't the most compelling story.

Queen of Spain. Prominence and novelty are the selling points here. It isn't every day that European royalty shows up in Lakedale, and the presence of the mayor and governor add prominence at the local level. The queen's visit is timely, and the visuals are potentially interesting. Apart from these factors, however, there's not much content to this story.

Teacher Fire. This is a story rich in conflict and emotional resonance, although the only new development is a preliminary court appearance. Because of its unusual nature, you can assume that local interest in this case is strong (novelty), and that the upcoming trial is likely to be a big deal. Visuals are reasonably interesting, as people are likely to be curious to see how the teacher handles herself in court.

Doctor Arrest. Like the teacher fire story, this item contains conflict, novelty, and proximity. The arrest is made an hour before the newscast begins, which validates the story's timeliness. The weakness of the story is in its relative lack of footage, although there is a shot of the doctor being taken into custody.

Employment. The story is strong on timeliness and proximity, but weak on visuals.

Doggie Day Care. Although strong on proximity and novelty, this feature is lacking in timeliness.

Police Chief. The suicide of the police chief is filled with conflict, timeliness, proximity, and prominence. Visuals are limited primarily to file footage and stills, but the gathering of friends and supporters at the home helps update the story pictorially.

Pileup. This is of obvious local interest, but by the time you go on the air at 5 p.m. the story is nearly 12 hours old.

Wings. This is a strong human-interest story, with elements of timeliness, proximity, conflict, and novelty. The visuals and sound bites are presumably compelling, as we have footage of the rescue and see the boy being reunited with his parents.

Vandalism. The visuals tell the story here, and proximity and timeliness are also key factors.

After you complete the exercise, take a look at the following rundown and read the rationale for it that follows:

DATE: 10 MAY 20XX
CAST: 5 PM
PRODUCER: SCHROEDER
TALENT: BAMBI WOODS

SLUG	TALENT	TIME	RUN TIME
OPEN/WIDE SHOT		:05	:00
A-1 POLICE CHIEF	BW/Reporter	1:50	:05
Live Remote/PKG			
A-2 DOCTOR ARREST	BW	:45	1:55
VO/SOT			
A-3 TEACHER FIRE	BW	1:20	2:40
PKG			
A-4 VANDALISM	BW	:20	4:00
VO			
A-5 WINGS	BW/Reporter	1:10	4:20
Short PKG			
A-6 EMPLOYMENT	BW	:15	5:30
Reader w/graphic			
A-7 GRAND OPENING	BW	:25	5:45
VO			
A-8 QUEEN OF SPAIN	BW	:45	6:10
VO/SOT/VO			
CLOSE/WIDE SHOT		:05	6:55
		TRT	7:00

Rationale. The prominence of the local police chief and the unexpectedness of his death make this an easy newscast for which to pick a lead. The ongoing gathering of family and friends at the chief's home provides the logical backdrop for a live remote, and the gravity of the story justifies a full package.

Doctor Arrest is a good story, something that on a different day might have played in the A-1 position. Because so much time has been devoted to Police Chief, the news about the dentist being taken into custody merits a VO/SOT rather than a full package. Teacher Fire, the third story in the lineup, does rate a package, for two key reasons: First, it involves a complicated chain of events that require expanded coverage, and second, running a package in A-3 after a VO/SOT in A-2 helps vary the story formats.

Why not put Teacher Fire in the A-2 slot? A case can be made that it's a better story than Dental Arrest. But Teacher Fire in A-3 is followed immediately by Vandalism in A-4, another story involving local schools. In turn, A-5, the story about the boy who wanted to fly, flows reasonably well out of the previous two items, which both deal with kids. That means three stories in a row can be thematically connected. Wings merits a short package because of its strong human-interest element and solid choice of sound bites and natural sound, whereas the more run-of-the-mill Vandalism story works best as a VO.

Employment and Grand Opening, in the A-6 and A-7 slots, relate to each other, because both deal with the local business climate. Because Employment is limited visually, it is presented as a reader with an over-the-shoulder graphic, followed by a VO about the opening of the mill. Queen of Spain is the more timely of the two kickers, and because the royal visitor offered remarks, the story functions nicely as a VO/SOT/VO. The other kicker, Doggie Day Care, will presumably be saved for a later newscast.

What is particularly effective in this rundown is the variety of story formats. This definitely helps keep the newscast from falling into too much of a structural rut.

PRODUCING A LONG-FORM NEWSCAST

For longer newscasts—programs lasting either 30 or 60 minutes—most of the same producing principles we have discussed so far still apply. The stories must be logically sequenced, the pace must flow, and there must be a variety of story formats and lengths. There are a few areas of difference, however.

Anchor Reads

Longer newscasts are more likely to involve two anchorpersons, which means that in addition to stacking the rundown, the producer assigns who reads which stories. The goal in making anchor assignments is to balance each person's contribution to the newscast. This does not mean both have to read the same number of stories, but rather that equity should be struck in a more general sense, so that neither anchor dominates.

Timing is one of the key challenges facing newscast producers. Every element of the program must be timed to the last second, and everything has to fit within the allotted running time.

As a rule of thumb, most news programs open on both anchors, then divide the reading assignments as the newscast continues. If there are two or three short, related stories, it might work best to give them to one anchor to read as a group, or it might make sense to change anchors after a single story. One caveat in assigning reads is to avoid "ping-pong" anchors, switching back and forth between anchors after every story.

Producers use anchor changes to help smooth otherwise rough transitions. Let's say you're going from a series of gruesome crime stories to some positive news about economic growth. Instead of writing a labored transition to get you from one topic to the next, a natural segue can be made by switching anchors. Ideally, of course, the producer is able to sequence the stories in a way that does not create too abrupt a shift in content in the first place.

Variety and Pacing

Variety is an overall goal of long-form newscast producing, not just in anchor reads, but also in story forms. Although it's likely that the first few stories in the newscast will merit a package or perhaps a package within a live remote, after that it is advisable to incorporate different story structures within each segment block. If the first couple of stories are packages, then go to a VO or VO/SOT/VO before running another package. When a segment block consists of 10 VO stories in a row and nothing else, the structure becomes too predictable and the pacing suffers.

A mixture of story forms is also helpful to the news anchors. According to WBAL's Tim Tunison, "VO/SOTs are a nice way to break up a long string of VOs. Your anchors will appreciate the opportunity to take a deep breath."

Variety can also be achieved by maintaining a high story count. This requires writers to keep their scripts tight to keep the pace moving.

Another means of adding variety to the newscast is to mix up the camera shots. For example, a one-shot of the anchorperson affords a couple of choices: You can show the person in either a head-and-shoulders framing or with an over-the-shoulder graphics box. By mixing both types of shots, along with the occasional two-shot of the co-anchors, the visual structure of the newscast becomes more interesting.

Standard editing transitions can also add interest, but they should be used judiciously. For newscasts the most common of these are wipes and dissolves. A wipe is when a new image appears to push the previous image off the screen, horizontally, vertically, diagonally, or in a pattern. A dissolve is a visual transition in which one image disappears as the next one comes on screen, with brief overlap between the two. Wiping and dissolving are used as standard transitions into taped stories and teases.

Segment Lengths

Newscasts adhere to a set structure, which means a set number of segments. For half-hour newscasts this might mean five or six segments. For hour-long programs the number will be around twice that.

Almost inevitably the first segment of the newscast will be the longest, for one simple reason: Postponing the commercial break means a greater likelihood of retaining viewers. As the newscast progresses, the segment blocks get shorter.

Weather and sports are allotted fixed segment times that must be closely observed, although the weather segment can run longer than normal when conditions merit. Sometimes weather functions as a news story, and in that situation it might make sense to bring the weather person into the mix at the top of the telecast, separate from the regular weather segment. Sports might need extra time on weekend newscasts, which usually works out because weekends tend to generate fewer breaking news stories.

The final, or kicker, segment might consist of only one or two short stories. Producers often use this last segment as padding in case the previous segments of the newscast have run long. It's not uncommon for the producer to program extra stories for the kicker segment, then end up killing them when the rest of the show goes long. By this same reasoning, a producer might be reluctant to run packages in the kicker slot, because these are fixed in length and cannot be cut down. VOs and VO/SOT/VOs, on the other hand, are shorter and can be trimmed if necessary because they are read live.

Thematic Organization

The same basic principles we discussed earlier in this chapter also apply to long-form newscasts. Look for stories with natural connections and group those together. Try to avoid sharp turns in the content. This might be more difficult when the program is longer, but on the other hand, the extra time allows producers to separate stories that don't logically belong together.

Although local newscasts emphasize local content, they can also include important national and international news items. These might be grouped together in a story roundup, in which case the organization is fairly straightforward. Late-evening newscasts, those that air at 10 p.m. or 11 p.m., are more likely to incorporate national and international stories than newscasts that run earlier in the day. If the story is significant enough, a nonlocal item can even lead the newscast. Generally speaking, however, the lead story should be local. It's best not to interweave too many national and international stories among the local news items, lest the audience end up confused about what's happening where.

Weather and sports often have their own segment blocks, but it might provide a nice transition to run a thematically appropriate news story at the beginning of those segments. If you've got a story about a local fisherman who reeled in a record catch, that could go as the first story in the sports block, before the sportscaster comes on with his or her own menu of items. Similarly, a national weather story, like an earthquake or hurricane on the other side of the country, might provide an appropriate start to the weather segment. Remember that if you program news stories inside the weather or sports segments, the time comes out of news, not out of weather or sports.

News Teases

Longer programs mean more news teases, all of which have to be coordinated by the producer. As a rule, there is an opening billboard tease about 30 seconds in length that promotes several of the top stories in the newscast, and also shorter teases going into each commercial break. The prebreak teases, which can run anywhere from 10 to 30 seconds, generally concentrate on stories coming up in the subsequent segment.

Internal news teases usually include video and sometimes sound. For stories that involve a live remote, the reporter often delivers that part of the tease live from the field. Weather and sports teases will most likely be delivered by the individuals who present those segments.

Live Remotes

Long-form newscasts typically contain one or more stories that are introduced live from a remote location in the field. Many news stations make it a policy to do a live remote for the lead story, and some stations have the technical capability for several live remotes within a single newscast. Live remotes add visual variety to the newscast and help pace the material.

The best live remotes are those that use the location as a storytelling element. Live remotes that take place during daylight hours have a somewhat easier time accomplishing this, because lighting conditions are more favorable. By late night it might be difficult for viewers to see much of a reporter's remote location unless the setting is indoors.

The structure of live remotes within newscasts can vary, but the standard setup goes like this: From the studio an anchorperson introduces the story and tosses to the reporter at the remote location. The reporter then speaks a few sentences on camera before his or her videotaped package runs. At the end of the package the shot comes back to the reporter live, who tosses back to the studio anchor. If there is time, or if the story needs further explanation, there may be a quick question-and-answer exchange between the reporter and anchor.

Not every live remote incorporates a package. It is also possible to stay with the reporter live on camera for the entirety of the remote, especially in the case of a breaking story for which there hasn't been time to prepare anything on tape. Remotes might also involve the reporter conducting a live interview with someone at the location.

Step by Step: Producing a Long-Form Newscast

Now let's put together a half-hour local Lakedale newscast that runs at 11 p.m. The following menu of stories represents your potential subject matter and specifies which elements of video and audio are available for each item. Please note that won't be able to use all of the stories. You also have the technical capability for two live remotes.

This newscast has two anchors (Bambi Woods and Chip Biffster), plus separate presenters for weather (Stormy Knight) and sports (Jock Dude). Your completed rundown should look like the previous sample rundowns, clearly showing the order of your stories, segment structure, how long each story will run, and what form it will take. Use the slugs that have been designated for each story.

Timing. You will have 28 minutes for the entire newscast. Of this, subtract the following amounts of time:

- 40 seconds for your opening billboard tease
- 10 seconds each for four internal prebreak teases (40 seconds total)
- 10 seconds for goodbye and closing credits
- three minutes for weather
- three minutes for sports
- eight minutes for four commercial breaks of two minutes each

This leaves 12 minutes, 30 seconds for your news and feature stories.

Newscast Structure. This half-hour newscast is divided into five segments (A-B-C-D-E) with four commercial breaks. Your two major news blocks will be the first two segments of the program (A and B). The C block is devoted primarily to weather, and the D block to sports. You will also have a quick final segment (E), which is appropriate for lighter, kicker stories. If you see an appropriate opportunity, you might want to run a short news story leading into the weather segment or the sports block.

Story Menu: International Stories

Mudslide. Huge mudslide kills dozens of shantytown residents in Rio de Janeiro. More rains are expected, with the potential for further devastation.

Available elements:

- Dramatic video with natural sound, no bites

Typhoon. A typhoon strikes New Guinea just before you go on air, but extent of the damage is unknown.

Available elements:

- Map of the area, no video

Kuwait. A suspicious bomb goes off in the capital of Kuwait. Minor injuries, no one claiming responsibility.

Available elements:

- Video with natural sound

French Riots. A demonstration in Paris turns violent when residents of a predominantly Muslim neighborhood clash with pro-Israel protestors in the street. Numerous injuries, some serious, but no deaths.

Available elements:

- Video with natural sound
- Angry bites (in English) from people on both sides

Story Menu: National Stories

Flood. A major city on the other side of the country from you is hit with an unusual flood. No deaths but hundreds of evacuations.

Available elements:

- Video of the soggy streets
- Bites from residents evacuated from their homes

Midair Collision. Two small planes collide in the air over a city 500 miles from you this afternoon. A local amateur videographer happened to be shooting pictures at the time. Four people dead, a house burns to the ground.

Available elements:

- Amateur video and natural sound of the crash
- Professional video of the burning house

Theme Park. An early-morning fire causes serious damage to a nationally known theme park several states away. The park was not open at the time so no injuries. The park will reopen within the week.

Available elements:

- Daylight video of the damage
- Bites from park officials

Capitol Evacuation. The U.S. Capitol in Washington, D.C., is briefly evacuated this afternoon after a suspicious package was discovered in a stairwell. Legislators and staff returned inside after about an hour.

Available elements:

- Video of the Capitol
- Sound bites from evacuees waiting outside, including a bite from one of your state's congressional representatives

Story Menu: Local Stories

Meat. A local butcher's shop is closed by the Department of Public Health at 3 p.m., after investigators find that bad meat was being sold.

Available elements:

- Video of shop exterior
- Angry bite from owner
- Bites from health inspector and customers

Zoo. Local schoolchildren serenade a family of chimps at the local zoo over the noon hour. The chimps are new arrivals.

Available elements:

- Video and natural sound
- Bites from kids

Hotel. Dedication ceremonies of a new luxury hotel, The Blueside, take place at 8 p.m. tonight with an appearance by the governor of the state. The Blueside is the city's tallest building and the first hotel to be built in central Lakedale in 50 years.

Available elements:

- Exteriors and interiors of the building
- Video and bite of governor at the ceremony

Chase. An early-afternoon high-speed chase briefly closes the heavily traveled Downtown Loop. A parolee who had stolen a car is forced off the road by police. There are no injuries.

Available elements:

- Video of the chase with natural sound
- Bites from police and eyewitnesses

Tornado. A tornado in the small town of Carvel, 30 miles south of Lakedale, injures 15 and levels three houses around 6:30 p.m. Several dozen residents remain in a temporary shelter at the local high school.

Available elements:

- Video of the tornado damage
- Home video of the funnel cloud
- Numerous bites from eyewitnesses and authorities

Note: It is also possible to include the station's weather person in news coverage of the tornado, separate from the regular weather segment.

Derailment. A freight train derails on the edge of town at 4 p.m., blocking a fairly heavily traveled street. The street reopened at 10 p.m.

Available elements:

- Video from the air and ground
- Bites from officials and train personnel

Deck Collapse. Six Lakedale residents are hospitalized after a wooden deck they were standing on collapses around 7:30 p.m. The second-story deck was attached to the rear of a home on the city's north side. Two of the injured individuals are in serious condition, and the others' injuries are described as minor.

Available elements:

- Video showing the collapsed deck and the exterior of the house
- Bites from eyewitnesses and police

Health Director. In an 11 a.m. news conference, Mayor Lyons appoints a new deputy director of public health.

Available elements:

- Video and bites from the mayor and the appointee

Missing Boy. A 5-year-old boy who had been missing since last night is found unharmed at a friend's house at 1 p.m. The boy and his friend said they were planning to run away.

Available elements:

- Video of the boy and his mother
- Bites from the mom and police

Special Olympics. Special Olympics athletes from throughout the state compete this afternoon in Municipal Stadium.

Available elements:

- Video of the competition
- Bites from participants and event sponsors

Robber. Police arrest a would-be robber who holds up a downtown bank at 4 p.m., then immediately has a flat tire in his getaway car. No injuries.

Available elements:

- Video of the suspect being taken into custody
- Exterior shots of the bank
- Shot of the vehicle with the flat tire

Pros and Cons of the Stories. As in the previous exercises, let's consider the pros and cons of the items on this story menu.

Of the international items, Mudslide is probably the strongest. Typhoon has the potential to be a major story, but it's too soon to tell. Kuwait and French Riots are about equal in importance, although the latter provides better visuals and sound.

The national stories all have merit. Flood is interesting because of the magnitude of the damage, but the fact that it happened on the other side of the country somewhat lessens the news value for a local audience. Capitol Evacuation is relevant owing to the prominence of the location and the people who work there. Midair Collision offers strong visuals, and Theme Park is of interest because the fire happened at a place familiar to viewers.

The menu offers several strong local stories. Storms do not happen in a vacuum, so the tornado that hit 30 miles from Lakedale would be of consequence to the wider viewing area. The tornado struck in the evening hours, so the news is still fresh. Deck Collapse is timely and the fact that six people were injured strengthens its newsworthiness. Meat is a story that many viewers can identify with, because everybody has to eat, although only a small segment of the audience would be directly affected. Hotel is newsworthy in that it's the city's tallest landmark and an unusual addition to the local skyline. The participation of the governor in the dedication ceremonies adds an element of prominence.

Derailment is timely in that the street reopened only an hour before your newscast begins, and the blocking of a major roadway means many in the audience have been inconvenienced. Chase also caused a street closing, but only briefly, although the story offers interesting visuals. Robber is interesting because of the way the story turned out, with a flat tire on the getaway car.

Health Director would be a better story if the appointment involved a new director of public health, instead of just a deputy director. Missing Boy is a decent human-interest story. Presumably it would have been included in the previous night's newscast, which makes it ripe for an update. Zoo and Special Olympics are both good features, with interesting visuals and sound.

Now let's look at the rundown for this half-hour newscast.

RUNDOWN
DATE: 10 MAY 20XX
CAST: 11 PM
PRODUCER: SCHROEDER
TALENT: BAMBI WOODS/CHIP BIFFSTER/STORMY KNIGHT (Wx)/JOCK DUDE (Sports)

SLUG	TALENT	TIME	RUN TIME
BILLBOARD OPEN VO/Live remote	BW/CB/Reporter A	:40	:00
A-1 TORNADO Live Remote/PKG	BW/ Reporter A	1:40	:40
A-2 WX UPDATE Stormy at wx map	Knight	:30	2:20
A-3 DECK COLLAPSE Live Remote/PKG	CB/Reporter B	1:40	2:50
A-4 ROBBER VO	BW	:20	4:30
A-5 CHASE VO/SOT/VO	BW	:40	4:50
A-6 DERAILMENT VO	CB	:25	5:30
A-7 MEAT VO/SOT/VO	BW	:40	5:55
A-8 MISSING BOY VO/SOT/VO	CB	:40	6:35
A-9 HOTEL PKG	BW/Reporter C	1:20	7:15
A-10 TEASE VO/On-cam	BW/CB	:10	8:35
BREAK #1		2:00	8:45
B-1 CAPITOL EVACUATION VO/SOT/VO	CB	:35	10:45
B-2 KUWAIT VO	BW	:15	11:20
B-3 FRENCH RIOTS VO	BW	:20	11:35

SLUG	TALENT	TIME	RUN TIME
B-4 THEME PARK VO/SOT/VO	CB	:45	11:55
B-5 MIDAIR VO	BW	:25	12:40
B-6 MUDSLIDE VO	CB	:15	13:05
B-7 TYPHOON Anchor Reader w/graphic	CB	:10	13:20
TEASE On-camera	CB/BW/Knight	:10	13:30
BREAK #2		2:00	13:40
C-1 FLOOD VO	BW	:20	15:40
C-2 WX	Knight	3:00	16:00
C-3 TEASE On-camera/VO	CB/Dude	:10	19:00
BREAK #3		2:00	19:10
D-1 SPORTS	Dude	3:00	21:10
D-2 TEASE VO	BW/CB	:10	24:10
BREAK #4		2:00	24:20
E-1 SPECIAL OLYMPICS PKG	CB/Reporter D	1:15	26:20
E-2 ZOO NATSOT/VO	BW	:15	27:35
E-3 GOODBYE/WIDE SHOT	BW/CB	:10	27:50
		TRT	28:00

Rationale. Choosing a lead for this newscast is fairly simple. Although the tornado struck only one small town, Tornado is an important story with implications for the entire audience. Everyone in the area will have gone through the same general weather pattern, more or less. The fact that some residents are still in a temporary shelter at airtime gives the story an up-to-the-minute angle and makes it suitable for a live remote, presumably from the shelter. It also makes sense to go to the weather person immediately after the news story to update viewers on the storm. Given the magnitude of this story, a package is definitely in order.

The second-best story of the newscast is Deck Collapse. Although it might be difficult at 11 p.m. to fully show the damage, this location still works for a live remote. The story merits a package, but not as much time as Tornado. Deck Collapse also has an ongoing element, in that the victims remain hospitalized.

After giving Bambi the anchor read on Tornado and Chip the anchor read on Deck Collapse, we cut back to Bambi for the next two stories, Robber and Chase, which work nicely back to back because both involve crimes in the downtown area. Robber goes first, because it's the fresher story, and it is a VO because no bites were available. Chase runs as a VO/SOT/VO to include the police reaction and natural sound.

We change anchors again for the next story, Derailment, which connects to Chase, because both stories entail the closing of downtown streets. Derailment might have been a package, but by 11 p.m. the blocked street has reopened and things are back to normal. Plus, there's plenty of other news, which means Derailment warrants only a 25-second VO.

Similarly, Meat might have gotten more attention on a slower news day, but in this case it works better as a VO/SOT/VO than as a package. Because of the sharp turn from Derailment to Meat, we make an anchor change here.

Missing Boy necessitates another shift in anchor reads because the content is so different. This is a good VO/SOT/VO story because viewers would be interested in hearing from the mother who was reunited with her missing son.

For the last story in the A block, Hotel works nicely in lightening the mood. It's a strong local story and something people in the audience would presumably be interested in, so for that reason it runs as a package. Note, too, that we return to Chip here for the anchor intro.

The B block begins with Chip, because Bambi started the A block. The goal is to distribute the anchor reads as equitably as possible. The B block consists entirely of national and international stories, none of which makes for an obvious segment lead. Capitol Evacuation gets the B-1 slot and a VO/SOT/VO simply because it's a U.S. story that deals with a subject of heightened audience interest. Capitol Evacuation provides a natural segue into the next two stories, Kuwait and French Riots, both of which run as VOs that are read by Bambi.

We then shift into Theme Park, which gets a VO/SOT/VO, and Midair Collision, a VO because of its strong video. With no particular connection between them, each story is read by a different anchor.

Finally, the B block ends with two international stories that involve natural phenomena: the Mudslide story from Brazil and the Typhoon from New Guinea. The availability of video footage makes Mudslide a VO, and the absence of pictures means Typhoon must run as an anchor reader with a graphic map. It might have been appropriate to precede these two stories with Flood, even though it deals with domestic, not international, news, but instead we have held back Flood for the C-1 position, immediately before the weather segment. Ending the B block with two weather stories helps set up a natural tease into the C block.

After the weather and sports segments, we are left with about two minutes for an E block kicker segment. The better of the two kicker stories is Special Olympics, so that runs as a short package, and Zoo runs as a VO with natural sound of the children singing.

The only story on the menu that did not make it into the newscast is Health Director. Because the announcement involved only a deputy health director, the item did not seem to merit inclusion.

CHECKLIST OF KEY POINTS

- Television newscasts are a combination of content (the stories), form (the structure), and timing (how long each item runs, and the overall running time of the program).

- A key task of newscast producers is choosing a lead story. Most of the time, this is fairly obvious, but on slow news days, the producer has latitude to make a more creative choice. When a station runs back-to-back newscasts, producers consult with each other to vary their leads. Because the audience composition is different for different times of day, the hour at which the newscast airs might also determine the choice of a lead.

- Sequencing the stories in a newscast, also called stacking, is another important responsibility of the producer. To the extent possible, producers group thematically related stories together. More serious stories tend to run earlier in the newscast, and kickers and features get played toward the end. Producers must also factor in national and international news, along with weather, sports, teases, and any other regular segments that are part of the newscast.

- Newscasts can involve a single anchor or more than one anchor. This affects how producers put together the format. Most newscasts also make use of live reports from journalists in the field. These live remotes are also coordinated by the producer.

- Producers draw up a rundown for each newscast that serves as a blueprint for everyone involved in its production. Rundowns include the date and time of the program; the names of the producers, anchors, and reporters; a listing of who reads which stories on camera; a roster of the stories that indicates structure (i.e., whether the story is a reader, VO, VO/SOT/VO, package, etc.); the running time of each segment in the program; and an overall running time for the entire program.

- Newscasts are fast-paced, with high story counts and short story lengths. In formatting a news program, producers rely on story structures, anchor reads, and visual techniques to propel the content forward. Producers must be particularly adept at timing while the show is on the air, because breaking stories often change the lineup at the last minute.

- Newscast producers work in a variety of program lengths, from short webcasts that might run only a few minutes to 30- and 60-minute newscasts. Producers of longer newscasts must pay special attention to pacing to keep the program moving along.

ASSIGNMENTS/ANALYSIS

Assignment: Producing a Short Newscast

From the following menu of stories, structure a three-minute television newscast for a local audience in the city of Lakedale. Assume that this segment functions as an insert within a network news program, airing at 8:25 on a Thursday morning. There is a single anchorperson.

Use the sample format in this chapter as a guide to how your rundown should look. Be sure to indicate the form each story will take, along with the correct order and timing. If a choice of video or bites is indicated, please specify which elements you are using. You are not writing a script for these stories, but organizing the material from a programming standpoint.

Because this is such a short newscast, you will not have time for any packages or live remotes.

Story Menu

COLLAPSE

A vacant three-story building in an industrial zone south of downtown collapses at around 6:30 a.m. Thursday. No injuries or fatalities, but one block of busy Central Avenue has been temporarily closed due to debris.

Available elements:

- Daylight footage of the collapsed building
- Shots of investigators sifting through the rubble
- Bite from the fire chief indicating that the cause is not yet known

STORM

A line of thunderstorms is approaching your town from the west. The storms are expected to arrive late this morning and last throughout the day, bringing intense rain with the possibility of flash flooding and isolated tornado activity.

Available elements:

- Meteorologist Stormy Knight with updated info at the weather desk
- Radar map and graphics of approaching storm
- Video of the same storm as it hit the states immediately to your west the previous evening

PUPPET WAGON

A van belonging to the Wee Pals Puppet Playhouse crashes into a tree near Prospect Park around 1 a.m. Thursday. The vehicle contained a troupe of puppeteers returning home after a show. All are in good condition at St. Mary's Hospital.

Available elements:

- Footage of the wrecked vehicle
- File footage of the Wee Pals in performance

MINI-MALL

A new seven-store mini-mall in the Universityville neighborhood of Lakedale has its official grand opening Wednesday night.

Available elements:

- Video of the ribbon-cutting
- Exteriors of mall

PANCHO

Ten-year-old Pancho Rodriguez is released from Mercy Hospital late Wednesday night. Pancho is a Peruvian boy brought to the United States by a local charity to have his sight surgically restored. The operation was a success, and Pancho will recuperate in a local private home until he returns to Peru in two weeks.

Available elements:

- Footage of Pancho waving on his way out of the hospital
- Still photo of the boy before his operation
- Bites from the surgeon who performed the operation

MUGGINGS

Two more muggings are reported in the South Bank neighborhood between 2 and 3 a.m. Thursday. Three previous muggings have been reported in the vicinity over the past week.

Available elements:

- Shots of crime locations
- Bite from police chief
- Bites from angry neighborhood residents

MAYOR

Mayor Norma Lyons is expected to be released from St. Mary's Hospital sometime today following surgery to reattach a finger accidentally severed in a cooking accident. The accident occurred Tuesday evening; the surgery took place on Wednesday.

Available elements:

- File footage of the mayor before the accident
- Exterior of hospital

Assignment: Producing a Medium-Length Newscast

You are a TV news producer for a station in Lakedale, in charge of putting together a seven-minute local news segment that airs at 5 p.m. today. The following menu of stories represents your choices and specifies which elements of video and audio are available. You also have the technical capability for one live remote.

Your completed newscast rundown should look like the sample rundowns in this chapter, showing the order of your stories, segment structure, how long each story will run, and what form it will take. Use the slugs that have been designated for each story.

Timing

You will have seven minutes for the entire newscast. Of this, subtract five seconds for your open and five seconds for goodbye and closing credits.

Story Menu

FIRST LADY

The First Lady of the United States arrives at Lakedale International Airport at noon. She is met by the mayor and governor, along with a children's choir. The First Lady will speak this evening at Lakedale University. Her appearance kicks off a three-day conference on early childhood development that will be attended by educators from around the world.

Available elements:

- Video of the plane landing
- Footage/natural sound of the First Lady emerging and being met by the officials and serenaded by the children
- Bites from the First Lady about the importance of childhood education

INDUSTRIAL ACCIDENT

Three employees of the Jordan Chemical Company are injured after an explosion in an industrial warehouse on the outskirts of town. The cause of the 10 a.m. explosion is believed to be an unstable chemical compound in a container inside the warehouse. The three victims are all in good condition at General Hospital and are expected to be released tomorrow. The warehouse will be closed for inspection for at least several weeks.

Available elements:

- Shots of the building after the explosion
- Shot of the ambulances carrying away victims
- Still photos of the accident victims
- Bites from the company spokesman and the head of the Lakedale Fire Department's hazardous materials team

WILDFIRE

A three-mile stretch of busy Route 5 is closed at 7 a.m., after a fast-moving grass fire jumps the road 12 miles east of Lakedale. Fire officials extinguish the blaze within an hour, and the road reopens at around 8:30. Route 5 is heavily used during the morning commute.

Available elements:

- Video of the fire
- Shot of "Road Closed" sign
- Bites from fire officials and frustrated commuters

BELL TOWER

Dedication at 2 p.m. of a new bell tower at St. Christopher's Cathedral in downtown Lakedale. This structure replaces the historic bell tower that burned to the ground one year ago.

Available elements:

- Video of the dedication ceremonies
- Bites from Gov. Smith and Bishop O'Callahan
- Footage inside the tower showing the bells
- File footage of the tower fire one year ago

PET STORE

Animal cruelty officers from the Lakedale Police Department close the Pretty Please Pet Store on the city's north side. The owners are arrested and charged with animal cruelty around 11:30 a.m. The police had been investigating reports that too many animals were confined in the facility under unsanitary conditions. Authorities also confiscated two rare birds that are on the list of endangered species. All the animals from the store were taken to the Lakedale Area Animal Shelter, where they will be kept pending litigation.

Available elements:

- Exteriors of the shop
- Interiors of the shop showing the unsanitary conditions
- Footage of the animals (including the rare birds)
- Shots of the owners being led into a police vehicle
- Bite from lead investigator describing conditions

PROTEST

Nurses at General Hospital stage a 15-minute demonstration on the grounds of the hospital to protest a proposed round of layoffs. About 75 nurses take part in the peaceful noon-hour protest. The layoffs are to begin next month.

Available elements:

- Various shots of the demonstrators and their signs, with natural sound
- Bites from the nurses involved in the protest
- Bite from hospital administrator defending the layoffs
- Bites from patients leaving the hospital
- Interior and exterior footage of the building

CHOPPER

A helicopter gets tangled in a power line, killing the pilot and temporarily knocking out power to a neighborhood in the southern part of Lakedale at around 4 p.m. The helicopter belonged to a local sightseeing company and had been rented by the pilot, who was from Montreal. No passengers were on board.

Available elements:

- Footage of the helicopter tangled in the power line
- Bite from police spokesman
- Map showing area affected by the outage

BUFFALO

A herd of buffalo briefly escapes from a nature preserve 15 miles west of Lakedale. When the buffalo get onto Route 5, a two-mile stretch of the highway is closed while the animals are rounded up. None of the buffalo are injured or do any damage themselves. One shocked motorist who gets caught on the road locks herself in her car until the herd is removed from the area. This all takes place around 2:30 in the afternoon.

Available elements:

- Video of the roundup, including numerous shots of the buffalo
- Shot of the fence where the animals broke through
- Bites from director of the nature preserve, the stranded motorist, and the local sheriff

SHOOTOUT

Police exchange gunfire with robbers who held up the Lakedale National Bank at 3 p.m. The shootout took place in an alley behind the bank, which is located downtown. One of the two robbers was injured and taken into custody. The second briefly escaped on foot and was captured 15 minutes later. As they hunted the suspect, police briefly cordoned off a 10-block area of downtown. The injured suspect is at Mercy Hospital in fair condition; the other is in lockup at the county jail. The district attorney plans an arraignment tomorrow.

Available elements:

- Exterior of the bank
- Footage from a distance of the police firing weapons and chasing through the streets
- Shot of the injured suspect being put into an ambulance
- Shot of the second suspect in police custody
- Bites from bank president, police chief, and several eyewitnesses
- Map of the affected area

RAIN FOREST

The Lakedale Zoo inaugurates a new facility, an indoor tropical garden that houses a variety of jungle flora and fauna. Visitors walk through the forest on a series of above-ground paths. The facility was donated by former Sen. Madison Morton, a Lakedale native and former ambassador to Tanzania. Sen. Morton leads the grand opening at 10:30 a.m.

Available elements:

- Video from inside the building, including footage of various birds and animals and natural sound
- Bite from the zoo director, opening-day visitors, and Sen. Morton

Assignment: Producing a Long-Form Newscast

You are a television news producer for a local station in Lakedale, in charge of putting together a half-hour 11 p.m. newscast. The following menu of stories represents your potential subject matter, and specifies which elements of video and audio are available for each item. Please note that you won't be able to use all of the stories. You also have the technical capability for two live remotes. This newscast has two anchors, plus separate presenters for weather and sports.

Your completed newscast rundown should look like the sample rundowns in this chapter, clearly showing the order of your stories, segment structure, how long each story will run, and what form it will take. Use the slugs that have been designated for each story.

Timing

You will have 28 minutes for the entire newscast. From this, subtract the following amounts of time:

- 40 seconds for your opening billboard tease
- 10 seconds each for four prebreak internal teases (40 seconds total)
- 10 seconds for goodbye and closing credits
- three minutes for weather
- three minutes for sports
- eight minutes for four commercial breaks of two minutes each.

This leaves 12 minutes, 30 seconds for your news and feature stories.

Newscast Structure

This half-hour newscast is divided into five segments (A–B–C–D–E) with four commercial breaks. Your two major news blocks will be the first two segments of the program (A and B). The C block is devoted primarily to weather, and the D block to sports. You will also have a quick final segment (E block), which is appropriate for lighter, kicker stories. If you see an appropriate opportunity, you might want to run a short news story leading into the weather segment or the sports block.

Story Menu: International Stories

TUNNEL FIRE

Fire in a Swiss tunnel traps motorists. At least 10 fatalities and dozens of injuries.
   Available elements:

- Dramatic video with natural sound, no bites

EIFFEL TOWER

The Eiffel Tower is evacuated after a terrorist threat in Paris. A small bomb goes off in a park near the tower, but no one is injured.
   Available elements:

- Video and natural sound of the evacuation
- Bites from American tourists

PLANE CRASH

An Argentine Airlines jetliner crashes in the Andes Mountains of South America, killing all 50 persons aboard. Two Americans were aboard, including a woman from the next state over from you.
   Available elements:

- Map of the region, no video or sound

SOUTH KOREA RIOTS

An anti-American demonstration in Seoul turns violent when demonstrators battle police in the streets—numerous injuries, some serious, but no deaths.

Available elements:

- Video with natural sound
- Angry bites (in English) from people on both sides

Story Menu: National Stories

VICE PRESIDENT

The Vice President of the United States is hospitalized after what White House spokesmen call minor heart palpitations. The announcement comes at 8:45 p.m. The VP is expected to be released tomorrow.

Available elements:

- Video/bites from the White House spokesman
- File footage of the vice president

SHIPWRECK

Divers off the coast of Puerto Rico announce the recovery of millions of dollars worth of Spanish treasure from a ship lost at sea in 1652.

Available elements:

- Video and bites from the divers, including shots of the gold treasure.

HURRICANE

Hurricane-force winds strike the U.S. Virgin Islands. No injuries or deaths, but thousands of dollars in property damage.

Available elements:

- Video and natural sound of the storm and its aftermath

Roller Coaster

A roller coaster goes off the track at a county fair in a state on the other side of the country, killing one passenger and injuring 15 others, none seriously.

Available elements:

- Footage of the accident aftermath
- Bites from police and eyewitnesses

KIDNAPPINGS

Two children from a small town in a neighboring state are kidnapped during their walk home from school. The parents appeal to the public for help in finding the missing kids.

Available elements:

- Footage and bites from the parents
- Video and still photos of the missing kids
- Exterior shot of the children's school

Story Menu: LOCAL STORIES

WATER RESCUE

A sheriff's department rescue boat retrieves 10 fishermen whose boat caught fire in Blue Lake. The rescue takes place around 4 p.m. One of the fishermen suffered from smoke inhalation; the others were OK.

Available elements:

- Video of the rescue boat returning to port
- Shot of the rescued men being taken away in an ambulance
- Bite from Sheriff Fred Wyatt

TENT COLLAPSE

Dozens of people suffer minor injuries when a party tent collapses on the grounds of the Lakedale Historical Museum. About 200 people were attending a fund-raising dinner when a security vehicle backed into a pole, knocking down the tent. The accident occurs at 8:30 p.m.

Available elements:

- Video of the aftermath, including shots of the collapsed tent
- Bites from eyewitnesses and police

ZOO FIRE

Monkeys at the Lakedale Zoo are evacuated after a fire breaks out in the Monkey House. Authorities believe the fire might have been set deliberately. One monkey is injured in the fire, which firefighters bring under control at 5 p.m.

Available elements:

- Video of the fire
- Shots of the evacuated monkeys
- Bites from zoo director Wilson Banderas and fire officials

SENATOR

One of your state's U.S. senators accepts a humanitarian award from the Mayor of Lakedale at a noontime ceremony at City Hall.

Available elements:

- Video and bites from the event

ILLEGAL IMMIGRANTS

Officials from the Immigration and Naturalization Service take two dozen illegal immigrants into custody at 2 p.m. The immigrants were discovered hiding in a boat in the Blue Lake Marina. All were Guatemalan citizens.

Available elements:

- Video of the immigrants and the boat
- Bite from INS official

AIRPORT

Lakedale International Airport is evacuated for two hours after a passenger runs through the security checkpoint and gets lost in the crowd. The incident occurs around 6:45 p.m. All flights are postponed, and everyone inside the gate area has to reenter security. Things are back to normal by 9 p.m. The suspect is not located.

Available elements:

- Footage of the crowds waiting outside the terminal
- File footage of the security checkpoint
- Bites from airport security and angry passengers

FIRE CHIEF MARRIAGE

Fire Chief Andy Edwards announced this morning that he will marry his longtime girlfriend, a local schoolteacher. The wedding will take place next month. Edwards was recently named "Lakedale's Sexiest Public Servant" by the Lakedale Ledger.

Available elements:

- Still photo of the couple

SPELLING BEE

A 10-year-old Lakedale boy becomes the state spelling champ in a competition held around 3 p.m. today. The boy has lived in America for only two years—his family immigrated here from Pakistan.

Available elements:

- Video and natural sound of the winning moment
- Bites from the boy and his parents

NUCLEAR

A citizens group called No Nukes for Lakedale holds a 4 p.m. press conference to call for the closing of the controversial Lakedale Nuclear Power Plant. Their report criticizes the plant as being vulnerable to terrorism.

Available elements:

- Video and bites from the press conference
- File footage of the plant

Analysis: TV Newscast Producing

- Record a local half-hour TV newscast and create a written rundown for it that lays out all the necessary elements.
- Compare two local newscasts that air at the same time and see how the producing decisions compare from one program to the next.
- Make a list of 20 local stories from your hometown newspaper and use them as content for creating a TV newscast rundown.

CHAPTER EIGHT

NEWS TEASES

TOPICS DISCUSSED IN THIS CHAPTER

- What Is a News Tease? • Challenges of Writing News Teases
- Mechanics of Writing News Teases • Rules for Writing News Teases
- Relating News Teases to Viewers • Using Titles in News Teases
- Examples of News Teases • Checklist of Key Points

ASSIGNMENTS/ANALYSIS

- Assignment: Writing News Teases • Analysis: TV News Teases

WHAT IS A NEWS TEASE?

A news tease is an effort to lure viewers to tune into an upcoming story, and by extension, the entire newscast. Teases are an acknowledgment that people watch television with their hands on the remote. If you expect viewers to keep watching, especially through long commercial breaks, you must give them an incentive; hence, the tease. With competition from hundreds of channels, news stations find themselves under increasing pressure to promote their product, and one of the ways of accomplishing this is with frequent (some might say overly frequent) news teases.

"People don't always have time to sit and watch the news from start to finish," says Tim Tunison, assistant news director at WBAL-TV in Baltimore. "Many of them aren't even watching the television—they're listening. And they're doing so while chasing their kids, making dinner, and cleaning the house. Teases are more important than ever."

Teases can take several forms: sound bite or no sound bite, on camera or VO, and titles or no titles. The common denominator is that teases are short, generally running five to 10 seconds per item. Teases tend to run in multiples, so that several stories are teased in quick succession. Like a microcosm of the newscast itself, these clusters are likely to include a mix of serious items, feature stories, weather, and sports.

Teases are found at several key points in a newscast:

- Preshow tease. This is the teasing of several stories back to back at the top of the newscast. It might also be called an open or billboard or even headlines, although that last term is something of a misnomer. Almost every newscast opens with a preshow tease of one kind or another.

- Internal teases before commercial breaks. These are teases that end a segment block, and they run just before the commercials begin. Internal teases promote what is coming up later in the newscast.

- Teases for upcoming newscasts. This type of tease occurs when a station airs back-to-back newscasts, because it promotes stories that will be seen in later programs. Typically these teases are delivered by the anchor or anchors of the newscast being highlighted.

In addition to these *cluster teases,* which promote several stories back to back, newscasts frequently include individual story teases that come in the form of anchor tags. These are short items that immediately follow a story, and they usually promote ongoing coverage of content that will be dealt with in a later newscast. For example, "We'll have further developments on that breaking story from downtown Lakedale tonight at 11." A variation of this is an anchor tag that directs viewers to the station's website for more information about the story in question.

Are news teases a form of journalism? In a way yes, and in a way no. In the competitive medium of television they function as necessary evils. If no one is watching, your journalistic efforts are for naught. As the circus barkers say, the first order of business is getting folks into the tent.

Teases might not qualify as journalism, but they are written by journalists. Producers handle most of them, but reporters often write teases for their own stories, especially in the case of on-camera teases being done from a remote location. Anchors, too, might take part in the writing. In larger markets and at the network level, promotions specialists are likely to handle at least some of the tease writing. Promotions specialists also write teases for news series or other programming that goes beyond the day-to-day stories.

As a rule, news teases are one of the last things in the script to be written, after the stories have been edited and the rundown put together. Still, because of their importance, teases should not be tossed off without planning. The task is more difficult than it looks.

CHALLENGES OF WRITING NEWS TEASES

The key objective of the tease writer is to keep the viewer tuned into the newscast. This is accomplished by playing up aspects of the story that are interesting and relevant to the lives of the people watching. What is there about a particular story that will make viewers want to stick around? How can the broadest possible audience be drawn into the content? Which visuals, sound, and narration can be used in packaging the information most effectively? These are the questions a tease writer must ask, because it is the tease writer's job to give the greatest number of people possible a reason not to change channels.

News teases typically run at the beginning of a newscast and at the end of each segment, just before the commercial break.

Tease writers have to strike a balance between providing enough information to make the story interesting and giving away every detail. If the tease answers all of a viewer's questions, that viewer has no reason to linger for the rest of the story. On the other hand, the tease has to be substantive enough for the audience to get hooked. The trick is to find the middle path.

"A good tease is something that delivers a promise," says Matt Gaffney, executive producer of WTTG-TV in Washington, D.C. "You are asking viewers to stay tuned, so you promise they'll get something if they do. Teases that give too much information do not work—they're basically a small version of the story and not really a tease."

Strong teases take advantage of video and sound. Producers should use their most vivid, interesting images in a tease and, when available, audio elements like memorable sound bites and natural sound. These ingredients greatly enliven a tease, and can break up the pattern of several teases in a row voiced by an anchor. Narration alone is not always sufficient to draw viewers into a story. Pictures, sound bites, and natural sound should be considered additional weapons in the writer's arsenal.

Another challenge of tease writing is the lack of context. A 20- or 30-second news story allows for a good deal more scene setting than a 5- or 10-second tease. The tease must make sense on its own terms in a very short amount of time. Each tease should therefore stress only one or two aspects of a story, those with the strongest audience appeal. There simply isn't time to provide details—that's the job of the story, not the tease.

Finally, bigger stories can generate more than one tease within a newscast, requiring the writer to come up with several different ways of promoting the same item. In that situation, the teases must not be repetitive. If something is teased at the top of the show and a couple of times internally, each version needs to be slightly different, both visually and in the language.

MECHANICS OF WRITING NEWS TEASES

Above all, news teases are short. The average tease length is between five and 10 seconds per individual story, including any sound bites or natural sound. This translates into only one or two sentences, although certain subject matter might justify a slightly longer tease.

Structurally speaking, there are three basic categories of teases, similar in nature to the different categories of news stories: VOs, teases with sound, and on–camera teases, also called stand-up teases. When stories are teased together in a cluster, as is usually the case, the mix is likely to include a variety of structures; for example, a VO, followed by a sound bite tease, followed by the anchor or reporter on camera, then back to a VO. This isn't always the case, as different news operations will have different procedures. The advantage of mixing structures is that it keeps the teases from becoming too formulaic.

VO Teases

VO teases are the most commonly used of the different structures. Like regular VO news stories, they consist of narration read by an anchorperson against complementary visuals. VO teases work best when driven by strong pictures. Good visuals can make the difference between someone deciding to watch a story or to change the channel. As with news stories, the writer should remember the importance of referencing, so that images and narration make sense in relation to each other.

Teases With Sound

Teases can include sound bites or natural sound, especially when the story offers strong audio elements. In such cases, it is important to carefully integrate those elements with the anchorperson's narration.

For teases with sound bites, there are two choices: running the bite first, and then a line or two of VO narration by the anchor (SOT/VO), or running the narration first and the bite second (VO/SOT). Placing the sound bite first is often a more dramatic way to structure the tease, especially when the content of the bite is particularly compelling.

Let's say you have a story about a deer that gets trapped inside a house after crashing through a picture window. The homeowner gives a bite that says, "I was sitting there watching my soap opera, and next thing I know a deer comes flying into the room." The tease could start with this bite, followed by a short anchor VO: "How one Lakedale resident got an unexpected visitor."

The opposite structure would put the anchor VO first: "A surprise visitor makes an unexpected house call." Then the homeowner's bite: "I was sitting there watching my soap opera, and next thing I know a deer comes flying into the room." Either version of the tease is acceptable; it's up to the writer to decide if one works better than the other.

Natural sound is another effective building block for creators of news teases. Nat sound is especially appropriate for certain kinds of stories, such as those that include chanting protesters, courtroom outbursts, claps of thunder, howling winds, noisy wild-life, musical performances, and the like.

As with sound bite teases, a tease built around natural sound can be structured either as an SOT/VO, with the nat sound first and narration second, or a VO/SOT, with narration first and nat sound second. There are no hard and fast rules governing the order. Each situation must be evaluated on a case-by-case basis.

As an example, let's take a story about a neighborhood group that marches at police headquarters against soaring crime rates. In this example you have several seconds of the protestors chanting, "Save our streets! Save our streets!" In the SOT/VO, you start the tease with this, then write an anchor VO that says, "Residents of South Bank march against crime at City Hall." Using the opposite structure, you start with an anchor VO: "Residents of South Bank make their voices heard at City Hall." Then the natural sound: "Save our streets! Save our streets!" Both versions work. In making the choice, you would want to look at other teases in the cluster to determine which structure better suits the overall flow.

Teases with sound must be approached with care. According to WTTG-TV's Matt Gaffney, "SOTs are difficult to include in teases because the viewer is not anticipating them and often the sound is so short the viewer is just beginning to comprehend the story when the sound and VO are over." With this thought in mind, writers must take extra care in setting up teases that include sound bites and natural sound.

On-Camera Teases

On-camera teases are used in several situations. Anchors will sometimes tease stories from the studio without any supporting video or recorded sound. This kind of tease is generally short and to the point. If it involves double anchors, it can be called a *tandem tease.*

Reporters in the field do on-camera teases from remote locations to increase the sense of immediacy. In this type of stand-up tease, the reporter should pick a visually interesting location. Recent years have seen a trend toward walking teases or teases in which the reporter is doing something while speaking on camera. Although action is a good thing on television, action for the sake of action can look awkward if not handled properly. Physical motion needs to be motivated, and teases are so short there isn't time for much activity.

Anchors and reporters are not the only ones delivering on-camera teases. Weather and sports anchors routinely tease their subject matter as well. On-camera teases are generally done live, but sometimes they are taped ahead of time. Pretaped teases are called *look-lives,* because they are meant to give the illusion of airing live.

On-camera news teases observe the same principles that apply to other forms of tease writing. The only difference is that the whole thing is delivered to the camera, without the benefit of additional visuals or sound.

Many news teases are delivered by reporters in the field. These can be done live or recorded on tape.

RULES FOR WRITING NEWS TEASES

Although effective tease writing does not follow a specific formula, certain rules can help you improve your skills.

• Avoid writing teases that read or sound like newspaper headlines. Headlines give a short but reasonably complete version of the story, whereas teases emphasize specific aspects of the situation without providing the big picture. To put it another way, headlines answer the audience's basic questions and teases leave the viewer wanting to know more.

• The language of news teases must be conversational. Toward that end, it is often a good idea to directly address viewers. For example: "Will you need to leave early for work tomorrow? Find out the latest on downtown construction." The wording here speaks in a personal way to whoever is watching.

• Although the previous example contains a question, resist the temptation to end all your teases with an interrogative. Teases written in the form of questions might be appropriate in some cases, but there's a risk involved: Instead of intriguing a viewer, a question that is too vague might not be compelling enough to keep him or her around.

• Because teases run for one or two sentences, each word has to count. Take out all unnecessary words and syllables. Make the text as crisp as it can be. Use vivid nouns and strong verbs. Don't hedge your bets with conditional verbs like could, maybe, and might; these tend to water down your message.

• Don't "telegraph" an upcoming commercial break by overusing phrases like "coming up next," "still ahead," "when we return," and so on. When you do use them, save the phrases for the very end of a tease, after the audience has heard a bit about the stories. Otherwise, if viewers are cued to expect a promotional message, they might be tempted to tune out.

• Be sure the story delivers what it teases. If the story fails to live up to its promise, viewers are likely to find themselves annoyed. By the same token, if the story contains exactly the same information as the tease, you've given the audience no reason to wait around for something more.

• Teases are often written with clever turns of phrase, but for certain subject matter cleverness might not be appropriate. If the story deals with a serious topic, avoid puns or other language that is too casual for the occasion.

• Teases usually come in clusters, as at the top of the newscast. Therefore writers need to think of them collectively. Language and sentence structure must be varied from one tease to the next, so as not to repeat words and phrases.

RELATING NEWS TEASES TO VIEWERS

To be truly effective, good teases should be as inclusive of the audience as possible. Don't hesitate to play to the self-interest of your viewers. Here's an example: "If you're headed to the beach this weekend, you won't want to miss our forecast." Obviously, not everyone watching the newscast will be headed to the beach, but to one degree or another, the forecast is bound to affect the entire audience.

Because viewers relate to people like themselves, use sound bites from interviewees in teases. Hearing a person make a point in his or her own words is often more compelling than having the anchor or reporter paraphrase the information. Strong sound bites from ordinary people can bring a tease to life.

Another way to pique audience interest is to write teases that emphasize the ironic twist. Consider this example: "A student gets kicked out of class for sexual harassment—a *kindergarten* class." The setup is fairly straightforward, but the payoff—the student in question is only in kindergarten—gives people something to come back for.

When appropriate, it might work to emphasize a story's emotional content as a means of interesting viewers. TV is an emotional medium; it's fine to take advantage of this in writing news teases, as long as the result does not descend into cheesiness.

That said, language in news teases too often goes over the top. As a rule of thumb, steer clear of terminology that cues the audience about how to feel: subjective nouns like nightmare and tragedy, or subjective adjectives like shocking, heart-wrenching, or terrifying. As with straight news stories, it is always best to let viewers come to their own decisions about how a story makes them feel. Anything less amounts to disrespect.

Take care that your language does not get too hyperbolic as you appeal to the audience. This means avoiding superlative words, or phrases like "We've got a story you won't believe." Tease the *content* of your stories, not the reactions viewers are supposed to have.

By the same token, it is not a good idea to attempt to scare the audience into watching. A tease that is deliberately frightening, like "Does your town's drinking water cause cancer?" toys with viewers' emotions. Unless you are on solid factual ground, you are better off steering clear of these kinds of scare tactics. Similarly, you don't want to raise the audience's hopes too high. Consider this example: "A new cure for baldness? We'll tell you about a breakthrough in hair-replacement products." Because this tease promises something the story is unlikely to deliver, it runs the risk of alienating those watching.

According to WBAL's Tim Tunison:

> You can't tease something and then not deliver. If you tease, "Beauty products in your bathroom that could kill you," you'd better be telling the truth. If you tease that something could kill you, only to say in the story that the product causes illness in people with severe allergies, you have a problem. Far too many television stations do this. And the viewers aren't dumb. We receive just as many viewer e-mails regarding our teases as we do about our stories. You have to be careful.

This is the bottom line: News teases must occupy the same ethical high ground as news stories.

USING TITLES IN NEWS TEASES

It is standard in many TV newsrooms to add titles to news teases. These titles are inevitably short—two or three short words at most—and they must be appropriate to both the mood and the subject matter of the story. For a thorough discussion of writing titles for television news stories, see Chapter 9, "TV News Graphics, Titles, and Supers."

EXAMPLES OF NEWS TEASES

Let's examine a few examples of news teases to see what works and what doesn't work. First, we concentrate on using language in teases, then we look at examples that add visuals, bites, natural sound, and titles.

Using Language in News Teases

Story #1: Hazardous Substances. Our first story deals with a report issued by a local environmental group critical of the way hazardous substances are transported through populated sections of Lakedale. The report alleges that city ordinances allow just about anything to pass through town in railroad freight cars, including nuclear waste and industrial chemicals.

Compare two versions of a tease for this story:

Weak
Next, we'll take a look at the transportation of hazardous materials through our city.

Better
Dangerous cargo—find out what's on board the railroad freight cars that pass through town.

This is a story with potentially strong audience appeal. Yet the first tease is written generically, addressing no one in particular. Its language is vague and does not engage the local residents who are its natural audience. The second tease relates the story more directly to viewers who live in the community of Lakedale. It also offers a reason to stay tuned by promising to tell them something they don't know. The wording is strong, but it does not cross the line into fear mongering, because the tease does not stray beyond the facts at hand.

Story #2: Heating Bills. The second story is a consumer report about saving money on winter heating bills. This piece includes interviews with energy experts who run through a list of easy cost-saving measures that any homeowner can undertake to weatherproof against the cold. Again, here are two versions of a news tease.

Weak
Many homeowners spend too much on winter energy bills because they fail to weatherproof their houses.

Better
Want to save money on your energy bills this winter? See how a few small steps can make a big difference.

A consumer story of this nature offers rich opportunities for tease writers. Version one, however, relies on a straightforward factual statement, with no attempt to involve the audience in the subject matter. Version two targets the viewers' self-interest and makes an appeal to the pocketbook. Who doesn't want to save money on utility bills? "A few small steps" cues the listener that these are tips that don't involve a great deal of effort, which is also attractive.

Story #3: Grand Opening. This story deals with the grand opening of a large office complex east of downtown. The complex occupies a 100-year-old local landmark originally constructed as a pharmaceutical factory. The imposing brick building, which sat empty for years, has been renovated as a center for biotechnology, with 15 companies and 350 employees.

Weak
An office complex has its grand opening in Lakedale, and dozens of new employees set up shop.

Better
Remember the old pharmaceutical factory on Highway 17? See how an eyesore got a high-tech makeover.

This is a slightly more difficult story to tease, in that it might not appeal to a wide range of viewers. The first example does little to address this problem, offering a not very interesting headline that summarizes more than it teases. The second version does a better job tying the story to a local audience by reminding them of something they have been driving by for years. The word makeover is also helpful, as most everyone enjoys seeing before-and-after images.

Story #4: Gang Violence. This is a news feature about the growing problem of gang activity in Lakedale, based on an in-depth interview with a former gang leader who now campaigns for peace on the streets. In the story, the former gang leader acts as a guide through parts of the city plagued by violence.

Weak
Gang violence is taking its toll on the local streets, as we learn from a one-time criminal.

Better
Step inside the violent world of hometown street gangs—with a one-time thug turned community activist.

The first version of this tease does little to draw in the viewer, and the reference to "one-time criminal" gives an incomplete description of the story's main character. The second version makes a more direct appeal to the audience by promising to take viewers inside a world they might not know much about. The main character of the story is more clearly identified in a way that ties him to the subject matter.

Using Visuals in News Teases

For the next example, let's add visual elements to create a VO tease. In addition to video, we will also be superimposing an on-screen title for each story.

Story #5: Teacher Fire. A 37-year-old grade school teacher is formally charged in court this morning for allegedly setting a fire at Barbara Bush Elementary School the previous afternoon. Authorities allege that she started the fire in a supply room after being terminated from her position because of absenteeism and complaints from parents. No students were in the building at the time. There were no injuries, and the fire caused only minor smoke damage to the supply room. The suspect had been a third-grade teacher at the school.

Available Visual Elements

- Video of the teacher in court as she listens to the charges
- File video of the fire, showing smoke coming out of the school building
- Close-up of sign outside the school that says "Welcome to Barbara Bush Elementary"
- School yearbook picture of the teacher

Weak

(Visuals)	(Sound)
	--------------------Anchor--------------------
Title: Day in Court File video of the fire, showing smoke coming out of the school building	THE CASE OF A LOCAL ELEMENTARY SCHOOLTEACHER FINDS ITS WAY TO COURT TODAY.

Better

(Visuals)	(Sound)
	--------------------Anchor--------------------
Title: Arson Charges Video of the teacher in court as she listens to the verdict File video of the fire, showing smoke coming out of the school building	A THIRD-GRADE TEACHER APPEARS IN COURT TODAY—CHARGED WITH SETTING FIRE TO A LOCAL ELEMENTARY SCHOOL.

The first version is bland. "Finds its way to court" does not single out any particular aspect of the case, and no mention is made of the fire that stands at the heart of the story. The use of the file footage here does offer an illustration of the fire, but not in a way that matches the script. Furthermore, the tease does not take advantage of the most interesting visual possibility, the image of the teacher herself as she appears in court. This is a story with a lead character. Why not show her?

The second version of the tease corrects these problems. The language is more specific and provides extra information. The visuals include a shot of the teacher, as well as a brief shot of the fire to remind viewers of the original story. As for the titles, "Day in Court" is too vague. "Arson Charges" gives a clearer idea of what happened.

Using Sound Bites in Teases

For the next story, let's add a sound bite to the tease, along with video and a title.

Story #6: Missing Boy. A 5-year-old boy who had been missing for several hours is rescued from a tree by the fire department. The boy is fine. He told firefighters he had run away from home and climbed the tree because he wanted to see if he could fly. Too frightened to jump, he finally called out for help and was discovered by a pedestrian, who summoned help on her cell phone.

Available Visual/Sound Elements

- Video of the rescue, with one firefighter handing the boy down from the tree to another rescuer
- Video of the boy being handed into his mother's arms
- Sound bite from the boy's mother: "He'll get a scolding all right—but first he gets a hug."
- Sound bite from the rescuer: "We're just happy we were able to help."

Weak

(Visuals)	(Sound)
Title: Rescue Mission Firefighter's on-camera bite	Bite: "We're just happy we were able to help."
	---------------------Anchor--------------------
Video of the firefighters handing the boy down from the tree	THE FIRE DEPARTMENT COMES TO THE RESCUE, AND ONE LAKEDALE FAMILY BREATHES A SIGH OF RELIEF.

Better

(Visuals)	(Sound)
Title: Up a Tree Mother's on-camera bite	Bite: "He'll get a scolding all right—but first he gets a hug."
	---------------------Anchor--------------------
Video of the boy being handed into his mother's arms	A MISSING FIVE-YEAR-OLD IS BACK IN HIS MOTHER'S ARMS—AFTER FIREFIGHTERS COME TO THE BOY'S RESCUE.

With two choices of sound bites, the trick is to pick the right one. Because the mother's bite shows more emotion, and because she has more at stake than the fire-fighters, it makes sense to select her over the rescuer. Similarly, the shot of the mother hugging her son packs more of an emotional punch than the boy with his rescuers. The language in the weak version relies on a cliché ("sigh of relief") and does not really shed much light on the story. It also poses a referencing problem, because the text talks about "one Lakedale family," but we're looking at firefighters, not the family. In the second version the anchor narration connects more logically with the sound bite, and the referencing works nicely with the pictures. The first title, "Rescue Mission," is adequate, but not very informative. "Up a Tree" is better because it works with the shot of the firefighters handing the boy down from the branches.

Using Natural Sound in Teases

For the final story, let's write a tease using natural sound, along with video and a title.

Story #7: Doggie Day Care. This is a feature about a new business in town that offers day care for canines. Among the services provided is home pickup and delivery for pet owners who can't drop off their animals. The story is structured as a "day in the life" of one pooch, a miniature schnauzer named Misty.

Available Visual/Sound Elements

- Shots of Misty and a couple of other dogs riding in the day care van

- Shots of Misty at the day care facility, running around with a toy in her mouth

- Shots and natural sound of Misty sitting up and barking before receiving a doggie treat

Weak

(Visuals)	(Sound)
Title: New Business Misty sitting up and barking	Natural sound for :03 of Misty barking --------------------Anchor--------------------
Misty running around with a toy in her mouth	HOW A NEW BUSINESS IN LAKEDALE IS PROVIDING DAY CARE FOR DOGS.

Better

(Visuals)	(Sound)
Title: Doggie Day Care Misty sitting up and barking	Natural sound for :03 of Misty barking --------------------Anchor--------------------
Shots of Misty and a couple of other dogs riding in the day care van	WHAT'S ALL THE BARKING ABOUT? HOW A NEW BUSINESS IN LAKEDALE HAS GONE TO THE DOGS.

Both versions start with three seconds of natural sound of Misty's barking. The first version follows up the natural sound with a generic line of narration that spells things out too literally. The second version does a better job teasing the story, as opposed to giving away too much information. The choice of shots also works better in the second tease, because it shows the dogs riding in the day care van, thus showcasing one of the more unusual aspects of the story. The first title, "New Business," is dull. "Doggie Day Care," by contrast, gives a clearer picture of what the story is about, and its lighter tone suits the mood.

CHECKLIST OF KEY POINTS

- News teases can run before a newscast or within a newscast, usually heading into a commercial break. Teases are often grouped together in clusters of three or four, although others run as brief anchor tags that immediately follow a story.

- The goal of the news tease is to keep viewers watching. Good teases give the audience a reason to stick around, which means withholding certain details to pique curiosity. Good teases also make use of strong visuals and sound.

- Most news teases are written as VOs. When there are compelling audio elements, teases can include natural sound or sound bites, although these need to be just a few seconds long. Sometimes teases are delivered on camera by an anchor or reporter.

- Teases are not headlines. Headlines give a summary of the story; teases highlight a promotable aspect of the story.

- The language of teases is direct, conversational, and vivid. Because they are so short, every word must count. Because they run in clusters, teases must be thought of collectively, as well as individually.

- Effective teases directly address the audience. One strategy is to tease the emotional content of a story, but teases should not scare the audience or promise more than they can deliver.

ASSIGNMENTS/ANALYSIS

Assignment: Writing News Teases

Based on the information provided, write news teases for the following stories. The first three are VO teases and the second group includes natural sound or sound bites. Assume you are writing for a 6 p.m. newscast. Make sure you follow proper script format, with visual elements listed in the left column and sound elements on the right. Give each story a brief title, no more than 16 characters in length (including punctuation and blank spaces).

Voiceover Teases (anchor narration without sound bites or natural sound)

POLICE CHIEF

Lakedale Police Chief Al Varden is found dead in his home at 3 p.m. by his wife. According to preliminary reports, he died from a gunshot wound to the head, an apparent suicide. Varden, who had been suffering from health problems, was a 20-year veteran of the force and had been chief for the past three years.

Available Visual Elements

- File footage of Varden at work
- Still pics of Varden alone and with his wife
- Exteriors of the Varden residence with police cars parked in the driveway

INTERSTATE PILEUP

A section of interstate highway about 10 miles north of Lakedale is briefly closed during the early-morning rush hour following an accident involving several cars and a semi trailer. The truck apparently jackknifed after its driver fell asleep, causing a chain collision. Injuries to motorists and passengers were minor, but authorities closed the highway in one direction for a half-hour, creating a major traffic jam.

Available Visual Elements

- Helicopter shot of the accident site, showing traffic backed up on the interstate
- Ground-level video showing the aftermath of the accident
- Close-up of signs that say "Road Closed"

LANDMARK THEATER

At a packed morning meeting the Lakedale City Council approves historic landmark status for the Dream Theatre, a 1920s-era movie palace. This designation means long-awaited plans can go forward to restore the facility as a performing arts center.

Available Visual Elements

- Footage from the meeting
- File video and historical stills of the theater
- Architectural sketches showing how the theater will look after renovations

TATTOO CONVENTION

An international convention of tattoo artists kicks off at the Union Hotel in downtown Lakedale. The convention began with a "Body Art Fashion Show" in which models displayed their tattoos for an enthusiastic audience. The conventioneers are in town for three days.

Available Visual Elements

- Numerous shots of the models at the "Body Art Fashion Show," including people with full-body tattoos
- Tight shot of the top of a man's bald head, displaying an American flag tattoo
- Shots of the audience at the fashion show as they enjoy the show
- Exterior of the convention hotel, with a sign that says "Welcome Tattoo Lovers"

KAHOLA DROWNING

A 36-year-old man drowns in a waterskiing accident around 2 p.m. at Lake Kahola, a recreational lake and county park outside of town. Police have identified the victim as Darwin Lamont, the founder and president of the city's largest real estate development company. The victim's father, also from Lakedale, is a former U.S. senator.

Available Visual Elements

- Video (from a distance) of police retrieving a body from the water
- Still photo of Darwin Lamont
- Still photo of Darwin Lamont with his father, Sen. Lamont
- Exterior of Lamont Real Estate, the corporate headquarters of Darwin Lamont's company

Teases With Sound Bites/Natural Sound

TOLLBOOTH CRASH

Three people are seriously injured when a moving van loses its brakes and slams into a turnpike tollbooth on Highway 17 at the eastern edge of town around 5 p.m. Two of the injured were in the van, and the third worked in the tollbooth. The on-ramp is closed for about 30 minutes.

Available Visual/Sound Elements

- Video of aftermath, including close-ups of the wrecked tollbooth and the moving van
- Video of an ambulance leaving the scene with the accident victims, natural sound of the sirens blaring
- Bite from an eyewitness: "The moving van was headed straight for the tollbooth, and the next thing I heard was a huge crash."
- Bite from a highway patrol officer: "The injuries are serious, but things could have been a whole lot worse."

SCHOOL VANDALISM

School officials at Benjamin Franklin Elementary report that all the building's south-facing windows had been shattered by vandals overnight. Classes began two hours late today to allow for cleanup. No suspects have been apprehended.

Available Visual/Sound Elements

- Video of the damage
- Shots of a janitor sweeping up broken glass, including natural sound as he pushes the shattered glass into a dustpan
- Shots of kids arriving late at school
- Bite from school principal: "Why anybody would want to do such a thing is beyond me."

CLOWN PARADE

The Clown Parade, an annual tradition in the Lakedale neighborhood of Greenside, takes place at 11 this morning. About 200 clowns from around the region participated, drawing several thousand spectators to a closed-off section of Highland Avenue. Today's parade marked the 20-year anniversary of Greenside's Clown Parade, and included the debut of a "toddler's parade," made up of preschool children dressed in clown costumes.

Available Visual/Sound Elements

- Video of the grown-up clowns marching through the streets, including natural sound of a marching band
- Tight shot of a clown who looks into the camera and pinches his nose, with natural sound of the nose making a loud honk
- Video of the toddler's parade
- Close-up shot of a crying clown baby, natural sound of the child wailing
- Bite from one of the parading clowns: "Look out, Lakedale—the Clown Parade is back in town."

PROM BAN

The principal of Lakedale Heights High School (LHHS) in suburban Lakedale bans nonstudents from attending the LHHS prom. LHHS students must attend with other LHHS students. The principal says he is trying to prevent a repeat of last year, when a nonstudent at the prom got into a fistfight with several LHHS students. Students quickly organize a protest at the end of the school day.

Available Visual/Sound Elements

- Exterior of Lakedale Heights High School
- Home video from last year's prom, including a brief snippet of the fistfight
- Shots of LHHS students demonstrating in front of the school building, with natural sound of the protestors chanting, "It's my prom and I'll bring who I want to!"

- Bite from the LHHS principal: "Prom night should be about having a good time, not about fighting."
- Bite from female student: "It's not fair—the school shouldn't be choosing our prom dates."

CONSTRUCTION

A Lakedale neighborhood is split over the proposed construction of a "big-box" discount store on the site of a former hospital. Opponents of the project say a park should be built on the land instead. Developers say they will go ahead with plans for the store in spite of the objections.

Available Visual/Sound Elements

- Exterior of the building site, which is basically an empty lot
- Architectural sketches of the proposed discount store
- Drive-by shots of the neighborhood where the controversy is taking place
- Bite from project opponent: "This land should be turned into a park, not a parking lot."
- Bite from project developer: "Our stores serve millions of customers—and add tax revenues to the local community."

Analysis: TV News Teases

- Record several local newscasts from the same day and compare how different stations promote the same story.
- Find and critique examples of the different structural types of news teases: VO teases, teases with sound bites, teases with natural sound, and on-camera teases.
- Watch a batch of news teases with the sound turned down and see if the visuals are interesting enough to draw you into the story.
- Compare the teases at the beginning of a newscast with those that come later in the program.
- Compare the writing of news teases for local TV news programs with news teases for network news programs.

CHAPTER NINE

TV NEWS GRAPHICS, TITLES, AND SUPERS

TOPICS DISCUSSED IN THIS CHAPTER

ASSIGNMENTS/ANALYSIS

NEWS GRAPHICS IN TELEVISION JOURNALISM

Modern technology makes possible virtually any graphic representation, animated or nonanimated, that a designer can envision. This opens up vast visual opportunities for television journalists, who use graphics to add nuance and detail to their stories while simultaneously enriching the aesthetic appeal of the news product. Reporters and producers still rightly regard video as the backbone of their coverage, but additional storytelling tools are now at their disposal.

No matter what medium they work in, good journalists share a common motto: "Show, don't tell." In other words, effective news stories inform the audience not just with words, but with examples and illustrations as well. TV news graphics offer precisely that ability. Although sometimes overlooked in a medium driven by video footage, these additional visuals should be thought of as powerful weapons in a television journalist's arsenal.

Graphics spice up newscasts and help fill the void in stories that lack pictorial elements. Charts, maps, and text graphics bring to life material that is otherwise difficult to illustrate, such as statistical data, or complicated spatial or organizational relationships. Research indicates that viewers are more likely to comprehend and retain information that is delivered through a combination of images and words. The creative use of graphics can therefore be of great service in clarifying the details of a story.

News graphics are a form of journalism that involves collaboration between two groups: editorial personnel like reporters and producers, whose emphasis is content, and designers, whose emphasis is presentation. For everyone involved, the goal is to operate within a journalistic framework, applying to graphic images the same standards that pertain to video footage. Accuracy, fairness, and objectivity matter just as much in news graphics as in writing, reporting, interviewing, shooting, and editing.

Graphics represent a rapidly growing area of the news business, not only in TV newsrooms but for web-based and print journalism as well. As society becomes increasingly oriented toward visuals, the use of pictorial elements in journalistic storytelling will undoubtedly increase. News professionals, especially those working in a visual medium like television, are well advised to master the basics of graphic design.

"The producers at WBAL-TV now have the ability to design many of the graphics on their own from the comfort of their desks," says Tim Tunison, assistant news director of the Baltimore station. "We still have an art department for more complex graphics. For producers, it's not just about words any more. Good producers weigh in on all key graphics in their newscast."

HOW TV NEWS GRAPHICS ARE CREATED

According to graphic artist Gary Stout of WBZ-TV, the CBS affiliate in Boston, designing television news graphics is "the process of using visual art to communicate a message." Like other forms of visuals, news graphics convey information in a way that goes beyond words. Unlike video footage, graphic images give their designers greater latitude for originality. Where videography depends on existing visuals, news graphics involve the creation of original visuals.

News graphics start with an idea. Several hours before a newscast airs, the show's producer meets with a graphic designer to discuss which stories will require visual representation beyond the standard video that serves as the backbone of most TV news coverage. Graphics almost always appear in story introductions, but they can also serve as internal elements within packages and shorter stories.

The key step in creating TV graphics is *preproduction,* or *prepro*—in other words, putting together a visual in advance of the newscast. Depending on their purpose and level of complexity, news graphics can take a few minutes to prepare or considerably longer. A graphic illustration that is on screen for only a few seconds requires less time to create than an explainer graphic that is used to clarify a detailed sequence of events. Graphics that consist of a freeze-frame with a caption require less time than something the artist creates from scratch. Still graphics require less time than animated graphics.

TV news operations commonly recycle graphics, particularly those that are not animated. Getting these ready for a newscast involves little more than calling up the images from a computerized database known as the still-storer. Anywhere from two-thirds to three-quarters of the graphics in a typical local newscast are repeats, but archival graphics might be altered or refreshed before they air again. Certain subject matter lends itself particularly well to archival graphics—stories about Christmas or other holidays, for example, in which the basic visual vocabulary does not change from year to year.

Where do designers find the visual building blocks for news graphics? A wide variety of source material is available to newsroom artists: video, still photos, drawings, maps, logos, icons, backgrounds, and so forth. Designers have access to footage shot by the station's photographers, as well as photos and video from subscription services like the Associated Press and the broadcast networks. For a business story about a well-known corporation, a designer might go to that company's website and download a logo.

Because many images are copyrighted and therefore off-limits, designers look for visual material that exists in the public domain. Photographs of celebrities like Marilyn Monroe and Elvis Presley, to name two, often require permission from the copyright holder before they can be used. A better source for newsroom artists would be images from public collections like the Library of Congress or the National Archives, which are easily accessible online.

After an artist tracks down the basic visual elements that will be incorporated into a news graphic, the process of creating the finished product begins. Depending on the situation, this might involve cropping an image, resizing, repositioning, enhancing the color, cleaning up the background, or whatever additional touch-up procedures are required to make the graphic as crisp, legible, and appropriate to the subject matter as possible. In most cases, the designer also adds captions, titles, labels, or other text that helps to explain an illustration's meaning.

USES OF TV NEWS GRAPHICS

TV news graphics can serve a variety of purposes in the newscast, some functional and some decorative. Let's look at the main types of graphics and how they are used.

Show-and-Tell Graphics

By show-and-tell we mean graphics with the main function of illustrating rather than delivering factual material. The over-the-shoulder boxes that appear on screen while an anchorperson is introducing a story are a prime example of show-and-tell graphics because their purpose is limited. They exist to help set up a story, but not really to explain or develop it.

Explainer Graphics

By contrast, explainer graphics have a more complicated objective. Their purpose is to serve as a storytelling element that helps the viewer understand information that might otherwise be difficult to follow. As such, explainer graphics tend to surface within stories, rather than in story introductions. They are also more likely to involve motion.

Let's consider a couple of examples. First, we have a story about a new underpass that has just opened on a downtown street. Due to an engineering error, it turns out the underpass was built too low to accommodate large trucks. An explainer graphic, either animated or still, can visually represent the problem by comparing the height of the underpass with the height of big semi trailers.

Here's a different example: Let's say a U.S. senator from your state steps down from office. As stipulated by law, the governor then appoints a replacement—in this case, himself—to fill the vacant seat, leaving the governorship open. The lieutenant governor steps in as governor, leaving that slot open until a special election can be held. These maneuvers could be somewhat difficult to explain in words, but an animated flowchart with images of the individuals easily illustrates how the shuffle will play out.

Explainer graphics can be employed in a variety of situations. They can be statistical or nonstatistical, they can deal with chronology or geography, and they can reenact events for which no video footage exists. As always, the journalistic goal of accuracy must apply.

Text Graphics

Some graphics exist primarily as a means of delivering textual information. For instance, a story about a 911 emergency call could include a text graphic with the caller's words transcribed onto the screen. In this example, the graphic serves two purposes: helping viewers follow the conversation and compensating for the lack of video footage. Text graphics can be used in a number of other nonvisual situations: quoting from court documents, press releases, e-mails, websites, newspaper stories, and other print sources.

Maps

Maps can be considered the first informational graphics, predating still photography and moving imagery in the mass media. In recent years maps have become a favorite visual device of news producers. Satellite technology has enabled newscasts to feature detailed and accurate maps of just about any spot on earth. Maps are frequently used in story introductions as a way of orienting the viewer to the material. They can also be helpful as explainer graphics in stories involving multiple locations.

Standard Graphics

These are generic graphics created for use on a repeat basis. They often take the form of brief animations with text, such as a "Breaking News" logo. They might be used to introduce regular segments like weather and sports. The animated introductions that begin newscasts are another example of standard graphics.

TO MOVE OR NOT TO MOVE?

Whatever their purpose, all television news graphics fall into two basic categories: *still graphics,* also called *nonmotion graphics,* and *motion graphics,* sometimes referred to as *animated graphics.* Newscasts mix both types of graphics to keep the visual side of the presentation from becoming too predictable.

Still Graphics

Still graphics typically involve a single image that summarizes the story at hand. Most of the time these are accompanied by a short caption or title. Nonanimated graphics can be constructed around video freeze-frames, still photographs, maps, logos, original artwork, typography, or just about any combination of these elements. The challenge is to keep the image simple enough to be quickly comprehended by even casual viewers of the newscast.

Because many still graphics are generic in nature, they are often archived for repeat use. This comes in handy when a story develops over several days, or with routine subject matter such as court appearances, legislative news, police reports, and the like. Still graphics are a major visual component of newscast production, most commonly during story intros, but also as illustrations within stories.

Motion Graphics

Motion, or animated, graphics take advantage of computer technology to put movement into TV news visuals. Motion graphics can be created with video footage and animation, or by adding motion to still images through such techniques as zooming, panning, dissolving, wiping, scrolling, and so on. As with still graphics, animated graphics involve a combination of elements that have been chosen and put together by the artist.

Motion graphics can appear during story introductions or as internal visuals within a story. When used in story introductions, animated graphics tend to be short and more concerned with illustration than explanation. Sometimes motion graphics are used to introduce regular segments or to label breaking news or teases. By comparison, internal motion graphics are more content oriented.

Some television news stories are better suited than others to animated graphics. For instance, a report about a tornado that sweeps through an area and touches down in several spots would be appropriate for graphic animation. So would news about a series of bomb attacks that unfold over one morning in a war zone. Both of these examples involve more than a single event in more than one place, making a motion graphic extremely useful for someone trying to make sense of the chronology and geography. Whatever the particulars, animated graphics must have a clear objective.

In some cases moving visuals are preferable to still graphics for aesthetic reasons. Artist Gary Stout cited the example of a story about spring flooding in New England. Photographers had shot dramatic footage of floodwaters rushing over a dam, but when Stout looked at the video as a freeze-frame, he realized it would work better as a motion graphic with the footage rolling. "All that rushing water looked great as moving video," Stout said, "but not so great as a frozen image."

In the competitive world of TV news, producers can find themselves under pressure to include animated graphics as a means of spicing up the newscast. However, motion graphics need a justification. Motion for the sake of motion might end up calling attention to itself. Furthermore, if all the graphics in a newscast are animated, they run the risk of becoming predictable. The most interesting approach is a mix of moving and nonmoving graphics.

ON-SCREEN PLACEMENT OF TV NEWS GRAPHICS

All television news graphics exist within a frame: either the frame of the TV screen itself or a separate frame within the TV screen. Designers of TV news graphics are keenly aware of the *aspect ratio* of the screen, a term that refers to its shape. Standard analog television has an aspect ratio of 3 by 4, meaning the screen occupies four horizontal lengths by three vertical lengths. High-definition television has a different aspect ratio: 9 by 16, which is closer to the dimensions of a movie screen. In creating visuals for television, aspect ratio is a fundamental compositional factor. For example, because TV is a horizontal medium, it can be difficult for graphics to show vertical objects such as a person standing up or the full expanse of a skyscraper.

Graphic images for television news appear on screen in several physical configurations. The following are a few of the standard placements.

Over-the-Shoulder Graphics

The most traditional of TV news graphics, these are boxes that appear over the shoulder of the anchorperson as a story is being read during a newscast. If the anchor is delivering news about a management shake-up at the police department, the graphic box might show a police badge with a short caption beneath: "Police Shake-Up," "Personnel Changes," or whatever fits the circumstances. These over-the-shoulder graphics are still images, and most stations have built up an archive of them that can be easily altered with updated text.

Over-the-shoulder graphics are illustrations rather than detailed designs, and as such qualify as show-and-tell graphics rather than explainers. Because they might be up on the screen for only a few seconds, the objective is a graphic that is instantly comprehensible to the viewing audience. Captions beneath these graphics need to be brief and simple. Typography needs to be legible.

Monitor Boxes

These are another type of show-and-tell graphics, designed to appear in a monitor on the news set. The shape of the monitor—either a standard or wide screen—determines the design. Graphics within a monitor might tend to look muddy, so bold and crisp images tend to work best. Monitor boxes often lack captions or other writing because text cannot be easily read in this situation.

Partial-Screen Graphics

Graphics displayed alongside anchorpersons need not be confined to a box. Some graphics can take up a portion of the screen, with the anchor occupying the rest of the space. Partial-screen graphics can serve as a background against which to scroll bullet points,

Graphics can be used in a range of situations. One common placement is in an over-the-shoulder graphic accompanying a story delivered by an anchorperson.

brief headlines, or other information like phone numbers, web addresses, and so forth. They can also serve as pure illustration.

Full-Screen Graphics

These graphics occupy the entire screen, either as backdrops for the anchorperson or as informational elements within stories. Full-screen graphics are often used to convey material that is not inherently visual. A story about rising gasoline prices, for instance, might include a full-screen graphic that depicts the increasing costs consumers have paid at the pump over the past few years. Full-screen graphics are also common within stories that call for the display of text.

AESTHETIC CONSIDERATIONS IN TV NEWS GRAPHICS

TV news graphics represent a marriage of content and design, and as such they are subject to a number of aesthetic considerations.

Size

A primary aesthetic consideration is the graphic's size. Over-the-shoulder or monitor graphics occupy a relatively modest portion of the television screen. This means the images they present must be bold, direct, and easy to decipher. Full-screen graphics offer more room for the designer to play with, and can therefore be more visually sophisticated. Because much of the audience watches television on a small screen, however, even full-screen graphics should not be overloaded with detail.

Simplicity

Every design should have a center of visual impact, which is to say one element that stands out from the others. Because still news graphics typically limit themselves to a single theme, the center of visual impact is usually fairly obvious.

Effective over-the-shoulder and monitor graphics do not attempt to tell a story in all its complexity. Instead they serve as a kind of visual shorthand for the material, providing viewers with a quick and easy reference point. These kinds of TV news graphics call for images that summarize the content and concentrate on a single idea.

News graphics should be set against an uncluttered background, which is why photographs and original designs often work better than video freeze-frames for over-the-shoulders and monitor boxes. Because TV graphics remain on the screen for only a few seconds, a simple image is most likely to register with viewers. Too much visual information can pose an obstacle to understanding.

At the same time, even a simple graphic can supply viewers with context. Imagine a story about Prince Harry of Britain in which a head-and-shoulders shot of Harry is the primary visual element of the graphic. If Harry's face is set against the backdrop of a British flag, the graphic helps to jog the audience's memory about who the prince is.

Explainer graphics, especially those that occupy the full screen, give designers an opportunity to create more complicated visual messages than over-the-shoulders and monitor boxes. Nonetheless, simplicity remains a key objective. Even full-screen explainer graphics do not afford viewers much time to assimilate the information.

Organization

An important responsibility of newsroom artists is to create graphics that organize information effectively. News graphics—particularly full-screen explainers—should be designed with the goal of leading a viewer's eye from one element to the next. Well-constructed graphics follow a sequence that mimics the natural order in which people assimilate information. In Western tradition this means working one's way from top to bottom and from left to right.

Still graphics in over-the-shoulder boxes or monitors on the news set do not occupy enough screen space to necessitate much visual sequencing. More complicated graphics, such as full-screen graphics that involve motion or in which text is scrolled onto the screen, require the artist to consciously build a sense of rhythm into the design. A wide range of organizational tools is available to facilitate this rhythm, including:

- Lines
- Boxes
- Columns
- Bullet points
- Arrows
- Icons
- Colored text
- Colored backgrounds
- Scrolling

These design tools can be still or animated, depending on the situation. In each case the objective is to employ the devices not as adornments, but as guideposts that help the audience along.

Color

Certain colors pose technical difficulties for designers of TV graphics. Orange might read better on camera than red, for instance, because red has a tendency to look black. Greens can be similarly tricky to work with. High-contrast colors tend to work best, although TV news graphics with too much splashy color could end up evoking the world of game shows and infomercials rather than journalism.

Screen Direction

News graphics must take screen direction into account. For example, if the graphic is an over-the-shoulder image of a gun, it is important to point the barrel of the weapon away from the anchor's head. Full-screen graphics, obviously, do not pose this problem.

Balance

Visual balance refers to the placement of elements within the frame of a design. A design is considered balanced if it equalizes the weight between two imaginary axes: the x (horizontal) and the y (vertical). A single visual element set midway within the frame along both axes results in a perfectly symmetrical design. Symmetry imbues a graphic with stability and formality, but it can also be dull, so designers sometimes deliberately opt for a less rigid arrangement. Whether symmetrical, or slightly off-axis, TV news graphics look better when they achieve a modicum of visual balance.

Contrast

Contrast refers to differences within an image in color, size, space, typography, and texture. In keeping with the mission of journalism as a serious enterprise, most news designers do not overdo contrast in their graphics. Nonetheless, it can be appropriate for graphics to make use of contrasting color schemes, type sizes, backgrounds, and so forth. Contrast might also mean keeping the design from becoming too cluttered with visuals and text.

Unity

The artistic principle of unity carries several meanings with regard to TV news graphics. Unity can refer to the idea that all the graphics aired on a particular television station, or within a particular newscast, will be visually consistent. It can refer to consistency within a design, so that contrasting elements like colors and typefaces do not clash. Unity can also describe the connection between a design and its subject matter.

A bright color background and a festive font, for example, would hardly be suitable for a text graphic listing the names of deceased soldiers. On the other hand, a Valentine's Day story about a mass wedding might feature flowery graphics that replicate the cover of a romance novel. The over-the-shoulder graphic for a story about real estate might mimic the look of a Monopoly board. It is up to the designer to find an appropriate visual expression of the content.

CHALLENGES OF CREATING TV NEWS GRAPHICS

Designers of TV news graphics face a range of challenges as they go about their work. Some of the challenges are journalistic in nature and some are aesthetic. The following section details a few potential problem areas to keep in mind.

Visual Clutter

Producers are under constant pressure to make their newscasts more visually stimulating, which can encourage an overemphasis on graphic elements. News graphics must have a readily understood reason for being. Color, sound, and motion are not ends unto themselves. Too often graphics in TV newscasts exist simply as decoration. Decoration is not necessarily a bad thing, except when it interferes with the larger journalistic mission of keeping the audience informed. As WBAL-TV's Tim Tunison puts it, "When the graphics become the story, you've got a problem."

Visual Redundancy

Designers of TV news graphics must take care not to be visually redundant. For a story about a school bus accident, the graphic might logically include a shot of the wrecked school bus. Therefore it would be unnecessary for the caption to also contain the words "school bus." If the central element of a news graphic is a logo that includes a company name, the caption should not repeat the name. TV news graphics should add a layer of new information, rather than being redundant with information that is already evident. The purpose of graphics is to clarify and expand, not duplicate.

Visual Clichés

Certain TV news graphics have been so overused they now fall into the category of visual clichés. Examples include the U.S. Capitol dome for stories out of Washington, George Washington's face on the dollar bill for financial news, and yellow police tape for a crime story. Sometimes, of course, there might be no escaping the cliché. Clichés can be effective because they register so readily with the audience. Clever designers and producers should nonetheless strive to find original ways of visualizing familiar stories, or at least original variations on the old standbys.

Working With Statistics

Because numbers can be difficult to visualize through words or video, TV newscasts routinely rely on graphics to explain statistical information. Numbers-based graphics demand creativity on the part of news designers. The artist should think of quantitative data along visual lines: a pile of money, a bag of groceries, or a yardstick showing snowfall amounts. In illustrating statistics, designers might find occasion to incorporate pictographs, which are visual representations of the thing being discussed. A pictographic chart showing the relative height of the world's tallest skyscrapers would include images of the actual buildings. Less literally, a chart that tracked the declining rates of smoking in the adult population might use cigarettes of varying lengths to pictographically display the change in numbers.

Sensitive Subject Matter

Like all journalists, news designers must approach delicate subject matter with care. Stories about death, for instance, call for graphics that show restraint and respect for the deceased, especially if no photographs are available. In the case of a soldier killed in a military operation, if you lack a photo it might work best to show empty boots against a flag background.

Artist Gary Stout cites a few other story topics that can be tricky to visualize. Abortion graphics, he says, are notoriously difficult to create, and he makes it a point to avoid images of babies and pregnant women in designing graphics on that subject. Rape is another sensitive topic that is best illustrated with abstract visuals. For stories about child abuse, Stout has created graphics that show a toddler's shoes but no actual child.

For controversial subject matter, Stout suggests illustrating with symbolic objects rather than human beings. Stout applied this principle during Boston's Catholic priest sex abuse scandal by designing graphics that showed things like a close-up of a clerical collar or generic church architecture with ecclesiastical typography. If graphics for controversial stories do include people, Stout recommends obscuring individual faces or isolating features so as not to reveal identity.

Attribution

To the extent possible, television news graphics should attribute information to the appropriate sources, just as print reporters use attribution to clarify the source of information in written news stories. Attribution is not necessary for simple, over-the-shoulder graphics or other show-and-tell visuals. However, for explainer graphics, particularly in controversial stories, it is a good idea to include a few words identifying the source of the information.

USING TYPOGRAPHY IN TV NEWS GRAPHICS

More often than not, TV news graphics are accompanied by text. In some cases the text is a matter of one or two short words that appear as titles or captions. In other instances the entire graphic is text based, as in the case of lengthy quotations, or bullet points that scroll onto the screen as an anchorperson narrates.

In creating text-based graphics, designers use typography as a subtle but important tool. Most TV stations stick to a standard set of typefaces for their news programs, a practice that promotes visual unity from one newscast to the next. These standard fonts tend to be bold and simple, easy to read, unadorned, and neutral. Plain type works better than italics. Capital letters work better than a combination of upper and lowercase letters.

The key consideration is legibility. Typefaces that lend themselves well to the printed page might not work as effectively on a TV screen, where the text competes with other visual material. Television news designers prefer sans serif typefaces, those without extra flourishes on the letters and numerals. On the printed page serifs can help distinguish one character from another, but on TV they can detract from legibility.

Full-screen graphics are particularly effective when conveying statistical information or material that is otherwise difficult to visualize.

Most typefaces used on television news are plain, even a little drab. Special occasions, however, might call for more creative use of typography. Certain typefaces suggest different time periods, for example. Think of the psychedelic opening credits in the Austin Powers movies, and how strongly that style of lettering evokes the 1960s, or the square, blocky, heavily serifed type on the old "Wanted: Dead or Alive" posters, which conjures images of the Old West. Such examples might not find their way into a television newscast, but they illustrate the difference typography can make in visual presentation.

Designers of TV news graphics do make frequent use of typefaces that visually reinforce particular subject matter. Typefaces like Courier or American Typewriter are appropriate for official documents. Stencil type works well with military stories. Gothic type suggests religion, or, in a different sense, heavy metal music. Florid, cursive script in which the letters are linked suggests romance; think of the typography you would find on a typical wedding invitation. Although news graphics should not be too extreme in their use of typography, creative designers will find numerous occasions in which it is appropriate to go beyond the standard lettering.

WRITING TITLES AND CAPTIONS FOR TV NEWS GRAPHICS

In July 2006 a frightening incident on a Boston highway generated widespread coverage on local New England newscasts. The episode offers a window into the challenges producers face in coming up with story titles. The incident involved a three-ton section of concrete ceiling paneling that fell onto a car as it traveled through a downtown tunnel, killing a woman and injuring her husband. In graphics that accompanied the news reports, local television stations offered several variations of a title for the story, including "Tunnel Collapse," "Tunnel Tragedy," and "Killer Collapse."

Each of the three choices presents its pluses and minuses. Of the three, "Tunnel Collapse" is the most straightforward and neutral, using language that does not cue the viewers' emotions. Yet the wording does not fully describe the scope of the problem. Yes, the tunnel collapsed, but the title gives no hint as to the fatal consequences of the event. "Tunnel Tragedy" gets closer to emphasizing the story's human dimension, but in doing so the title is telling the audience how it is supposed to feel. Furthermore, by avoiding the word collapse, "Tunnel Tragedy" gives viewers only a vague idea of what actually happened. "Killer Collapse" references the fatality, and also describes what happened. Like "Tunnel Tragedy," its two words alliterate. However, of the three titles, this one is the most sensational. To some viewers, "Killer Collapse" might come across as disrespectful of the human beings at the center of the accident.

So what's the solution? "Tunnel Death" accurately summarizes the essence of the story, without crossing the line into exploitation. It might not be as flashy as some of the other choices, but it suits the mood of the situation without compromising journalistic objectivity. "Tunnel Death" would also lend itself well to accompanying visuals.

This example shows the level of consideration that goes into creating an appropriate title for a show-and-tell news graphic. Although the writing of titles and captions might seem like an easy task, it can be more difficult than it looks. The following are some rules to consider.

Brevity

Each station will have its own policy on a maximum title length, but a good rule of thumb is to limit your title or caption to 16 characters, including spaces and punctuation. This is why one- or two-word caption lines are so frequently used: because they are short.

Accuracy

The title needs to reflect the facts of the situation. In such a brief amount of space, this is not always possible, at least not with any degree of thoroughness. The writer must do the best he or she can to accurately summarize the story in a way that makes sense to someone watching the newscast on television.

Tone

The wording must match the tone and mood of the story. A story involving death and injury is not the place to show off one's gift for clever wordplay. Here's a rule of thumb: The more somber the story, the less flashy the word choice should be. Feature stories, on the other hand, give writers an opportunity to have fun with titles and captions.

Referencing

Titles and captions must work in relation to the accompanying visuals. If the words do not make sense with the images, the viewer might end up confused. By the same token, words and pictures should not be redundant with each other. Consider as an example a story about an antiwar protest. If the graphic shows a sign emblazoned with the phrase "Stop the War," it would not make much sense to use a caption or title that repeated that same wording. The graphic and the text should offer complementary layers of information.

STEP BY STEP: CREATING GRAPHICS FOR TV NEWS STORIES

Keeping the preceding points in mind, let's walk through the process of creating of television news graphics. We will concentrate on two types of visuals: over-the-shoulder still graphics and animated graphics that function as full-screen explainers.

Over-the-Shoulder Still Graphics With Captions

For each story on the following menu, we will create an over-the-shoulder still graphic box that includes a visual and a one-line caption. Because of space limitations, the caption line cannot exceed 16 characters, including punctuation and blank spaces.

For the first story, because the available visual elements are limited, let's design a graphic that uses original artwork.

Robber in Disguise. Police shoot and wound an alleged armed robber disguised in a nun's habit as he runs out of a downtown bank that had just been held up. Nobody else was harmed, and the would-be robber's injuries are minor.

Available Visual Elements. The video for this story is limited to exteriors of the bank after the holdup, showing the front entrance blocked off with yellow police tape. There are no visuals of the suspect, either in or out of his disguise.

Analysis. With no video or stills of the suspect, we must rely on a computer-generated image. Because of the unique nature of the robbery, and the lack of serious injuries, it is possible—in fact, preferable—to go with a less serious graphic. A stylized figure in a nun's outfit holding a gun would be the obvious choice.

Captions. The offbeat nature of this story cries out for a clever caption. Among the possibilities: "Holy Holdup" (11 characters), "Robed Robber" (12 characters), or "Ungodly Arrest" (14 characters). Because religion can be a sensitive issue, we must take care not to cross the line into sacrilege, but all three of these possibilities remain safely within bounds.

For the next story, instead of original artwork, we will build a graphic using the available visual elements.

Rescue Dog. A golden retriever named Gridley pulls a baby in a car seat from the fast-moving Blue River. The baby's mother had accidentally driven the family Blazer off a bridge into the water. Just at that moment, the dog had been cavorting on shore. Mother, baby, and dog all are fine.

Available Visual Elements

- Video of the dog after the rescue including full-body shots and close-ups of the animal's face
- Professionally shot still portrait of the baby
- Still snapshot of the mother holding her baby
- Video that shows the vehicle after it plunged into the river
- Video of the vehicle being pulled from the river by a towline

Analysis. There are two key elements to this story: the dog and the baby. Unfortunately, we lack a shot that includes them both. We could go with the dog alone, specifically the close-up of the dog's face in a freeze-frame. We could go with the shot of the baby. The problem with using the baby is that the picture is a professional studio portrait that would look pretty generic in a graphics box. The shot of the mother and child together is less formal, but it doesn't really get at what is unique about the story. It might be possible to use a freeze either of the vehicle in the river or the vehicle being pulled from the river, although neither of these adequately summarizes the facts at hand. The best option is either a close-up of the dog, who in the final analysis qualifies as the lead character in this little drama, or a composite of the dog and the baby.

Captions. Focusing the visual on the dog also helps with captioning. This is a story with a happy ending, so it's fine to have a little fun with the title. "Golden Hero" works pretty well, because it gives a hint of what happened. "Golden Gridley" alliterates nicely, but the audience probably would not get the "Gridley" reference until they heard the whole account. The best choice: "Golden Retrieval," which succeeds both as a pun and in summarizing the story.

Animated Explainer Graphics With Text

For the last story in this section, we will design an animated explainer graphic that takes up the full screen. Available visual elements are listed, but essentially we will need to create original visuals. We will also add text, as appropriate.

High-Speed Chase. At 3 a.m. police pursue a stolen delivery truck on a 20-minute chase through the streets of Lakedale's South Bank neighborhood. Along the way the truck crashes into a parked car on South Main Street, hits a fire hydrant at the corner of Lincoln Boulevard and 79th Street, knocks down a row of mailboxes along Hamburg Lane, and finally comes to a stop after crashing into a tree in Murdock Park. The driver runs into the woods and briefly escapes before being apprehended and arrested.

Available Visual Elements

- Video footage of the delivery truck after it crashed into a tree
- Video footage of police cars racing down the street
- Mug shot of the suspect after his arrest

Analysis. The objective of this explainer graphic is to visually break down the sequence of events. Because the story has a strong geographical component, it makes sense to use a map of South Bank as the graphic's key full-screen element. We can animate the map to show the progress of the police chase, pausing briefly at each of the steps along the way—the parked car, the fire hydrant, the mailboxes, and the crash into the tree. The route that the truck traveled gives us a path for our animation to follow.

Text. A story title like "Overnight Chase" or "Police Pursuit" should be present for the full duration of the graphic. As each location is highlighted, the coordinates for that location should appear on the screen. By the end of the animated graphic, these four location captions and the story title will constitute the on-screen text.

ON-SCREEN SUPERS IN TV NEWSCASTS

Supers, sometimes referred to as *lower thirds* because of their placement on the screen, are a standard feature of television news stories. (Some newsrooms also refer to supers as *keys.*) Because newscasts include so many interviewees and changes of location, supers are used to help viewers keep track of who and what they are seeing.

TV news producers use two main types of supers: *identifying supers,* which include the name of the person on screen along with a brief description of his or her relevance to the story, and *locator supers,* which pinpoint location. Identifying supers typically occupy two lines, one for the name and a second for the descriptor. Most locator supers run for only a single line.

Identifying supers are used over interview sound bites, with the exception of man-on-the-street bites in which the identity of the speaker is not vital. For all other interviews, it is standard to run a super that lists the person's name on the top line, and a few words of description on the second line. This description could be a title, such as "PTA Chairperson"; the name of the interviewee's employer, such as "Jones Corporation"; or sometimes just a brief bit of biographical information pertinent to the story. In the case

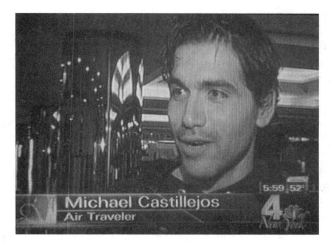

Michael Castillejos
Air Traveler

Identifying supers are usually found in the lower third of the frame, and identify the person on screen as well as his relevance to the story.

of a neighborhood dispute over a plan to widen a residential street, the descriptor line might say something like "Project Supporter" or "Project Opponent."

Whatever the choice, the second-line descriptor needs to be short (20 characters is a typical maximum) and easily comprehensible to the general audience. Abbreviations, because they can be confusing, might not always work. Let's say an interviewee has the official title of Assistant Director of Programming for the Lakedale University School of Education. Obviously, that title is too long to fit into the allotted space. However, an abbreviated version might be difficult to understand: Asst. Prog. Dir, LUSOD is both confusing and, at 21 characters, one character over the limit. In this case it might be better to go with something more generic: School of Education (19 characters), LU School of Ed (15 characters), Lakedale U (10 characters), or Lakedale Univ. (14 characters).

In coming up with second-line descriptors, writers should avoid clichés. Some TV news operations have been known to routinely identify accident survivors with the descriptor "Lucky to be Alive." This is both cheesy and subjective. Better to go with a straightforward description: "Accident Survivor."

Unlike identifying supers, locator supers are easy to write, because they their only purpose is to label where a story takes place. Locators can be particularly helpful when the story jumps around to different locations. If there has been flooding in your area, for example, a number of different localities are likely to be affected, and in a "roundup" package that gives an overview of the situation, the locator supers help the viewer keep track of what's happening where.

One final word of warning about using supers in TV newscasts: Spelling errors are not acceptable. If viewers spot mistakes in how a word is spelled, the credibility of the entire product gets called into question. Any text that goes up on the screen must be checked and double-checked ahead of time, whether it's being used in a graphic, a title, or a lower third. Much of this text involves names and other proper nouns, so computer spell-check programs cannot be trusted as the final arbiters of how something is spelled. When in doubt, look it up or make a phone call.

STEP BY STEP: WRITING
ON-SCREEN SUPERS

For each of the individuals named in italics (eight people in all), let us come up with a two-line descriptive super to use with a sound bite. The top line is the person's name. The second line should be a brief (20-character maximum) description that explains who the person is.

ENGLISH TEACHER

Jerome Moler, an English teacher at Lakedale Central High School, angrily denounces parents at a packed school board meeting. A group of parents led by *Daisy Arthur* has been seeking to get Moler dismissed because of his 50 percent failure rate. Arthur's 15-year-old daughter, *Wendy Arthur*, was among the students who failed Moler's sophomore English class.

Analysis

The most obvious second-line caption for Jerome Moler is "English Teacher." This is an accurate, neutral description of who he is, and at 15 characters it fits within the allotted space. On the negative side, "English Teacher" does not supply a context for why Moler is at the center of controversy. Given the complicated nature of the story, however, it might not be possible to incorporate additional details into the super.

Daisy Arthur presents a more difficult captioning problem. Describing her as "Parent" would be accurate, but not very informative. "Angry Parent" or "Upset Parent" might work, although each of these makes a judgment about Daisy that would have to be backed up by the facts of the story. "Wants Teacher Fired" is another option. Although it is longer (19 characters), it provides more insight into Daisy's role.

For Wendy Arthur, the descriptor "High School Student" (19 characters) is probably the safest way to go, even though that description says little about Wendy's involvement in the story. "Failed English Class," at 20 characters, just fits into the space, and in one sense it is accurate. However, it could also cause confusion: Wendy herself is not a failed English class, as the text seems to imply. If the audience can't read the super and immediately understand what is going on, it's better to stick with the version that is bland and accurate.

PARNASSUS PROTEST

A neighborhood group called HUSH (Help Us Save History) stages a sit-in protest outside the offices of The Parnassus Group (TPG), a local real estate development company. Parnassus is planning to raze the 125-year-old Empire Hotel in Lakedale's Greenside neighborhood to build an upscale shopping mall. The protestors are led by HUSH president *Arnie Melcher*. The public relations spokesperson for Parnassus is *Mary Ann Duval*.

Analysis

The first thought might be to identify Arnie Melcher as "Leader of HUSH," but the problem there is that most people in the audience won't have any idea what HUSH is. At 20 characters, it would be possible to spell out the full name of the group— "Help Us Save History"—beneath Arnie's name, but again, a viewer reading that caption might be more confused than enlightened. In this case it is better to go with a more generic description of Arnie such as "Community Activist" (18 characters) or "Preservationist" (15 characters). Another possibility might be "Mall Opponent" (13 characters).

As with the preceding example, the abbreviated name of the company is not well enough known to justify inclusion in the caption, so "TPG Spokesperson" won't work for Mary Ann Duval. "Parnassus Group Spokesperson" would be better, but it exceeds the space limitations. In this case, because Ms. Duval is appearing on camera in her capacity as a company representative, it is acceptable to limit the caption to "Parnassus Group" (15 characters). Alternately, if Arnie Melcher is identified as "Mall Opponent," Mary Ann Duval could be captioned as "Mall Supporter."

CHECKLIST OF KEY POINTS

- Graphics are an important element of television journalism, adding nuance and detail to all kinds of stories. As the motto says, "Show, don't tell."

- News graphics are a collaborative effort between designers and journalists. Although some graphics are created fresh each day, most are recycled from previous newscasts. Graphic designers maintain extensive archives of visuals they can use and reuse.

- Different types of graphics are used in different situations. Show-and-tell graphics are simple, easily understood illustrations. Explainer graphics help viewers make visual sense of complicated information. Text graphics are word-based, used to display quotations on the screen. Maps are another widely used form of television news graphics.

- TV news graphics can be divided into two broad categories: still and motion. Still graphics work particularly well as show-and-tell illustrations. Motion, or animated, graphics generally deliver more substantive information.

- Graphics run in various on-screen configurations. Over-the-shoulder graphics appear next to the anchorperson, usually as simple illustrations. Other uncomplicated graphics are displayed within monitor boxes on the news set. Partial-screen graphics take up a portion of the screen, whereas full-screen graphics occupy the entire frame.

- A number of aesthetic considerations must be taken into account when designing TV news graphics. These include size of the graphic, simplicity of the image, organization of the visual elements, color, screen direction, balance, contrast, and unity.

- TV news graphics can be challenging to create. Designers must avoid clutter, clichés, and visual redundancy.

- Graphics can be helpful in conveying quantitative information, but they must do so in a way that makes sense to the audience. Try to think of numerical data along visual lines, such as a bar graph in which the bars are represented by stacks of coins.

- Graphics that deal with sensitive subject matter must be approached with care. When the topic is controversial, visuals should not be cheesy or inflammatory. Generic or abstract imagery might work better than pictures of specific individuals.

- To the extent possible, designers should attribute information in graphics to the appropriate sources.

- The majority of TV news graphics include text as well as visuals. Captions and titles that accompany graphics should be brief, accurate, and appropriate to the topic and mood of the story.

- In addition to graphics, TV news producers make extensive use of supers, the descriptive captions that run at the bottom of the screen during stories. Supers fall into two main categories: identifying supers, which describe the individuals who are speaking on screen, and locator supers, which clarify locations.

- Identifying supers typically consist of two lines: the person's name on the top line, and a brief description of the individual on the bottom line. The description must be short—about 20 characters in length, including blank spaces. These second-line descriptions need to be accurate, and they should avoid clichés.

ASSIGNMENTS/ANALYSIS

Assignment: Creating Over-the-Shoulder Still Graphics

For each story on the following menu, create an over-the-shoulder still graphic box that includes visuals and a one-line caption. Because of space limitations, the caption line cannot exceed 16 characters, including punctuation and blank spaces. In some cases you will be able to use visuals from the existing video footage and still photos. In others you will need to come up with original artwork.

Drowning

A 36-year-old man drowns in a waterskiing accident around 2 p.m. at Lake Kahola, a recreational lake in a county park outside of town. Police have identified the victim as Darwin Lamar, the founder and president of the city's largest real estate development company. The victim's father, also from Lakedale, is a former U.S. senator.

Available visual elements

- Video (from a distance) of police retrieving a body from the water

- Still photo of Darwin Lamar

- Still photo of Darwin Lamar with his father, Sen. Lamar

- Exterior of Lamar Real Estate, the corporate headquarters of Darwin Lamar's company

Gas Line

A gas line explosion closes a two-block stretch of street in an industrial park on Lakedale's south side. The street is not a major route. No injuries or fatalities.

Available visual elements

- The only usable visual is a "Road Closed" sign. Otherwise you will need to create something original for the graphic.

Lightning

The Lakedale Bible Baptist church catches fire after its steeple is struck by lightning. The fire is quickly contained, and damage is confined to the roof.

Available visual elements:

- Video of the aftermath of the fire. Because of trees in the background, the shot of the steeple does not lend itself very well to a freeze-frame.

Prom Ban

The principal of Lakedale Heights High School (LHHS) in suburban Lakedale bans nonstudents from attending the LHHS prom. LHHS students will be required attend with other LHHS students. Students quickly organize a protest at the end of the school day.

Available visual elements:

- Exterior of Lakedale Heights High School

- Home video from last year's prom (this footage is grainy and not very well-lit)

- Shots of LHHS students demonstrating in front of the school building, some with signs that say "It's my prom!"

Mayoral Candidate

A popular candidate for mayor, radio talk-show host Dude Winters, withdraws from the race after a local newspaper reports that Winters was convicted of the armed robbery of an out-of-state liquor store in 1990.

Available visual elements:

- Publicity still of Dude Winters

- Mug shot of Dude Winters from his 1990 arrest

- Shot of "Dude Winters for Mayor" yard sign

Grand Opening

Today marks the grand opening of the Century Center, a large office complex near downtown Lakedale. The 100-year-old landmark, built originally as a pharmaceutical factory, has been renovated as a center for biotechnology, with 15 companies and 350 employees occupying what had been an empty shell.

Available visual elements:

- Exterior of the building (wide shot)

- Exterior of the entrance to the building, including the name of the complex

- Historical photo of the building when it was a pharmaceutical factory

Puppet Fire

The Wee Pals Puppet Playhouse burns to the ground in an overnight fire. No injuries, but dozens of puppets were destroyed. Arson is suspected.

Available visual elements:

- The only available visual is file footage from a puppet show at the theater taken some years earlier, but the shots do not isolate any individual puppets.

Tattoo Convention

An international convention of tattoo artists kicks off at the Union Hotel in downtown Lakedale. The convention began with a "Body Art Fashion Show" in which models displayed their tattoos for an enthusiastic audience. The conventioneers are in town for three days.

Available visual elements:

- Numerous shots of the models at the "Body Art Fashion Show," including people with full-body tattoos
- Tight shot of the top of a man's bald head, displaying an American flag tattoo
- Numerous other tight shots of specific tattoos
- Shots of the audience at the fashion show as they enjoy the show
- Exterior of the convention hotel, with a sign that says "Welcome Tattoo Lovers"

Assignment: Creating Animated Explainer Graphics

For each of the next two stories, create an animated explainer graphic that takes up the full screen. The graphics should be accompanied by the appropriate text. Bear in mind, however, that any text you write must be brief.

Housing Prices

A report released today by the Lakedale Association of Realtors shows a sharp increase in housing costs for Lakedale residents. The report compares prices for the current year with prices from three years ago, and also five years ago. The statistics are divided into three categories: sales of single homes, sales of condominium units, and monthly rentals.

Available visual elements:

- Because the information comes from a written report, no video footage has been shot specifically for this story. However, you can assume that there are plenty of archival images of different kinds of housing to work with.

Trolley Line

The Lakedale Transit Authority (LTA) releases a preliminary proposal for a trolley line that will run from Downtown to the suburb of Lakedale Heights. The route will begin at Central Station Downtown (the major hub for the city bus lines) and end seven miles away at the Lakedale Heights Mall, with a total of 15 stops along the way.

Available visual elements:

- Computer-generated renderings of the trolley
- Logo of the LTA
- Shot of Central Station
- Shot of the Lakedale Heights Mall
- You also have a variety of maps to work with

Assignment: Writing Identifying Supers

For each of the individuals named in the following story descriptions (10 people in all), come up with a two-line descriptive super to use over a sound bite. The top line should be the person's name. The second line should be a brief (20-character maximum) description that explains who the person is. Use all capital letters.

- *James Jasperson* is honored in an award ceremony for rescuing an elderly woman from a burning building. Jasperson is presented with the "Community Hero Award" by *Pamela Crowne*, president of an organization called the Lakedale Community Association, which sponsors the award. The woman who was rescued, 80-year-old *Fanny Marie Minson*, is also on hand for the ceremony.

- The trial of a man accused of poisoning his next door neighbor's German shepherd dog gets underway in District Court. The defendant is *Vernon Macaroni*, 49, charged with animal cruelty. His attorney is *Penny Powell*. The attorney for the prosecution is *Stewart L. Capps*. The chief witness against Vernon Macaroni is the dog's owner, *Thelma Granger*, 38, who testified that she saw Macaroni sneaking out of her garage around the time of the killing.

- *Horace Tate*, 40, a former astronaut with NASA, is named superintendent of schools for the Lakedale School District. He is welcomed to the job by *Amelia Winston*, acting chairwoman of the Lakedale Parent Teacher Association. Among Tate's first orders of business is a meeting with *David Juarez*, chief negotiator for the Lakedale Teachers Union.

Analysis: TV News Graphics, Titles, and Supers

- Record a local or network newscast and analyze the news graphics used at the beginning of each story. Are they visually interesting? Are they easily understood? Are their captions effective?

- Record a local or network newscast and analyze the news graphics used within the first few stories. Are they visually interesting? Are they easily understood? How well do they advance the storytelling?

- Take the front page of your city's daily newspaper or a national newspaper like USA Today and create over-the-shoulder news graphics for each of the main stories. Your graphics should include captions no more than 16 characters in length.

- Record a local or network newscast and analyze the identifying supers used in the first few stories. Were the second-line descriptors clear? Did they fairly describe the person's involvement in the story?

- Choose 10 stories from a daily newspaper that include quotes from interviewees. For each of the interviewees write a second-line descriptor no more than 20 characters in length.

CHAPTER TEN

TELEVISION NEWS ON THE WEB

TOPICS DISCUSSED IN THIS CHAPTER

- The Growth of TV News on the Web • The Responsibilities of Web Journalists
- Contents of TV News Websites • Writing for TV News Websites
- TV News Webcasts • Checklist of Key Points

ASSIGNMENTS/ANALYSIS

- Assignment: Writing and Producing for the Web
- Analysis: TV News Websites

THE GROWTH OF TV NEWS ON THE WEB

Online journalism is the newest and fastest growing branch of television news. Over the course of a few short years, websites have joined on-air newscasts as standard fixtures of TV journalism. This has opened up a plethora of job opportunities, especially for young journalists with the skills and imagination to successfully tell stories across a variety of media.

To one degree or another, every journalist in a modern television newsroom is already a web journalist. Although each station and network has its own staffing pattern, TV-based websites reflect the full range of journalistic specialties: writing, producing, reporting, anchoring, shooting, editing, graphics, teases—everything that goes into making a television newscast also goes into the online product. Reporters who put together packages for on-air newscasts routinely prepare web versions of their stories as well. Video that does not make it on the air finds an outlet on the website. Producers who organize half-hour news programs for broadcast produce shorter versions of their shows as webcasts. Anchors and weatherpersons write their own blogs and conduct online chats.

Television newsrooms also have employees who devote themselves exclusively to the website. These individuals serve as producers, writers, and designers, coordinating information from sources both internal and external. Some web journalists gained their experience on the television side of the operation, some come from a print background, and some have spent their entire careers working on the web. Like all news practitioners, they observe the established rules of the profession: accuracy, fairness, and a strict adherence to ethical standards. The delivery platform might be different, but the underlying principles are the same.

In many newsrooms, web operations exist hand in hand with the station's assignment desk. This makes for a convenient setup, because it is in the nature of web-based news to be as up-to-the-minute as possible. By pairing the web operation with the assignment desk, web producers can stay on top of breaking developments and update their sites accordingly. As stories unfold, the online side of the newsroom works in tandem with the broadcast side to report the latest details.

Whatever the structural arrangement, TV news outlets at both the local and network level are expanding rapidly into web-based journalism. Watch any TV newscast and you are bound to see heavy cross-promotion of the online product. After some initial resistance to the idea, television news organizations have realized that websites are an extension of the on-air product, not a threat to it.

According to veteran reporter Beth Parker of WTTG-TV in Washington, D.C., online journalism is "the present and the future." Says Parker: "Over the years I've grown accustomed to young kids running up to the live truck yelling, 'Hey, lady, can I be on TV?' A few months ago, a boy who was about eight years old came running up as I was about to do a live shot. I've heard it so many times, I thought I knew what was coming. He surprised me, though. He ran up and said, 'Hey, lady, can I be on the internet?' Now that's a turning point!"

THE RESPONSIBILITIES OF WEB JOURNALISTS

Web journalists perform many of the same functions handled by other journalists in the TV newsroom: making news judgments, producing, reporting and writing, editing video, designing graphics, and so forth. However, they also have specialized duties unique to their medium.

Because online news must be turned around as quickly as possible, web producers and reporters tend to rely more heavily on secondary sources than their print and on-air counterparts. This does not mean that online journalists relinquish their responsibility to check information, just that there is not always as much time for original reporting. As a rule, web journalism is primarily newsroom based, as opposed to field based.

One online journalist described the difference this way: "Web-based journalism is a process of news *gathering* more than news reporting." Using a wide variety of sources— wire services like the Associated Press, network video feeds, the station's own assignment desk, the reporting of in-house reporters and videographers, and so on—web producers evaluate material and make editorial decisions about what to post on the site and how to package content for the local audience.

Web journalists who work out of TV newsrooms spend a good deal of time on the telephone, checking out tips and verifying information before writing their stories. Against never-ending deadlines, they constantly update everything on the site, adding new details to already-posted stories, taking down items that are no longer fresh, and putting up breaking stories as they develop.

Internet journalists also execute a number of producing functions: coordinating with external sources such as news wires and network video feeds, dealing with the station's own reporters about local stories, working with graphic artists to create visuals, and staying on top of newsworthy developments from the weather and sports departments. Web-based journalists must also come up with creative ways to make the site interactive, whether it's soliciting photos from viewers, devising features called *web extras,* setting up message boards that allow the audience to comment on stories, or creating online polls.

TV news websites cover a vast range of material, from hometown happenings to national and international stories. This breadth of subject matter gives web producers an opportunity to feature stories that would probably receive just a passing mention in a station's on-air newscasts. For instance, a major flood in Pennsylvania might rate only a few seconds of airtime in a local California newscast, but thanks to video-sharing arrangements with station affiliates around the country, the California website can offer extended video clips of the Pennsylvania flood to interested consumers. The possibilities are nearly limitless.

A fundamental challenge of online journalism is knowing how to take full advantage of online storytelling tools. Web producers therefore need fluency in all the different modes of journalistic communication: from text to images, from video to graphics. At bottom, working as an online journalist for a TV station website calls for a broad combination of skills and an understanding of which methods are best suited to a particular story.

CONTENTS OF TV NEWS WEBSITES

Visit the websites of 20 different local television stations, and you'll find 20 different versions of what a TV news website should be. Some are elaborate, providing local, national, and international news content, along with sports, weather, consumer information, health updates, entertainment listings, travel tips, community calendars, and the like. Others focus more narrowly on news stories in the immediate viewing area.

Whatever the structure, all TV news websites share certain common denominators. They highlight current stories, particularly those that are local. They tie the online product to the on-air product, cross-promoting the station's TV newscasts and personalities. They offer stories in a range of formats that incorporate text, video, stills, and graphics. They also provide a vehicle for advertising.

The typical TV news website posts several dozen stories a day, some in the video/audio format and others that are primarily text based. The video packages might be duplicates of what ran on the newscasts, or stories that have been put together exclusively for the web. Online video postings might also offer viewers the chance to check out raw footage or extended clips that go beyond what the on-air story contained. For example, an interview with a local celebrity might have run in abbreviated form on a newscast, with only a handful of sound bites included. Online, by contrast, it can run in its entirety.

Extended video clips are just one type of web extras that TV news websites provide. A story about a complicated legal case might give visitors to the site a chance to read detailed court documents. A story involving a controversial exchange of e-mails could include the full text of those e-mails. News from a war zone might be accompanied by detailed maps that show where fighting has taken place.

Stories that appear on TV news websites almost always include a pictorial element—if not video, then still photos, informational graphics, or maps. Slide shows are a regular component of online news sites, especially for stories that generate interesting visuals. Web producers can easily create slide shows using still images supplied by wire services, or by stringing together video freeze-frames. Some slide shows revolve around a specific theme, whereas others are more general, like the "This Week in Pictures" feature that many websites post on a routine basis.

Station websites regularly invite viewers to submit original photos or videos, the best of which are then posted. More often than not these images depict happenings in the local area. Let's say there has been a major snowstorm in your town. The website for a hometown TV station can run a batch of amateur photos showing what various sections of the city look like under a blanket of snow. A number of TV news websites highlight a "picture of the day," chosen from images submitted by audience members.

Interactivity is a hallmark of TV station websites. Almost all sites run a daily poll question, usually about a current issue in the news, and many online sites invite the audience to participate in discussions about the important stories of the day. Some station websites also offer a "Build your own newscast" option that allows users to choose video clips from a menu of current stories.

A growing number of TV news websites now feature blogs. These might take the form of first-person videos, with narration by a reporter, anchor, or photographer. Or they might be short, diary-like essays written by members of the newsroom staff. The award-winning website of KGW-TV in Portland, Ore., offers an extensive array of mostly text-based blogs that cover a range of subject matter: weather, sports, health, entertainment, business, and even a "manager's blog" in which news executives discuss the decision making behind coverage of sensitive stories.

The KGW site also carries regular blogs by station anchors and reporters. Sometimes the topics are personal: an on-air personality's thoughts about child rearing, for instance, or plans for running a local marathon. Other times these blogs give KGW journalists a chance to take viewers "behind the headlines" by describing how a particular story was covered.

The goal in all of these offerings is to attract an audience. Just as television newscasts are subject to ratings, so do websites closely track the number of hits from consumers. As is the case with any journalistic operation, visits to websites fluctuate greatly, rising dramatically when major breaking news occurs. The more impressive the numbers,

The growth of TV news websites means new opportunities for journalists. Many reporters and anchors now write their own blogs or columns that describe the behind-the-scenes process of newsgathering.

the more stations can charge for advertising, making online journalism just as competitive as standard television.

TV news on the web is viewed as an increasingly important source of revenue, as evidenced by the numerous advertisements that run alongside the news stories. These commercial announcements take several forms, from interactive display ads on the home page to pop-ups to video-streamed commercials that play before a consumer can watch a video clip. As the internet grows in popularity as an information medium, online advertising will become an increasingly significant underwriter of TV news.

WRITING FOR TV NEWS WEBSITES

Much of the web-based journalism produced by TV stations is text oriented, requiring writing skills that would not be out of place in a newspaper setting. "As a web journalist I'm writing constantly," says Chuck McKenney, an online producer for WBZ-TV, the CBS station in Boston. McKenney estimates that he writes an average of 15 stories a day for WBZ's internet news site. Basic writing skills, he says, are critical. According to McKenney, "it's much easier to take a journalist and teach him the technical aspect than someone with a strong technical background and teach him news judgment and how to write."

Writing for the web brings a certain degree of freedom because stories need not adhere to a particular length, as is inevitably the case for TV news reports. Despite this freedom, most online stories are short. Standard news stories on the web—crime, accidents, disasters—follow a concise and straightforward writing style, closer in feel to the writing that appears in daily newspapers than TV scriptwriting. The objective is to distill a great deal of information into a clear and compressed form. As in print journalism, the essence of the story must be captured in the first sentence or two. The details must be conveyed quickly and crisply. The tone must be neutral and fair.

Because TV news websites deal with both local and nonlocal material, online news writers need to be conversant with stories outside their immediate viewing area. Although the writing style is the same whether it's a hometown, national, or international story, it is up to the web journalist to recognize which nonlocal stories will matter to a local audience, and why. Whenever possible, the writer should seek out a hometown angle on a major national or international story.

Writing for online news sites involves a fair amount of summarizing. Summary sentences at the beginning of a story are common, which means writers must know how to boil a story down to its bare bones. The classic "inverted pyramid" style of newspaper writing, in which the most important information goes at the top of the piece, is a reasonable model to follow. The key questions—Who? What? When? Where? Why? How?—should be answered within the first few paragraphs.

Online news requires constant updating, because there are no fixed deadlines. Depending on the shop, TV station websites might be updated as frequently as every 30 minutes, or even more frequently in the case of a breaking story. Writers must grow accustomed to the realities of constantly revising their copy to keep the material as fresh as possible.

Not all stories on journalistic websites qualify as hard news. As an antidote to the serious subject matter, online news sites feature a good many lighter stories as well. This lighter material offers more room for creative writing, especially when it comes to headlines. Headline writing is a prized skill, on the web as in print, because a catchy phrase can make the difference in attracting readers. Chuck McKenney recalls a story about a truck loaded with strawberries that crashed on a New England highway, causing an enormous traffic tie-up. The headline he came up with was "Strawberry Jam."

As with television and print, headlines for online news stories must fit within specific space constraints. Writer-producers at Boston's WBZ-TV work with 50 characters per headline, including punctuation marks and blank spaces between words. "I can't tell you how many times I've come up with the perfect headline that's 51 characters long," McKenney says, "meaning I have to come up with something else."

Of course, web-based journalism goes well beyond the use of text. Online news takes advantage of the full range of audiovisual building blocks: text, video, still photos, graphics, animation, audio clips, and whatever else might contribute to making a story interesting. The challenge for web producers is to figure out creative ways of integrating these visual elements into the coverage.

TV NEWS WEBCASTS

As supplements to the on-air newscasts, a growing number of TV stations are producing separate, shorter webcasts for posting on the website. Typically these are compressed versions of the standard 30- or 60-minute newscasts, composed of many of the same elements. Webcasts can run any length, but they tend to be short: anywhere between three and 10 minutes. Depending on the frequency with which they are produced, webcasts can be posted on a station's website for several hours or longer, until they are replaced by a more up-to-date program.

The rudiments of writing and producing a webcast are essentially the same as they would be for a long-form newscast. Producers select a mix of stories, beginning with

TV news websites allow journalists to go beyond the time constraints of traditional broadcasting and allow viewers to watch stories when it is most convenient.

a lead item that represents the most significant story at the time of production. The webcast is likely to include VO/SOT/VOs, VOs, and readers. Fully edited packages are less common because of time limitations.

As with longer newscasts, there are several principles to keep in mind:

- The lead story should be something that affects a broad audience, or that is particularly timely and local.

- Stories should be sequenced in a logical order. This means grouping stories according to their thematic content: crime, accidents, national and international headlines, entertainment news, and so on.

- Because webcasts are so short, they are likely to be delivered by only a single anchorperson, although this might vary from station to station.

- Webcasts tend to have a news-you-can-use feel, so they generally include brief weather forecasts in addition to the top news items. There might also be quick sports segments, especially on the weekends or on game nights.

Beyond the internet versions of standard newscasts, some TV stations produce webcasts in alternative programming formats. For instance, a reporter might appear on a live webcast to conduct a real-time chat with readers. A sports anchor might do an exclusive online interview with a local athlete. Special occasions could call for special webcasts on hot topics in the news.

As technological boundaries fall, TV news is finding innovative ways of reaching audiences: From webcasts to podcasts to text messages, the reach of television journalism is constantly expanding. What seems futuristic today will be taken for granted tomorrow. For young journalists with an ability to tell stories, the horizon looks bright.

CHECKLIST OF KEY POINTS

- As the fastest growing branch of television news, online journalism offers a range of job opportunities for journalists skilled in storytelling across media.

- TV newsrooms include personnel who devote themselves exclusively to the station's web operation, but to an increasing extent everyone in the newsroom is expected to be an online journalist.

- Web journalists fulfill many of the same functions as traditional TV news producers, serving as coordinators of information from a variety of sources. Generally speaking, television news websites concentrate more on gathering and packaging information than original reporting.

- Although TV news websites highlight local stories, they have the capability to include news from national and international sources as well.

- News stories on the web take advantage of a combination of storytelling elements: text, still images, moving images, and graphics. Websites might post stories that ran during the regular newscasts, or additional material that could not be included on the air because of time constraints.

- In addition to the major stories of the day, TV station news sites offer a range of web extras. These take a number of forms: raw video footage, extended interview excerpts, slide shows, and interactive features like polls, message boards, and photo contests.

- Blogs are standard features on many TV news websites. Blogs can be written by anchors, reporters, newsroom executives, or other station personnel, and they deal with everything from personal essays to behind-the-scenes details about the news of the day.

- Newswriting on the web calls for strong journalistic skills and an ability to use text concisely and accurately. Online writers must distill information into summary sentences and headlines. Because there are no fixed deadlines, writers need to frequently update their stories.

- Most TV news websites carry regular webcasts, which are shorter versions of a station's full-length newscasts. Some stations give viewers the chance to create their own newscasts by selecting stories they would like to watch from a menu of items.

ASSIGNMENTS/ANALYSIS

Assignment: Writing and Producing for the Web

- Go back to the VO and VO/SOT/VO assignments at the end of Chapter 3, and write a headline and summary sentence for each of them that might appear on a TV news website. Limit your headlines to 50 characters, including punctuation and blank spaces.

- Go back to the package assignments at the end of Chapter 4, and turn each of them into a 500-word text story for the web. After you've finished writing, choose several visuals (stills, video clips, or both) for each story to be posted along with your text.

- Go back to the long newscast producing assignment at the end of Chapter 7, and reduce the half-hour of news to a seven-minute webcast that includes one minute of weather and one minute of sports.

- Compile a list of five topics in your local area that might be turned into interactive web extra features. The list might include current issues in the news, annual events in your area, upcoming political races, the doings of local celebrities, and so on. Indicate what form is most appropriate for each idea.

- Using current stories in the news as your inspiration, come up with a list of 10 interactive poll questions that might work on a TV news website.

Analysis: TV News Websites

- Visit the websites of the local TV news stations in your area and compare their effectiveness. What are the pros and cons of each site? Which offers the best information? The strongest writing? The most interesting visuals and graphics?

- Visit the websites of five local TV news stations around the country and compare their web extras. Which station is generating the most creative ideas? Which web extras interactively involve the viewers? Which ideas seem to fall flat?

- Visit the websites of the major TV news networks—ABC, CBS, NBC (which shares a site with MSNBC), CNN, and Fox News Channel—and compare their effectiveness. What are the pros and cons of each site? Which offers the best information? The strongest writing? The most interesting visuals and graphics?

TV News Terms

Anchor: The person delivering the news on camera.

archival footage: Visual material for a news story that already exists and therefore does not need to be shot. Archival footage may come from a TV station's library of previous stories, or from an outside source. Also called *file footage*.

aspect ratio: A term that refers to the shape of a TV screen. Standard analog television has an aspect ratio of 3 by 4, meaning the screen occupies four horizontal lengths by three vertical lengths. High-definition television has an aspect ratio of 9 by 16, which is closer to the dimensions of a movie screen.

assignment editor: The person in a newsroom who monitors day-to-day news events and dispatches reporters and crews to stories.

backtiming: Figuring out how much time remains during a live newscast.

break: A pause for commercials.

B-roll: Supplementary video that is run over narration, interview bites, and so on.

bug: A station logo that appears in the corner of the screen and usually remains in place throughout the newscast. Bugs might also show the time and temperature, especially during early-morning newscasts.

cold open: When a newscast or segment begins on something other than a shot of the anchors.

crawl: The line of text that scrolls horizontally across the bottom of the screen during some newscasts.

credit: Acknowledgment by name of someone involved in the newscast, generally run at the end of the program. A courtesy credit is sometimes given to companies or individuals who contribute to the production in some way, like hair and wardrobe consultants.

CU: Close-up, as in a talking head shot. Also called a *tight shot*.

dissolve: An editing transition in which one image disappears as the next one appears, with overlap between the two. If the dissolve is slow enough, you can actually see the first picture trailing off and the second one coming into view. Dissolves can happen at any speed, depending on the situation. In news, most dissolves are quick.

edit points: The precise beginning and ending of sound bites or shots that are being edited into taped stories.

end break: The commercial break at the end of a program.

ENG: Electronic newsgathering. This usually refers to the technical side of TV journalism, particularly live shots from the field.

enterprise stories: Nonbreaking news stories that are developed by reporters, producers, and assignment editors. These are usually original stories that other media have not covered.

explainer graphics: Television graphics that add detail and explanation to a news story. Explainer graphics usually serve as internal elements within a story. They can be full-screen and they are often animated.

file footage: Another term for archival footage.

IFB: An earpiece worn by anchors and reporters that allows them to hear instructions from producers and directors while a program is in progress.

infographic: An on-screen graphic designed to offer factual information about a news story.

internal break: A commercial break within a program.

key: A title or image that is superimposed over the main shot.

kicker: A soft feature story, usually placed toward the end of a newscast.

lead-in: An introduction, as in the anchorperson's introduction of a taped news package.

lip flap: This occurs when an interviewee is shown speaking on camera at the same time an anchor or reporter is delivering voice-over narration. Lip flap is something to be avoided.

lip microphone or lip mic: A microphone that filters out background noise. These are used when reporters record their narration tracks at remote locations in the field.

live remote: A live report from a journalist in the field. Also called a *live shot*. Live remotes are most often used to introduce stories on tape.

locator super: Text displayed on the screen that indicates the location of the reporter or story.

logging: The process of making a list of video and sound elements that have been recorded in the field. Reporters log their field tapes before writing a script to have a complete record of the available shots, sound bites, and natural sound.

look-live: An anchor or reporter appearing on camera in a brief taped segment that is meant to look like it is being delivered live. Look-lives are usually short pieces like intros, tags, and teases.

lower third graphic: Text that is superimposed on the bottom of the screen, usually either the name and identification of an interviewee or a locator super.

mic: An abbreviation for microphone. Although the word is pronounced "mike," TV professionals do not spell it that way.

monitor box: A graphic that appears inside a TV monitor on the news set.

motion graphics: Animated news graphics.

natural sound: Sound recorded at the scene of a story that is organic to the situation. Also called *nat sound*, *natsot*, or *natural sound on tape*. Natural sound differs from sound bites in that it does not come from interviews, but rather from the environment.

one-shot: A shot framed to show only one person, such as an anchor or interviewee.

open: The preproduced opening of a newscast, including animated titles, music, and so on.

outro: The opposite of an intro. Outros, also called *tags*, come at the end of a story and are delivered by either an anchor or reporter.

over-the-shoulder graphic: An image, either still or moving, that appears in a box placed over the shoulder of the anchorperson during a newscast.

package: A fully edited, self-contained story on videotape, complete with visuals, sound bites, reporter narration, reporter stand-ups, and natural sound.

preproduction (pre-pro): Advance preparation of visual materials for a newscast or story.

reader: The shortest, most basic form of studio-based TV news story. Also called *anchor reader*. It is read by an anchorperson who remains on camera for the brief duration of the script, usually in the 10- to 20-second range.

remote: A shot, usually done live, that originates from a location in the field and is transmitted back to the TV station.

roll cue: The last few words an anchor or reporter says before a videotaped story begins. During a live newscast the director listens for the roll cue to know when to start the tape.

rundown: A blueprint for the newscast that lists all the stories in their proper sequence and includes additional information about timing, anchor reads, story formats, graphics, and so forth.

segment block: The period of programming between commercial breaks.

show-and-tell graphics: Graphics that serve to illustrate a story rather than deliver factual material.

slug: A short name given to a news story for the purpose of internal reference. Slugs are usually only a word or two long.

SOT: Sound on tape, which usually means a sound bite.

sound bite: A quote from an interviewee.

stacking: Deciding on the order of stories that will run in a newscast.

stand-up: The reporter on camera, delivering information to the camera.

still graphics: News graphics that are not animated.

still-storer: A device that stores thousands of still images that are used as news graphics.

super: A brief bit of text or other visual material that is superimposed over the dominant on-screen image.

tag: The opposite of a lead-in or introduction, a tag is a bit of additional information given at the end of a taped story by an anchorperson or reporter. Tags are sometimes called outros.

talent: Anyone who works on camera; in television news this would be anchors and reporters.

tease: A short promotional item about an upcoming news story, designed to entice viewers to keep watching.

teleprompter: A device attached to a studio camera from which anchorpersons read their scripts. The words of the script scroll down the teleprompter screen to make the delivery appear seamless and natural.

text graphics: On-screen news graphics that deliver textual information such as transcripts of 911 calls, quotations from court documents, and the like.

time-code: A time stamp that is automatically embedded onto videotape as it records in the field. In logging tapes, reporters note the time-code for shots and sound bites to quickly access these elements during the editing process.

title: A few words of on-screen text. These may be titles in a literal sense, but sometimes the word is used synonymously with super.

total running time (TRT): Length of either a complete program or an individual story. Also referred to as *running time* or *run time*.

two-shot: A shot showing two people, such as co-anchors on a news set, or a reporter and an interviewee.

VNR: Video news release. VNRs are edited packages with video and sound, produced by corporations, organizations, and government agencies in the hope of generating favorable television publicity.

voice-over (VO): Narration that accompanies video. VO stories, also called *reader/voice-overs* (R/VO), add a visual layer to the storytelling by incorporating video, full-screen graphics, or other illustrations to the anchorperson's words. These stories usually run in the 10- to 30-second range. More generically, the term VO describes any instance within a story in which narration is being read against visuals.

VO/SOT: A studio-based news story that adds the element of sound bites from interviewees. Also called *SOTs,* for sound on tape. The standard structure for this type of story is the VO/SOT/VO. Think of these as a sound bite sandwich: first the anchorperson reads a voice-over, then there's the sound bite, then another anchor voice-over. VO/SOT/VO stories run in the 20- to 50-second range, depending on the length of the bite.

wide shot: A shot showing a general view of its subject, usually taken from a distance.

wipe: An editing transition in which a new image appears to push the previous image off the screen. Wipes can be done horizontally, vertically, diagonally, or in a pattern.

Information About the City of Lakedale

All of the exercises and assignments included in this textbook have been set in the fictitious city of Lakedale, a medium-sized American community. This appendix includes details about Lakedale and its institutions and citizens. This information is designed to provide context as you complete the work.

COMMUNITY PROFILE

Location

You can assume that Lakedale is located somewhere in your general region of the country. Like *The Simpsons'* Springfield, our mythical community is Anytown USA, but to keep things simple, think of it as being close to wherever you live. This will give you a better understanding of how the place works.

Demographics

Lakedale has a population of 200,000 people, with another 50,000 in the immediate surrounding area. The demographic profile of Lakedale reflects that of the United States as a whole, with about the same racial and ethnic breakdowns, socioeconomic levels, range of religious affiliations, and so on.

Geography

The city of Lakedale is the county seat of Lakedale County. As the name suggests, Lakedale is located on a large body of water called Blue Lake. The Blue River runs from the lake through the city and beyond.

Neighborhoods

Lakedale's central business district is referred to as Downtown, and the area is circled by a freeway called the Downtown Loop. Other neighborhoods include River Bluffs, a wealthy residential area on the fashionable west side; South Bank, an economically

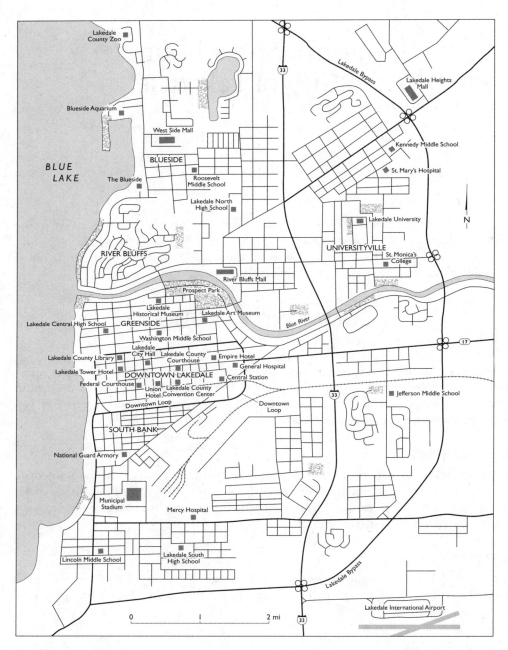

Map of the city of Lakedale.

BLUE
LAKE

BLUESIDE

RIVER BLUFFS

GREENSIDE

DOWNTOWN LAKEDALE

SOUTH BANK

UNIVERSITYVILLE

Lakedale County Zoo

Blueside Aquarium

West Side Mall

The Blueside

Roosevelt
Middle School

Lakedale North
High School

Lakedale
Historical Museum

Lakedale Art Museum

Prospect Park

River Bluffs Mall

Blue River

Lakedale Central High School

Washington Middle School

Lakedale County Library

Lakedale
City Hall   Lakedale County
Courthouse

Empire Hotel

General Hospital

Lakedale Tower Hotel

Central Station

Federal Courthouse

Union   Lakedale County
Hotel   Convention Center

Downtown Loop

Downtown
Loop

National Guard Armory

Municipal
Stadium

Mercy Hospital

Lincoln Middle School

Lakedale South
High School

Kennedy Middle School

St. Mary's Hospital

Lakedale University

St. Monica's
College

Jefferson Middle School

Lakedale Heights
Mall

Lakedale Bypass

Lakedale Bypass

Lakedale International Airport

33

17

33

33

N

0   1   2 mi

disadvantaged area south of downtown; Greenside, an older neighborhood north of downtown containing many architectural landmarks; Blueside, an economically mixed section along the shores of Blue Lake; and Universityville, generally referred to as U-Ville, which surrounds Lakedale University on the city's east side.

Suburbs and Outlying Communities

Four suburbs lie just beyond the city limits of Lakedale. The largest and most important of these is Lakedale Heights, with a population of about 20,000. The others are Rock City (8,000), Pandora (7,000), and Finchester (5,000). A number of other small towns lie further out in Lakedale County, including Vanderwood, Mintern, and Carvel. These towns are more rural in character, although many of their residents commute to jobs in Lakedale.

Transportation

Lakedale's major transportation routes include the Downtown Loop, which encircles the downtown area; the Lakedale Bypass, a ring road that goes around the outskirts of the city; Interstate 33, a major north–south highway that is part of the federal interstate highway system; Highway 17, a four-lane toll road that runs east–west and connects Lakedale to the state capital; and Route 5, which crosses the county diagonally.

Public transportation is provided the Lakedale Transit Authority (LTA). LTA operates a network of bus lines throughout the city and suburbs. A trolley line from downtown to the suburb of Lakedale Heights is in the planning stages.

Other important transportation landmarks are Lakedale International Airport, located south of the city off Interstate 33, and Central Station, a rail and bus terminal located downtown.

Media Market

Lakedale is a medium-to-small television market. The city of Lakedale is at the center of the viewing area, which extends about 75 miles in every direction from downtown. All the major television networks have local affiliates in Lakedale.

There is also a daily newspaper, the Lakedale Ledger, and numerous radio stations. All the local news outlets operate extensive websites.

COMMUNITY DIRECTORY

Major Civic Institutions

Lakedale City Hall
Lakedale County Courthouse
Federal Courthouse
Lakedale County Convention Center
National Guard Armory

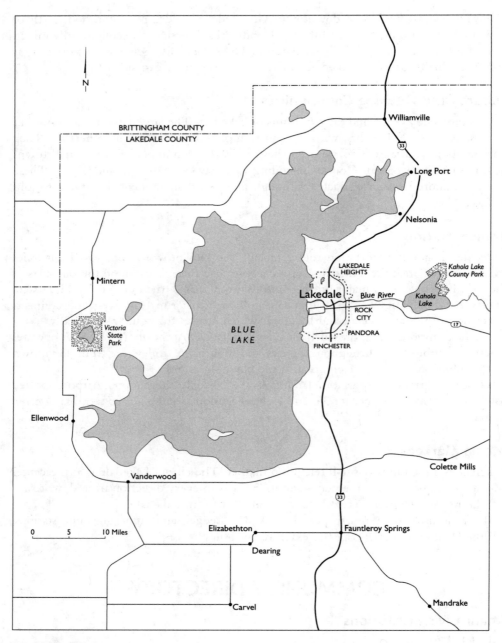

N

BRITTINGHAM COUNTY
LAKEDALE COUNTY

Williamville

Long Port

Nelsonia

Mintern

LAKEDALE
HEIGHTS

Kahola Lake
County Park

Lakedale

Blue River

Kahola
Lake

Victoria
State
Park

BLUE
LAKE

ROCK
CITY

PANDORA

FINCHESTER

17

Ellenwood

Colette Mills

Vanderwood

33

0   5   10 Miles

Elizabethton

Fauntleroy Springs

Dearing

Carvel

Mandrake

Map of Lakedale County.

Major Cultural Institutions

Lakedale Art Museum
Lakedale Historical Museum
Lakedale County Zoo
Lakedale County Library
Blueside Aquarium
Majestic Theater
Dream Theater
Wee Pals Puppet Playhouse
Lakedale Symphony Orchestra
Lakedale Summer Theater

Educational Institutions

- Lakedale University: This is a four-year state university with about 10,000 students, located in the neighborhood known as Universityville. Lakedale University's mascot is a lion.
- St. Monica's College: This is a four-year Catholic college for female students.
- High schools: There are three high schools in the city: Lakedale North High School, Lakedale Central High School, and Lakedale South High School.
- Middle schools: There are five middle schools: Washington, Jefferson, Lincoln, Roosevelt, and Kennedy.
- Elementary schools: There are 15 elementary schools.
- Parochial schools: There is one Roman Catholic high school, Holy Cross High School. Two other Catholic schools, Bishop Academy (male) and St. Teresa's (female), serve students through the eighth-grade level.

Suburbs like Lakeport Heights operate their own school districts.

Medical Facilities

General Hospital
Mercy Hospital
St. Mary's Hospital

Religious Institutions

All the major religious denominations are represented in Lakedale.

Recreational Facilities

Municipal Stadium is the Lakedale's main outdoor venue for sporting events.

The city of Lakedale is home to several dozen parks. The largest of these is Prospect Park, in the Greenside neighborhood north of downtown. A number of parks lie along the shores of Blue Lake, and others are scattered throughout the city.

Lake County maintains a park system outside the city limits as well. The most popular of the county parks is Kahola Lake.

The Lakedale County Fairgrounds host a number of local events, including the annual celebration known as Lakedale Heritage Days.

Victoria State Park, known for its beautiful scenery, is 30 miles west of Lakedale.

Public Utilities

Lakedale Energy Corporation supplies power to the city and region. It operates the controversial Lakedale Nuclear Power Plant, which is located east of the city.

Major Hotels

Union Hotel
Empire Hotel
Lakedale Tower Hotel
The Blueside

Major Shopping Areas

Downtown Lakedale
Lakedale Heights Mall
River Bluffs Mall
West Side Mall

Community Organizations

Lakedale Area Animal Shelter

COMMUNITY DIRECTORY

This directory lists the major governmental departments and key public servants in the community.

City Administration

Mayor Norma Lyons
City Council

Other City Departments and Officials

City Manager's office
Public Works Department
Parks and Recreation Department
City Engineering Department
City Transportation Department

Department of Public Health
Abby Mantz, City Historian

Lakedale Police Department (LPD)

Al Varden, Chief of Police
Leon Sanders, Acting Chief of Police (after Varden's death)
Angela Porroni, Community Liaison Officer for the LPD
Sgt. Alice Sweeney, media spokesperson for the LPD
Capt. John diPraia, head of the LPD bomb squad

Lakedale Fire Department (LFD)

Andy Edwards, Fire Chief
John Arthur, media spokesperson for the LFD

Lakedale School District

Superintendent of Schools

Lakedale University

Professor Lyndon Carthage, Criminal Justice Department
Professor Andy Snyder, Art Department

Lakedale International Airport

Sheila Clover, media spokesperson

County Government

Roberta Philpot, District Attorney
Fred Wyatt, Sheriff
June Harper, Animal Control Officer

State Government

Gov. Chet Smith
Lt. Gov. Sally Jones
Alexander Clayton, Secretary of Education
Robert Bryan, State Parks Commissioner
Sgt. Jerry Garten, media spokesperson for the State Highway Patrol
Melvis Ansonia, State Lottery Director

Town of Vanderwood

Mayor John Winborn

Radio–Television News Directors Association Code of Ethics and Professional Conduct

The Radio-Television News Directors Association [RTNDA], wishing to foster the highest professional standards of electronic journalism, promote public understanding of and confidence in electronic journalism, and strengthen principles of journalistic freedom to gather and disseminate information, establishes this Code of Ethics and Professional Conduct.

PREAMBLE: Professional electronic journalists should operate as trustees of the public, seek the truth, report it fairly and with integrity and independence, and stand accountable for their actions.

PUBLIC TRUST: Professional electronic journalists should recognize that their first obligation is to the public. Professional electronic journalists should:

Understand that any commitment other than service to the public undermines trust and credibility.

Recognize that service in the public interest creates an obligation to reflect the diversity of the community and guard against oversimplification of issues or events.

Provide a full range of information to enable the public to make enlightened decisions.

Fight to ensure that the public's business is conducted in public.

TRUTH: Professional electronic journalists should pursue truth aggressively and present the news accurately, in context, and as completely as possible.

Professional electronic journalists should:

Continuously seek the truth.

Resist distortions that obscure the importance of events.

Clearly disclose the origin of information and label all material provided by outsiders.

Professional electronic journalists should not:

Report anything known to be false.

Manipulate images or sounds in any way that is misleading.

Plagiarize.

Present images or sounds that are reenacted without informing the public.

FAIRNESS: Professional electronic journalists should present the news fairly and impartially, placing primary value on significance and relevance.

Professional electronic journalists should:

Treat all subjects of news coverage with respect and dignity, showing particular compassion to victims of crime or tragedy.

Exercise special care when children are involved in a story and give children greater privacy protection than adults.

Seek to understand the diversity of their community and inform the public without bias or stereotype.

Present a diversity of expressions, opinions, and ideas in context.

Present analytical reporting based on professional perspective, not personal bias.

Respect the right to a fair trial.

INTEGRITY: Professional electronic journalists should present the news with integrity and decency, avoiding real or perceived conflicts of interest, and respect the dignity and intelligence of the audience as well as the subjects of news.

Professional electronic journalists should:

Identify sources whenever possible. Confidential sources should be used only when it is clearly in the public interest to gather or convey important information or when a person providing information might be harmed. Journalists should keep all commitments to protect a confidential source.

Clearly label opinion and commentary.

Guard against extended coverage of events or individuals that fails to significantly advance a story, place the event in context, or add to the public knowledge.

Refrain from contacting participants in violent situations while the situation is in progress.

Use technological tools with skill and thoughtfulness, avoiding techniques that skew facts, distort reality, or sensationalize events.

Use surreptitious newsgathering techniques, including hidden cameras or microphones, only if there is no other way to obtain stories of significant public importance and only if the technique is explained to the audience.

Disseminate the private transmissions of other news organizations only with permission.

Professional electronic journalists should not:

Pay news sources who have a vested interest in a story.

Accept gifts, favors, or compensation from those who might seek to influence coverage.

Engage in activities that may compromise their integrity or independence.

INDEPENDENCE: Professional electronic journalists should defend the independence of all journalists from those seeking influence or control over news content.

Professional electronic journalists should:

Gather and report news without fear or favor, and vigorously resist undue influence from any outside forces, including advertisers, sources, story subjects, powerful individuals, and special interest groups.

Resist those who would seek to buy or politically influence news content or who would seek to intimidate those who gather and disseminate the news.

Determine news content solely through editorial judgment and not as the result of outside influence.

Resist any self-interest or peer pressure that might erode journalistic duty and service to the public.

Recognize that sponsorship of the news will not be used in any way to determine, restrict, or manipulate content.

Refuse to allow the interests of ownership or management to influence news judgment and content inappropriately.

Defend the rights of the free press for all journalists, recognizing that any professional or government licensing of journalists is a violation of that freedom.

ACCOUNTABILITY: Professional electronic journalists should recognize that they are accountable for their actions to the public, the profession, and themselves.

Professional electronic journalists should:

Actively encourage adherence to these standards by all journalists and their employers.

Respond to public concerns. Investigate complaints and correct errors promptly and with as much prominence as the original report.

Explain journalistic processes to the public, especially when practices spark questions or controversy.

Recognize that professional electronic journalists are duty-bound to conduct themselves ethically.

Refrain from ordering or encouraging courses of action that would force employees to commit an unethical act.

Carefully listen to employees who raise ethical objections and create environments in which such objections and discussions are encouraged.

Seek support for and provide opportunities to train employees in ethical decision-making.

In meeting its responsibility to the profession of electronic journalism, RTNDA has created this code to identify important issues, to serve as a guide for its members, to facilitate self-scrutiny, and to shape future debate.

Adopted at RTNDA national convention in Minneapolis September 14, 2000.

Ten Questions for Ethical Decision Making

The following questions, compiled by Bob Steele of the Poynter Institute, are a good starting point for journalists as they set out to report a story.

Ask These 10 Questions to Make Good Ethical Decisions

1. What do I know? What do I need to know?
2. What is my journalistic purpose?
3. What are my ethical concerns?
4. What organizational policies and professional guidelines should I consider?
5. How can I include other people, with different perspectives, in the decision-making process?
6. Who are the stakeholders—those affected by my decision? What are their motivations? Which are legitimate?
7. What if the roles were reversed? How would I feel if I were in the shoes of one of the stakeholders?
8. What are the possible consequences of my actions? Short term? Long term?
9. What are my alternatives to maximize my truth-telling responsibility and minimize harm?
10. Can I clearly and fully justify my thinking and my decision? To my colleagues? To stakeholders? To the public?

Reproduced with the permission of Bob Steele.

INDEX